LEISURE ARTS PRESENTS

Big Book of
Best-Loved
Quilt Patterns

Join us in congratulating Jo-Ann Stores, Inc., on their 60th anniversary! Throughout
its years of expansion since 1943 — from a single fabric shop in Cleveland, Ohio, to
nearly a thousand fabric and craft supply stores nationwide — this family-run business
has upheld the old-fashioned values of vision, quality, and service. To make your own
version of the commemorative Medallion Celebration Quilt, turn to page 10.

Oxmoor
House®

Big Book of
Best-Loved
Quilt Patterns

©2003 by Oxmoor House, Inc.
Book Division of Southern Progress Corporation
P.O. Box 2463,
Birmingham, Alabama 35201

Published by Oxmoor House, Inc., and Leisure Arts, Inc.

Library of Congress Control Number: 2002113359
ISBN: 0-8487-2850-5
Printed in the United States of America
First Printing 2003

Editor-in-Chief: Nancy Fitzpatrick Wyatt
Executive Editor: Katherine M. Eakin
Art Director: Cynthia R. Cooper
Copy Chief: Catherine Ritter Scholl

Big Book of Best-Loved Quilt Patterns
Editor: Rhonda Richards
Contributing Copy Editor and Technical Writer: Laura Morris Edwards
Designer/Illustrator: K. Davis
Senior Photographer: John O'Hagan
Photo Stylist: Katie Stoddard
Publishing Systems Administrator: Rick Tucker
Director, Production and Distribution: Phillip Lee
Book Production Manager: Theresa L. Beste
Production Assistant: Faye Porter Bonner

For more books to enrich your life, visit:
www.oxmoorhouse.com

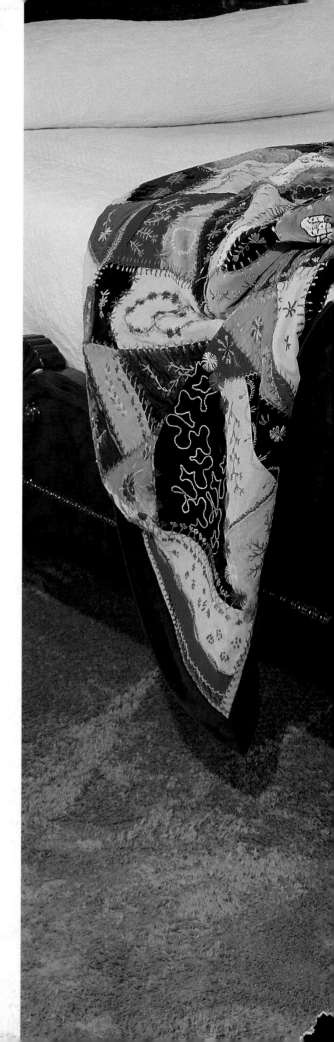

Contents

Chapter 1: Squares & Rectangles

Road to Oklahoma, page 18

Chapter 2: Diamonds & Stars

Hands All Around, page 72

Chapter 3: Circles & Curves

Love Ring, page 129

Friendship Album, page 187

Chapter 4: Patchwork Mosaics

Chapter 5: Medallions & More

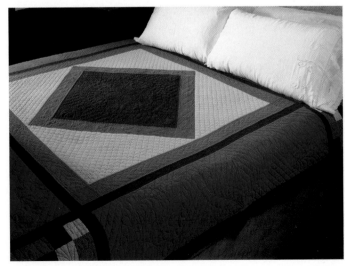

Diamond In A Square, page 220

Chapter 6: Picture Blocks

Cherry Basket, page 238

Country Hearts, page 280

Chapter 7: Appliqué

Chapter 8: Special Techniques

Rail Fence, page 336

Organizing A Signature Quilt, page 352

Chapter 9: Quiltmaker's Workshop

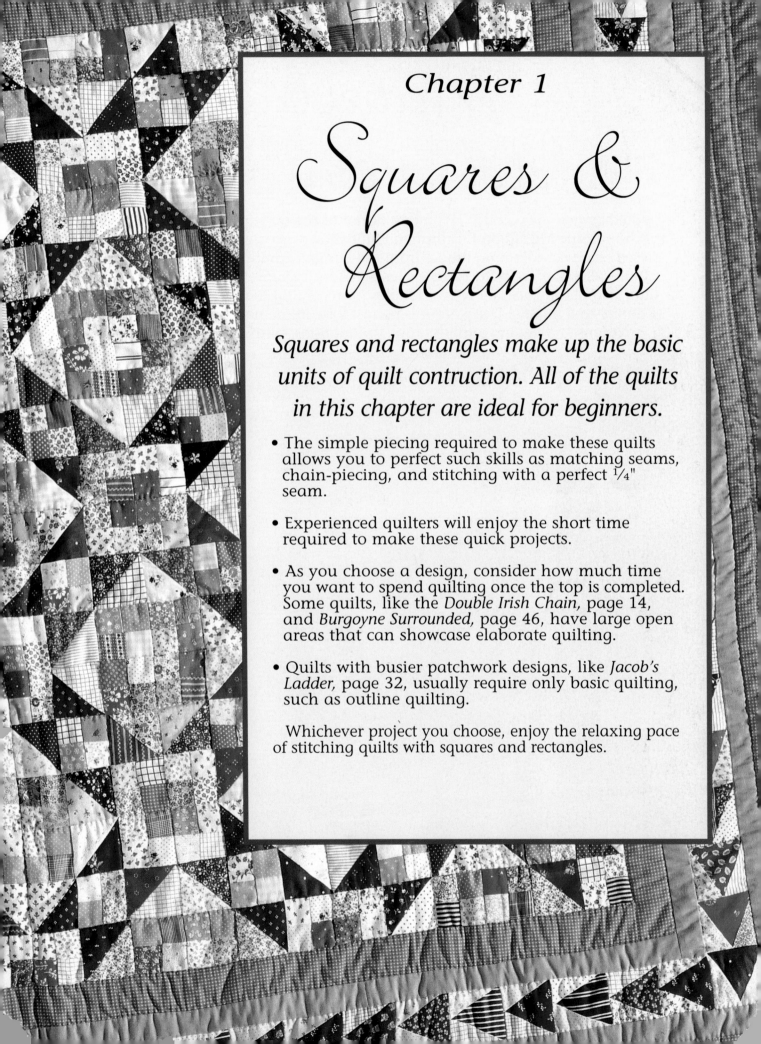

Chapter 1

Squares & Rectangles

Squares and rectangles make up the basic units of quilt contruction. All of the quilts in this chapter are ideal for beginners.

• The simple piecing required to make these quilts allows you to perfect such skills as matching seams, chain-piecing, and stitching with a perfect $\frac{1}{4}$" seam.

• Experienced quilters will enjoy the short time required to make these quick projects.

• As you choose a design, consider how much time you want to spend quilting once the top is completed. Some quilts, like the *Double Irish Chain,* page 14, and *Burgoyne Surrounded,* page 46, have large open areas that can showcase elaborate quilting.

• Quilts with busier patchwork designs, like *Jacob's Ladder,* page 32, usually require only basic quilting, such as outline quilting.

Whichever project you choose, enjoy the relaxing pace of stitching quilts with squares and rectangles.

Medallion Celebration Quilt

Created by designer Cindy Casciato in honor of the 60th anniversary of Jo-Ann Stores, this handsome Medallion Celebration Quilt showcases a central photo transfer and is pieced using coordinating fabrics from the Limited Edition Anniversary Album Circa 1943 collection, manufactured exclusively for Jo-Ann's by Springs Industries. The quilt's border includes 64 open triangles for recording the names and reminiscences of family and friends. The pattern is perfect for commemorating your family's special occasions — wedding anniversaries, graduations, births, or milestone birthdays.

Members of the Jo-Ann's family shown on the quilt include (standing) Alma Zimmerman, CEO Alan Rosskamm, Fred Zimmerman, and (seated) Martin and Betty Rosskamm.

Finished Quilt Size
51" x 51"

Number of Blocks and Finished Size
16 (6") Signature Blocks

Materials
Photograph sized to $8^{1}/_{8}$" to $8^{1}/_{8}$"
10" square white solid and photo transfer paper _or_ photo transfer fabric
$^{1}/_{2}$ yard large print
1 yard tan print
$^{3}/_{4}$ yard blue print #1
$^{3}/_{4}$ yard blue print #2
$^{1}/_{2}$ yard burgundy print #1
$^{3}/_{8}$ yard burgundy print #2
$^{1}/_{2}$ yard gold print
$1^{3}/_{4}$ yard border stripe print for outer border*
$3^{1}/_{2}$ yards fabric for backing*
56" x 56" square of batting*
Fusible web
*Outer border on quilt shown has $4^{1}/_{4}$" finished width. If wider border is desired, additional fabric for border and backing and batting may be needed.

Cutting
Measurements include $^{1}/_{4}$" seam allowances.

From large print, cut:
- 1 ($13^{1}/_{4}$") square. Cut square twice diagonally to make 4 D triangles.

From tan print, cut:
- 1 ($2^{1}/_{2}$"-wide) strip. Cut strip into 2 ($2^{1}/_{2}$" x $8^{1}/_{2}$") B rectangles and 2 ($2^{1}/_{2}$" x $12^{1}/_{2}$") C rectangles.
- 1 ($3^{5}/_{8}$"-wide) strip. Cut strips into 8 ($3^{5}/_{8}$") squares. Cut squares twice diagonally to make 32 I triangles.
- 4 ($3^{7}/_{8}$") strips. Cut strips into 32 ($3^{7}/_{8}$") squares. Cut squares once diagonally to make 64 M triangles.
- 2 ($8^{1}/_{8}$") squares. Cut squares once diagonally to make 4 E triangles.
- 4 ($2^{7}/_{8}$") F squares.

From blue print #1, cut:
- 4 (1"-wide) strips. Cut strips into 4 (1" x $12^{1}/_{2}$") flange #1 strips and 4 (1" x $17^{1}/_{2}$") flange #2 strips.
- 1 ($3^{1}/_{4}$"-wide) strip. Cut strip into 4 ($3^{1}/_{4}$") squares. Cut squares once diagonally to make 8 G triangles.
- 1 ($5^{1}/_{8}$"-wide) strip. Cut strip into 6 ($5^{1}/_{8}$") squares. Cut squares once diagonally to make 12 P triangles.
- 1 ($9^{3}/_{4}$"-wide) strip. Cut strip into 3 ($9^{3}/_{4}$") squares. Cut squares twice diagonally to make 12 Q triangles.

From blue print #2, cut:
- 4 ($1^{1}/_{4}$"-wide) strips. Cut strips into 2 ($1^{1}/_{4}$" x $24^{1}/_{2}$") K strips and 2 ($1^{1}/_{4}$" x 26") L strips.
- 2 (2"-wide) strips. Cut strips into 28 (2") N squares.
- 6 ($2^{1}/_{4}$"-wide) strips for binding.

From burgundy print #1, cut:
- 1 ($9^{3}/_{4}$"-wide) strip. Cut strip into 3 ($9^{3}/_{4}$") squares. Cut squares twice diagonally to make 12 Q triangles.
- 2 ($5^{1}/_{8}$") squares. Cut squares once diagonally to make 4 P triangles.

From burgundy print #2, cut:
- 2 (2"-wide) strips. Cut strips into 36 (2") N squares.
- 2 (6") squares. Cut squares twice diagonally to make 8 J triangles.

From gold print, cut:
- 1 ($2^{1}/_{4}$"-wide) strip. Cut strip into 16 H squares.
- 3 ($3^{3}/_{8}$"-wide) strips. Cut strips into 32 ($3^{3}/_{8}$") squares. Cut squares twice diagonally to make 128 O triangles.

From border stripe print, cut:
- 4 ($4^{3}/_{4}$"-wide) lengthwise outer border strips.

Center Square Assembly
1. Following manufacturer's instructions, transfer photo to center of white fabric square or photo transfer fabric. Trim square to $8^{1}/_{2}$" x $8^{1}/_{2}$" (square A), making sure photograph is centered.
2. Sew B rectangles to top and bottom of A square, and C rectangles to sides of A square to make unit 1 *(Unit 1 Diagram)*.

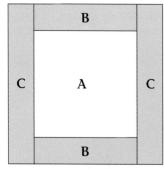

Unit 1 Diagram

3. With wrong sides together, press flange #1 strips in half lengthwise. Matching seam allowances and right sides, sew flange strips to sides, then top and bottom of unit 1.
4. Sew 4 D triangles to unit 1 to make unit 2 *(Unit 2 Diagram)*. Press flange toward center of quilt top.

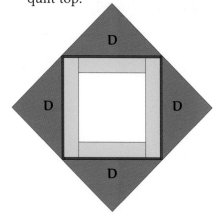

Unit 2 Diagram

5. Sew #2 flange strips to sides of unit 2 in the same manner as #1 flange strips (Step 3).
6. Sew 2 I triangles to 1 H square to make unit 3 *(Unit 3 Diagram)*. Make 16 unit 3's.

Unit 3 Diagram

7. Sew 2 Unit 3's, 1 J triangle, 1 G triangle, and 1 F square together as shown in *Unit 4 Diagram*. Make 4 unit 4's.

Unit 4 Diagram

8. Sew 2 unit 3's, 1 J triangle, and 1 G triangle together as shown in *Unit 5 Diagram*. Make 4 unit 5's.

Unit 5 Diagram

9. Sew 1 unit 5 to 1 E triangle, then 1 unit 4 to make pieced triangle unit *(Pieced Triangle Unit Diagram)*. Make 4 pieced triangle units.

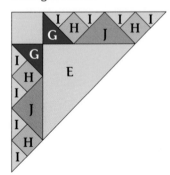

Pieced Triangle Unit Diagram

10. Sew 1 pieced triangle unit to each side of Unit 2 to complete center square.

Signature Block Assembly

1. Referring to Corner and Side Block Diagrams, sew 2 O triangles to 1 N square to make triangle unit. Sew 1 triangle unit to 1 M triangle to make patch. Sew 4 patches together to make block. Make 4 corner blocks and 12 side blocks.

Corner Block Diagram

Side Block Diagram

Quilt Assembly

Refer to *Borders*, page 358, to add borders to quilt top center.

1. Add K strips to top and bottom of center square, then L strips to sides to complete inner border.
2. Referring to *Side Pieced Border Diagram*, sew 4 P triangles, 4 Q triangles, and 3 blocks together to make side pieced border. Make 2 side pieced borders.

Side Pieced Border Diagram

3. Referring to *Top/Bottom Pieced Border Diagram*, sew 4 P triangles, 8 Q triangles, and 5 blocks together to make top pieced border. Repeat to make bottom pieced border.

Top/Bottom Pieced Border Diagram

4. Sew side pieced borders, then top and bottom pieced borders to quilt top.
5. Center 1 outer border strip on each side of quilt and join. Miter corners.

Optional Embellishment

1. Following manufacturer's instructions, fuse web to wrong side of large print fabric. Cut out desired motifs from print fabric and fuse to quilt top as desired.
2. Appliqué motifs using a Satin Stitch or decorative stitch and matching or invisible thread.

Quilting and Finishing

1. Divide backing fabric into 2 (1³/₄-yard) lengths. Cut 1 piece in half lengthwise. Sew 1 narrow panel to each side of wide panel. Press seam allowances toward narrow panels.
2. Layer backing, batting, and quilt top; baste. Quilt as desired. Quilt shown was machine quilted. Blocks were quilted in-the-ditch, outline quilted around fabric designs, echo quilted around appliqués, with a swirl design added around photo.
3. Join 2¹/₄" wide blue strips into 1 continuous piece for straight-grain French-fold binding. Add binding to quilt.

Quilt Top Assembly Diagram

Quilt designer Cindy Casciato (far right) of Jo-Ann's exchanges ideas with Sue Hausmann (far left), host of *America Sews with Sue Hausmann,* and Karen Good, host of *America Quilts creatively.*

Double Irish Chain

"Two-block" pattern quilts are made up of two different square blocks that are alternated to make an overall pattern. Double Irish Chain is one of these. Traditionally stitched in green and white, this example has a shamrock quilting pattern to add an Irish touch.

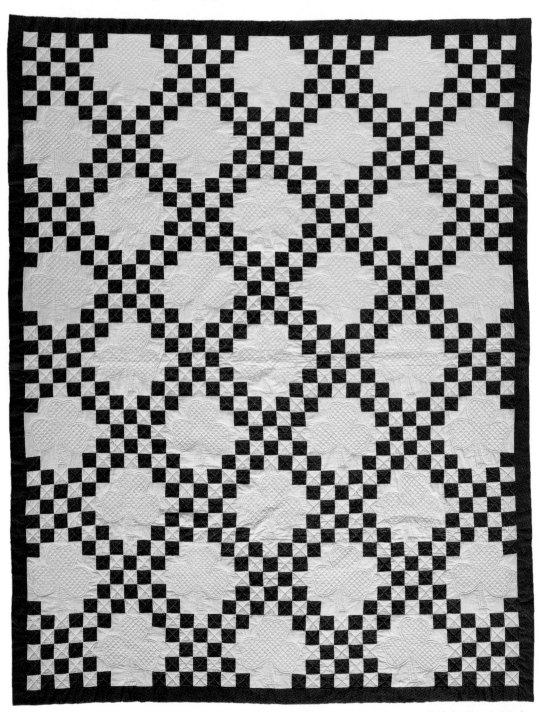

Quilt by Peggie Morley

Finished Quilt Size
74" x 94"

Number of Blocks and Finished Size
32 (10") Checkerboard Blocks
31 (10") Corners Blocks

Materials
3¾ yards navy pindot
4½ yards muslin
5½ yards fabric for backing
Full-size batting

Cutting
Measurements include ¼" seam allowances. Border strips are exact length needed. You may want to cut them longer to allow for piecing variations.

From navy pindot, cut:
• 24 (2½"-wide) strips for checkerboard strip sets.
• 8 (2½"-wide) strips for corners strip sets.
• 9 (2½"-wide) strips. Piece strips to make 2 (2½" x 70½") top and bottom border strips and 2 (2½" x 94½") side border strips.
• 10 (2¼"-wide) strips for binding.

From muslin, cut:
• 26 (2½"-wide) strips for checkerboard strip sets.
• 4 (6½"-wide) strips for corners strip sets.
• 6 (10½"-wide) strips. Cut strips into 31 (6½" x 10½") D rectangles for corners blocks.

Checkerboard Block Assembly
1. Join 3 muslin and 2 navy strips as shown in *Strip Set A Diagram* to make 1 strip set. Make 6 Strip Sets A. Press seam allowances toward

navy. Cut strip sets into 96 (2½"-wide) A segments for checkerboard blocks.

2. Join 3 navy and 2 muslin strips as shown in *Strip Set B Diagram* to make 1 strip set. Make 4 Strip Sets B. Press seam allowances toward navy. Cut strip sets into 64 (2½"-wide) B segments for checkerboard blocks.

3. Alternate 3 A segments and 2 B segments as shown in *Checkerboard Block Assembly Diagram*. Join to make 1 Checkerboard block (*Checkerboard Block Diagram*).

4. Make 32 Checkerboard blocks.

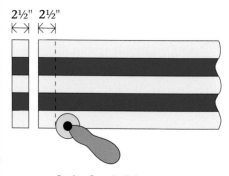

2½" 2½"

Strip Set A Diagram

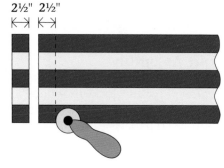

2½" 2½"

Strip Set B Diagram

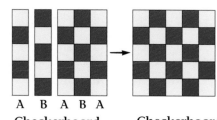

A   B   A   B   A
Checkerboard Block Assembly Diagram

Checkerboard Block Diagram

Quilt Top Assembly Diagram

Corners Block Assembly

1. Join 1 navy strip to each side of 1 muslin 6½"-wide strip as shown in *Strip Set C Diagram* to make 1 strip set. Make 4 Strip Sets C. Press seam allowances toward navy. Cut strip sets into 62 (2½"-wide) C segments.

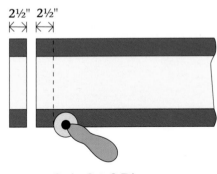

Strip Set C Diagram

2. Referring to *Corners Block Assembly Diagram*, join 1 C segment

to each side of 1 muslin D rectangle to make 1 Corners block *(Corners Block Diagram)*.

3. Make 31 Corners blocks.

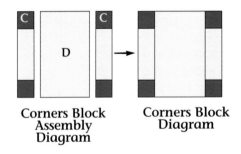

Corners Block Assembly Diagram

Corners Block Diagram

Quilt Assembly

1. Referring to *Quilt Top Assembly Diagram*, lay out blocks in 9 horizontal rows of 7 blocks each. Join into rows; join rows to complete center.

2. Add top and bottom borders to quilt. Add side borders.

Quilting and Finishing

1. Divide backing fabric into 2 (2¾-yard) lengths. Cut 1 piece in half lengthwise. Sew 1 narrow panel to each side of wide panel. Press seam allowances toward narrow panels.

2. Layer backing, batting, and quilt top; baste. Quilt as desired. Quilt shown was quilted in Xs in small squares. Large muslin areas were filled with a shamrock pattern. (See pattern on facing page.)

3. Join 2¼"-wide navy pindot strips into 1 continuous piece for straight-grain French-fold binding. Add binding to quilt.

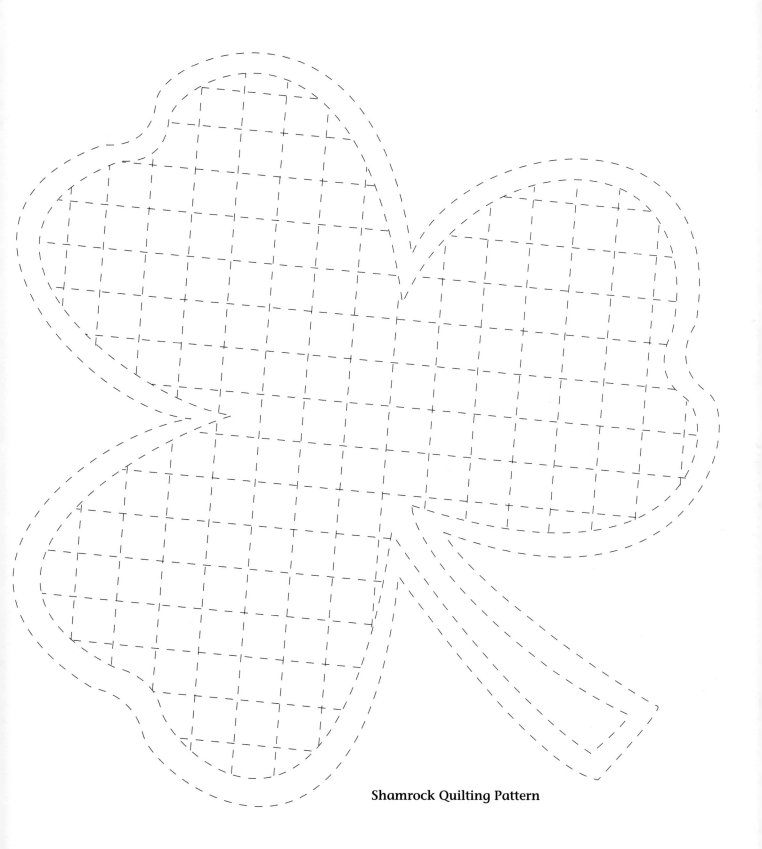

Shamrock Quilting Pattern

Road to Oklahoma

In 1880, the United States government opened up two million acres of Indian Territory land in the west for settlement. Settlers from the east poured into the Oklahoma Territory. Perhaps one of those pioneer women, stitching along the trail, named this pattern.

Finished Quilt Size
97³⁄₈" x 97³⁄₈"

Number of Blocks and Finished Size
64 (9¹⁄₂") Road to Oklahoma Blocks

Materials
2¹⁄₄ yards blue print for blocks
2 yards light brown print for blocks
5 yards dark brown print for blocks, sashing, and binding
2³⁄₄ yards cream print for blocks
9 yards fabric for backing (or 3 yards 108"-wide backing)
King-size batting

Cutting
Measurements include ¹⁄₄" seam allowances.

From blue print, cut:
- 12 (2⁷⁄₈"-wide) strips. Cut strips into 168 (2⁷⁄₈") A squares.
- 11 (3¹⁄₄"-wide) strips. Cut strips into 128 (3¹⁄₄") squares. Cut squares in half diagonally to make 256 B triangles.

From light brown print, cut:
- 22 (2⁷⁄₈"-wide) strips. Cut strips into 297 (2⁷⁄₈") A squares.

From dark brown print, cut:
- 7 (2⁷⁄₈"-wide) strips. Cut strips into 96 (2⁷⁄₈") A squares.
- 3 (3¹⁄₄"-wide) strips. Cut strips into 32 (3¹⁄₄") squares. Cut squares in half diagonally to make 64 B triangles.
- 36 (2⁷⁄₈"-wide) strips. Cut strips into 144 (2⁷⁄₈" x 10") sashing strips.
- 11 (2¹⁄₄"-wide) strips for binding.

From cream print, cut:
- 21 (2⁷⁄₈"-wide) strips. Cut strips into 288 (2⁷⁄₈") A squares.
- 8 (3¹⁄₄"-wide) strips. Cut strips into 96 (3¹⁄₄") squares. Cut squares in half diagonally to make 192 B triangles.

Inner Block Assembly

1. Join 1 blue and 1 cream B triangle to make 1 triangle unit (*Blue/Cream Triangle Unit Diagram*). Make 4 triangle units.

Blue/Cream Triangle Unit Diagram

2. Referring to *Inner Block Diagram*, lay out triangle units with 2 blue, 4 light brown, and 6 cream As. Join into rows; join rows to make 1 Inner Block.

3. Make 36 Inner Blocks.

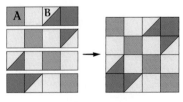

Inner Block Diagram

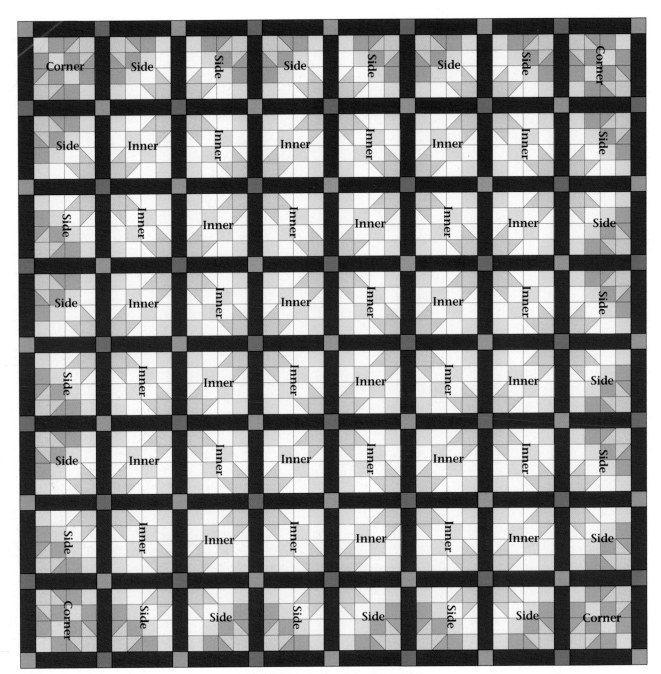

Quilt Top Assembly Diagram

Side Block Assembly

1. Join 1 blue and 1 cream B triangle to make 1 triangle unit (*Blue/Cream Triangle Unit Diagram*). Make 2 triangle units.

2. Join 1 blue and 1 dark brown B triangle to make 1 dark brown triangle unit (*Brown/Blue Triangle Unit Diagram*). Make 2 dark brown triangle units.

Brown/Blue Triangle Unit Diagram

3. Referring to *Side Block Diagram*, lay out triangle units with 2 blue, 4 light brown, 3 dark brown, and

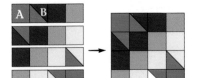

Side Block Diagram

3 cream As. Join into rows; join rows to complete 1 side block.

4. Make 24 side blocks.

Corner Block Assembly

1. Join 1 blue and 1 dark brown B triangle to make 1 triangle unit (*Brown/Blue Triangle Unit Diagram*).

Make 4 triangle units.

2. Referring to *Corner Block Diagram*, lay out triangle units with 2 blue, 4 light brown, and 6 dark brown As. Join into rows; join rows to make 1 corner block.

3. Make 4 corner blocks.

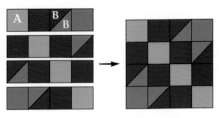

Corner Block Diagram

Quilt by Mary Eucolano Chapman; owned by Mark Alan Chapman

Quilt Assembly

1. Referring to *Quilt Top Assembly Diagram,* lay out sashing strips, sashing squares, and blocks, rotating blocks as shown.

2. When you are satisfied with placement, join into rows. Join rows to complete quilt.

Quilting and Finishing

1. Divide backing fabric into 3 (3-yard) lengths. Cut 1 piece in half lengthwise. Sew 1 narrow panel between wide panels. Press seam allowances toward narrow panel. Remaining panel is extra and may be used to make a hanging sleeve.

Seams will run horizontally.

2. Layer backing, batting, and quilt top; baste. Quilt as desired. Quilt shown was outline-quilted.

3. Join 2¼"-wide dark brown strips into 1 continuous piece for straight-grain French-fold binding. Add binding to quilt.

Churn Dash

You may recognize this traditional block
by one of its other familiar names: Monkey Wrench, Old Mill,
Hole in the Barn Door, Indian Hammer, or Quail's Nest.

Quilt from Hannah Antiques, Birmingham, Alabama

Finished Quilt Size
84" x 99"

Number of Blocks and Finished Size
30 (12") Churn Dash Blocks

Materials
30 fat eighths* assorted prints for block backgrounds
30 fat eighths* assorted solids for blocks (or 30 (5" x 22") strips)
3¼ yards cream for sashing and binding
½ yard rust print for sashing squares
1¼ yards solid medium brown for border (2⅞ yards for unpieced borders)
7½ yards fabric for backing (or 3 yards 90"-wide backing)
Queen-size batting
*Fat eighth = 9" x 22"

Cutting
Measurements include ¼" seam allowances.

From each print, cut 1 background set of:
- 1 (5" x 22") strip. Cut strip into 1 (4½") A square and 2 (4⅞") squares. Cut 4⅞" squares in half diagonally to make 1 set of 4 C triangles.
- 1 (2½" x 22") strip. Cut strip into 4 (2½" x 4½") B rectangles.

From each solid, cut 1 block set of:
- 1 (5" x 22") strip. Cut strip into 4 (2½" x 4½") B rectangles and 2 (4⅞") squares. Cut squares in half diagonally to make 1 set of 4 C triangles.

From cream, cut:
- 24 (3½"-wide) strips. Cut strips into 71 (3½" x 12½") sashing strips.
- 10 (2¼"-wide) strips for binding.

From rust print, cut:
- 4 (3½"-wide) strips. Cut strips into 42 (3½") sashing squares.

From solid medium brown, cut:
- 10 (3½"-wide) strips. Piece to make 2 (3½" x 87") top and bottom border strips and 2 (3½" x 102")

Quilt Top Assembly Diagram

side border strips. If you prefer unpieced borders, cut 4 (3½"-wide) lengthwise strips from alternate yardage.

Block Assembly
1. Choose 1 background set and 1 block set. Join 1 C triangle from each set to make 1 C unit. Make 4 C units.
2. Join 1 B from each set to make 1 B unit. Make 4 B units.
3. Referring to *Block Assembly Diagram*, lay out A, B units, and C units. Join into rows; join rows to complete 1 Churn Dash block (*Block Diagram*).
4. Make 30 Churn Dash blocks.

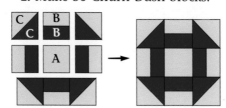

Block Assembly Diagram

Quilt Assembly
1. Referring to *Quilt Top Assembly*

Diagram, lay out sashing strips, sashing squares, and blocks. Join into rows; join rows to complete center.
2. Center 1 medium brown border strip on each side and join to quilt. Miter corners.

Quilting and Finishing
1. Divide backing fabric into 3 (2½-yard) lengths. Cut 1 length into 1 (30"-wide) lengthwise panel. Sew 30" panel between wide panels. Press seam allowances toward narrow panel. Remaining panel is extra and may be used to make a hanging sleeve. Seams will run horizontally.
2. Layer backing, batting, and quilt top; baste. Quilt as desired. Quilt shown was outline-quilted.
3. Join 2¼"-wide cream strips into 1 continuous piece for straight-grain French-fold binding. Add binding to quilt. (*Note:* The original quilt has backing turned to the front for 1"-wide self-binding. This preserves the look, but is less durable. See page 364 for instructions on making self binding.)

Slice of Pine

The traditional Pineapple Block has numerous ⌐ triangle pieces. This innovative quiltmaker simplified ⌐ pattern by making fewer, larger triangles—hence the name *Slice of Pineapple*. The block center features a Four-Patch unit rather than a simple square.

Finished Quilt Size
95" x 115"

Number of Blocks and Finished Size
20 (15") Slice of Pineapple Blocks

Materials
3½ yards pink for blocks and sashing squares
3½ yards green for blocks and sashing squares
5½ yards muslin for blocks and binding
9 yards fabric for backing
King-size batting

Cutting
Measurements include ¼" seam allowances.

From pink, cut:
- 11 (3"-wide) strips. Piece strips to make 2 (3" x 95") inner top and bottom borders and 2 (3" x 98") inner side borders.
- 6 (5½"-wide) strips. Cut strips into 40 (5½") A squares.
- 7 (3⅜"-wide) strips. Cut strips into 80 (3⅜") squares. Cut squares in half diagonally to make 160 B triangles.
- 3 (3"-wide) strips. Cut strips into 40 (3") C squares.
- 5 (3"-wide) strips for sashing square strip sets.

From green, cut:
- 11 (3"-wide) strips. Piece strips to make 2 (3" x 98") inner top and bottom borders and 2 (3" x 118") inner side borders.
- 6 (5½"-wide) strips. Cut strips into 40 (5½") A squares.

- 7 (3⅜"-wide) strips. Cut strips into 80 (3⅜") squares. Cut squares in half diagonally to make 160 B triangles.
- 3 (3"-wide) strips. Cut strips into 40 (3") C squares.
- 5 (3"-wide) strips for sashing square strip sets.

From muslin, cut:
- 7 (15½"-wide) strips. Cut strips into 49 (5½" x 15½") sashing strips.
- 14 (3⅜"-wide) strips. Cut strips into 160 (3⅜") squares. Cut squares in half diagonally to make 320 B triangles.
- 11 (2¼"-wide) strips for binding.

Block Assembly
1. Join 1 green and 1 muslin B triangle to make 1 green triangle unit *(Triangle Unit Diagram)*. Make 8 green triangle units.

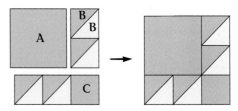

Triangle Unit Diagram

2. Join 1 pink and 1 muslin B triangle to make 1 pink triangle unit. Make 8 pink triangle units.
3. Referring to *Quadrant Assembly Diagram*, join 2 green triangle units. Add to side of 1 green A square. Join 2 green triangle units and 1

Quadrant Assembly Diagram

...square. Add to bottom of A ...e to make 1 green quadrant. ...e 2 green and 2 pink quadrants.
4. Lay out quadrants as shown in *Block Assembly Diagram.* Join into rows; join rows to complete 1 Slice of Pineapple block. Make 20 Slice of Pineapple blocks *(Block Diagram).*

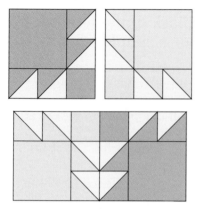

Block Assembly Diagram

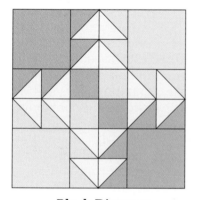

Block Diagram

Sashing Square Assembly

1. Referring to *Strip Set Diagram,* join 1 pink and 1 green strip to make 1 strip set. Make 5 strip sets. Cut strip sets into 60 (3"-wide) segments.

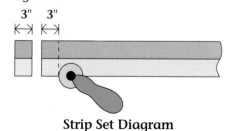

Strip Set Diagram

2. Join 2 segments as shown in *Four-Patch Assembly Diagram* to make 1 sashing square.
3. Make 30 sashing squares.

Four-Patch Assembly Diagram

Quilt Assembly

1. Referring to *Quilt Top Assembly Diagram,* lay out sashing strips, sashing squares, and blocks. Join into rows; join rows to complete center.
2. Join 1 pink and 1 green strip to make 1 border strip. Make 4 border strips, matching lengths.
3. Center 1 border strip on each side of quilt and join. Miter corners, if desired. Alternately, trim corners as shown, leaving ¼" seam allowance, using 45° mark on your ruler.

Quilt Top Assembly Diagram

Quilting and Finishing

1. Divide backing fabric into 3 (3-yard) lengths. Join to make backing. Seams will run horizontally.
2. Layer backing, batting, and quilt top; baste. Quilt as desired. Quilt shown was outline-quilted in blocks and sashing squares, and has Flying Geese in sashing.
3. Join 2¼"-wide muslin strips into 1 continuous piece for straight-grain French-fold binding. Add binding to quilt.

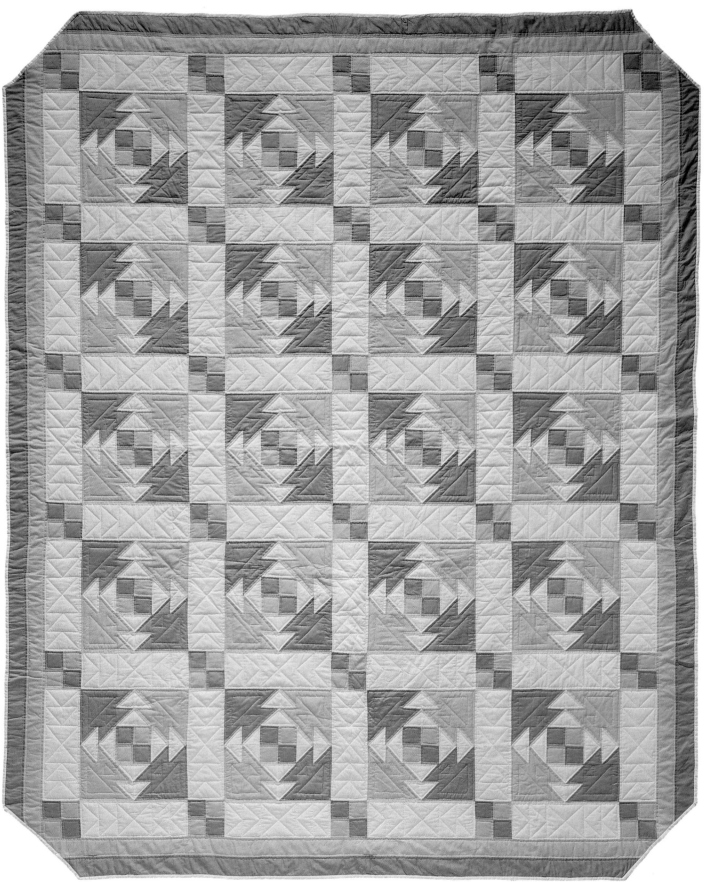

Quilt by Harlene Rose

Double T

This pattern became popular in the 1920s during Prohibition. It was designed by the Women's Christian Temperance Union (WCTU) to support the temperance movement against the legal sale of alcohol.

Quilt by Mary Eleanor Arrowsmith Keller,
Mary Elizabeth Keller Brading, and Jennifer C. Rozens

Finished Quilt Size
72" x 72"

Number of Blocks and Finished Size
32 (6¾") Double T Blocks

Materials
30 (3¼" x 22") strips light prints for T block backgrounds

32 (5" x 22") strips dark prints for blocks

2 (3¼" x 6½") strips light prints for star blocks

2 (3½" x 14") strips solids to coordinate or contrast with prints for star blocks

1 yard navy for inner border and binding (1¾ yards for unpieced borders)

2⅜ yards rose for setting squares and middle border (2¼ yards for unpieced borders)

1¼ yards blue for outer border (2⅛ yards for unpieced borders)

4½ yards fabric for backing

Twin-size batting

Cutting
Measurements include ¼" seam allowances. You may want to cut borders longer to allow for piecing variations.

From each light print, cut 1 set of:
- 2 (3⅛") squares. Cut squares in half diagonally to make 4 A triangles.
- 8 (1⅝" x 2¾") B rectangles.

From each of 30 dark prints, cut 1 set of:
- 2 (3⅛") squares. Cut squares in half diagonally to make 4 A triangles.
- 1 (2¾") D square.
- 16 (1⅝") C squares.

From each of 2 dark prints, cut 1 set of:
- 2 (3⅛") squares. Cut squares in half diagonally to make 4 A triangles.
- 1 (2¾") D square.
- 8 (1⅝" x 2¾") B rectangles.

From each of 2 light prints, cut 1 set of:
- 2 (3⅛") squares. Cut squares in

half diagonally to make 4 A triangles.

From each solid, cut:
- 16 (1⅝") C squares.

From navy, cut:
- 6 (1¾"-wide) strips. Piece to make 4 (1¾" x 58") inner border strips. (If you prefer unpieced strips, cut 4 lengthwise strips from alternate yardage and trim to above length. Cut 5 lengthwise binding strips when using this option.)
- 8 (2¼"-wide) strips for binding.

From rose, cut:
- 8 (3¾"-wide) strips. Piece to make 4 (3¾" x 65") middle border strips. (If you prefer unpieced strips, cut 4 lengthwise strips from alternate yardage and trim to above length. When using this

option, cut remainder into 11 (7¼") strips; cut strips into 32 (7¼") setting squares.)
- 7 (7¼"-wide) strips. Cut strips into 32 (7¼") setting squares.

From blue, cut:
- 8 (5"-wide) strips. Piece to make 4 (5" x 74") outer border strips. (If you prefer unpieced strips, cut 4 lengthwise strips from alternate yardage and trim to above length.)

Block Assembly
1. Choose 1 set each light and dark prints.

2. Join 1 light and 1 dark A triangles to make 1 A unit. Make 4 A units.

3. Referring to *Diagonal Seams Diagram*, place 1 dark C square atop 1 end of 1 light B rectangle, right sides facing. Stitch diagonally from corner to corner as shown. Trim excess fabric ¼" from stitching and press open to reveal triangle. Repeat on opposite end to make 1 Flying Geese unit. Make 8 Flying Geese units. Join 2 Flying Geese units to make 1 side unit. Make 4 side units.

Diagonal Seams Diagram

4. Referring to *Double T Block Assembly Diagram*, lay out A units, side units, and 1 dark D square. Join into rows; join rows to complete 1 Double T block (*Double T Block Diagram*).

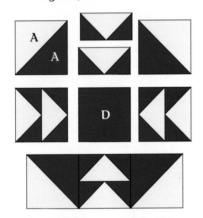

Double T Block Assembly Diagram

Double T Block Diagram

5. Make 30 Double T blocks.
6. For Wild Goose Star blocks, substitute 1 set of contrasting or coordinating C squares for dark C squares (*Wild Goose Star Diagram*). Make 4 light/dark A units and 4 side units with dark Bs and substitute C squares.

Wild Goose Star Block Diagram

Quilt Assembly

1. Referring to *Quilt Top Assembly Diagram*, join 4 blocks and 4 setting squares to make 1 row. Make 8 rows. Alternate direction of rows and join to complete center.
2. Center 1 navy border strip on each side of quilt and join. Miter corners.
3. Repeat with rose and blue borders to complete quilt.

Quilting and Finishing

1. Divide backing fabric into 2 (2¼-yard) lengths. Cut 1 piece in half lengthwise. Sew 1 narrow panel to each side of wide panel. Press seam allowances toward narrow panels.
2. Layer backing, batting, and quilt top; baste. Quilt as desired. Quilt shown was outline-quilted in blocks. Setting squares feature the Rose Leaf pattern shown on the facing page. Borders are grid quilted.
3. Join 2¼"-wide navy strips into 1 continuous piece for straight-grain French-fold binding. Add binding to quilt.

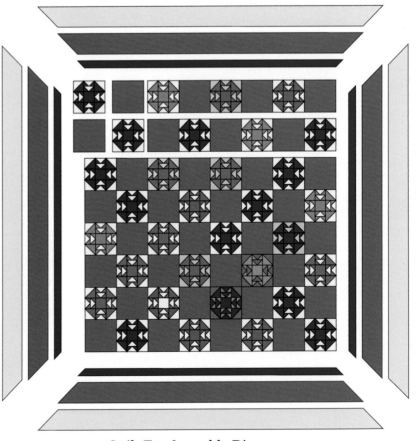

Quilt Top Assembly Diagram

Rose Leaf Quilting Pattern

Quilt Label
Trace, scan, or photocopy this quilt label to finish your quilt.

Jacob's Ladder

The name for this quilt pattern comes from Jacob's dream as described in Genesis 28:10–16. The dark triangles are set so that they appear to form ladders across the quilt top.

Quilt by Carol Olson; owned by Christie Kelly

Finished Quilt Size
Lap: 54" x 66"
King: 108" x 132"

Number of Blocks and Finished Size
48 Jacob's Ladder Blocks
6" Lap Size, 12" King Size

Materials
Lap size:
2½ yards total assorted light prints for blocks and pieced border
1 yard total assorted medium prints for blocks
1¼ yards total assorted dark prints for blocks and pieced border
1¼ yard blue pindot for borders
1 yard gray for borders and binding
4 yards fabric for backing
Twin-size batting

King size:
6 yards total assorted light prints for blocks and pieced border
2½ yards total assorted medium prints for blocks
3½ yards total assorted dark prints for blocks and pieced border
4 yards blue pindot for borders
2½ yards gray for borders and binding
12 yards fabric for backing
King-size batting

Measurements include ¼" seam allowances. Border strips are exact length needed. You may want to make them longer to allow for piecing variations.

Cutting for Lap-size Quilt:
From light prints, cut:
- 480 (1½") A squares.
- 96 (2⅞") squares. Cut squares in half diagonally to make 192 B triangles.
- 96 lap size Ds or 96 (2" x 3") rectangles for paper piecing.
- 96 lap size Ds rev. or 96 (2" x 3") rectangles for paper piecing.

From medium prints, cut:
- 480 (1½") A squares.

From dark prints, cut:
- 96 (2⅞") squares. Cut squares in half diagonally to make 192 B triangles.

- 96 lap size Cs or 96 (3") squares for paper piecing.

From blue pindot, cut:
- 5 (1½"-wide) strips. Piece as needed to make 2 (1½" x 48½") inner side borders and 2 (1½" x 38½") inner top and bottom borders.
- 6 (4½"-wide) strips. Piece as needed to make 2 (4½" x 66½") outer side borders and 2 (4½" x 46½") outer top and bottom borders.

From gray, cut:
- 11 (1½"-wide) strips. Piece as needed to make 2 (1½" x 50½") inner side borders, 2 (1½" x 40½") inner top and bottom borders, 2 (1½" x 44½") outer top and bottom borders, and 2 (1½" x 58½") outer side borders.
- 7 (2¼"-wide) strips for binding.

Cutting for King size quilt:
From light prints, cut:
- 480 (2½") A squares.
- 96 (4⅞") squares. Cut squares in half diagonally to make 192 B triangles.
- 96 king size Ds or 96 (3" x 5") rectangles for paper piecing.
- 96 king size Ds rev. or 96 (3" x 5") rectangles for paper piecing.

From medium prints, cut:
- 480 (2½") A squares.

From dark prints, cut:
- 96 (4⅞") squares. Cut squares in half diagonally to make 192 B triangles.
- 96 king size Cs or 96 (5") squares for paper piecing.

From blue pindot, cut:
- 9 (2½"-wide) strips. Piece as needed to make 2 (2½" x 96½") inner side borders and 2 (2½" x 76½") inner top and bottom borders.
- 12 (8½"-wide) strips. Piece as needed to make 2 (8½" x 132½") outer side borders and 2 (8½" x 92½") outer top and bottom borders.

From gray, cut:
- 20 (2½"-wide) strips. Piece as needed to make 2 (2½" x 100½")

inner side borders, 2 (2½" x 80½") inner top and bottom borders, 2 (2½" x 88½") outer top and bottom borders, and 2 (2½" x 116½") outer side borders.
- 13 (2¼"-wide) strips for binding.

Block Assembly
Instructions and diagrams are the same for both sizes. Choose 1 size group throughout.

1. Join 1 dark and 1 light B triangles to make 1 triangle unit *(Triangle Unit Assembly Diagram)*. Make 4 triangle units.

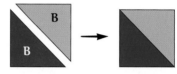

Triangle Unit Assembly Diagram

2. Join 2 medium and 2 light print As to make 1 center Four-Patch unit *(Center Four-Patch Assembly Diagram)*.

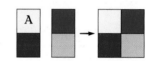

Center Four-Patch Assembly Diagram

3. Join 3 light and 1 medium print As to make 1 light print unit *(Light Print Four-Patch Assembly Diagram)*. Make 2 light print units.

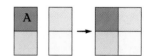

Light Print Four-Patch Assembly Diagram

4. Join 3 medium and 1 light print As to make 1 medium print unit *(Medium Print Four-Patch Assembly Diagram)*. Make 2 medium print units.

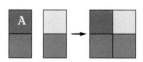

Medium Print Four-Patch Assembly Diagram

5. Lay out units carefully as shown in *Block Assembly Diagram*. Join into rows; join rows to com-

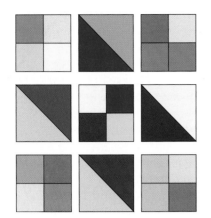

Block Assembly Diagram

to make side pieced border and add. Repeat for opposite border.

5. Join 22 border units to make top pieced border and add. Repeat for bottom border, turning 1 unit as shown.

6. Add outer gray top and bottom borders. Add outer gray side borders.

7. Add outer blue top and bottom borders. Add outer blue side borders.

plete 1 Jacob's Ladder block *(Block Diagram)*.

6. Make 48 Jacob's Ladder blocks.

Block Diagram

7. To make pieced borders, you may paper piece or use templates at right. Join 1 D and 1 D rev. to each side of 1 C to make 1 border unit. Make 96 border units *(Border Unit Diagram)*.

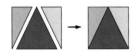

Border Unit Diagram

Quilt Assembly

Refer to *Quilt Top Assembly Diagram* throughout.

1. Lay out blocks in 8 horizontal rows of 6 blocks each, alternating direction of ladders as shown. Join into rows; join rows to complete center.

2. Add inner blue side borders. Add inner blue top and bottom borders.

3. Add inner gray side borders. Add inner gray top and bottom borders.

4. Join 26 border units as shown

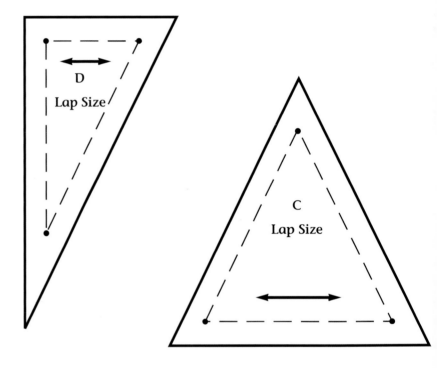

D
Lap Size

C
Lap Size

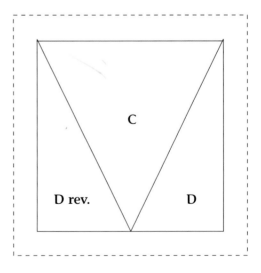

Paper Piecing Pattern Lap Size

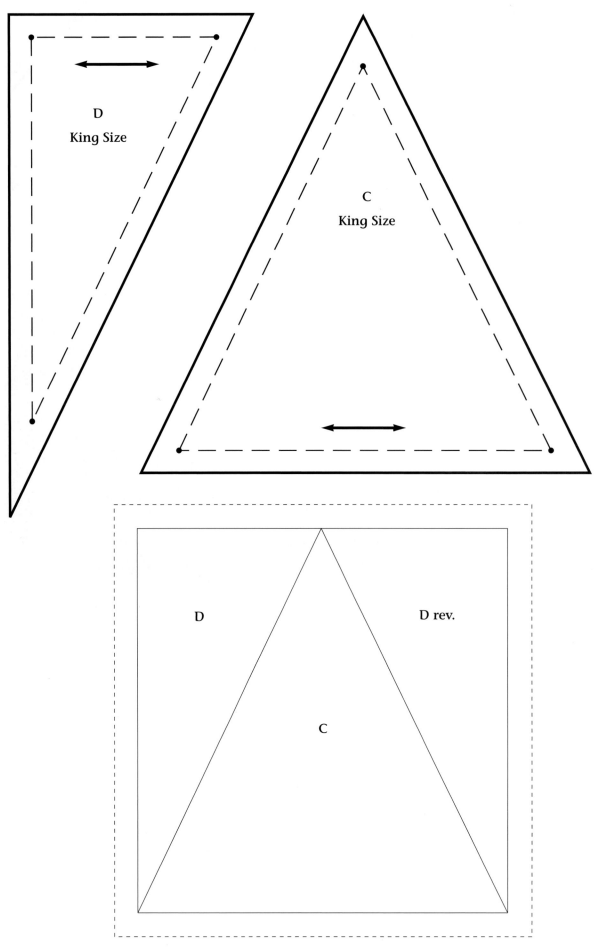

D
King Size

C
King Size

D

D rev.

C

Paper Piecing Pattern King Size

Quilting and Finishing

1. Lap size: Divide backing fabric into 2 (2-yard) lengths. Cut 1 piece in half lengthwise. Sew 1 narrow panel to 1 side of wide panel. Press seam allowance toward narrow panel. Remaining panel is extra and may be used to make a hanging sleeve.

2. King size: Divide backing fabric into 3 (4-yard) lengths. Join to make backing.

3. Layer backing, batting, and quilt top; baste. (Piece excess from side of batting to end as needed for king size.) Quilt as desired. Quilt shown was outline-quilted in blocks, with double stripes in border.

4. Join 2¼"-wide gray strips into 1 continuous piece for straight-grain French-fold binding. Add binding to quilt.

Quilt Top Assembly Diagram

Shoo-Fly

Shoo-Fly is a simple, pleasing pattern often found in quilts of the Amish regions of the upper Midwest. The name probably comes from shoo-fly pie, an incredibly sweet and delicious traditional dessert of the Pennsylvania Dutch.

Quilt by Jennifer C. Rozens

Finished Quilt Size
97" x 115"

Number of Blocks and Finished Size
30 (15") Shoo-Fly Blocks

Materials
4 yards total assorted light prints for blocks
4 yards total assorted medium prints for blocks
5 yards dark print for sashing, border and binding
9 yards fabric for backing
King-size batting

Cutting
Measurements include ¼" seam allowances. Border strips are exact length needed. You may want to cut them longer to allow for piecing variations.

From light prints, cut:
- 60 (5⅞") squares. Cut squares in half diagonally to make 120 A triangles. Sort into 30 sets of 4 matching triangles.
- 75 (5½") B squares. Sort into 15 sets of 4 matching squares and 15 single squares.

From medium prints, cut:
- 60 (5⅞") squares. Cut squares in half diagonally to make 120 A triangles. Sort into 30 sets of 4 matching triangles.
- 75 (5½") B squares. Sort into 15 sets of 4 matching squares and 15 single squares.

From dark print, cut:
- 2 (15½"-wide) strips. Cut strips into 24 (3½" x 15½") sashing strips.
- 12 (2¼"-wide) strips for binding.
- 3 yards. Cut yardage into 4 (5½"-wide) lengthwise strips. Trim to make 2 (5½" x 105½") side borders and 2 (5½" x 97½") top and bottom borders.
- From remainder, cut 5 (3½"-wide) lengthwise strips. Trim strips to make 5 (3½" x 87½") horizontal sashing strips.

Block Assembly

1. Choose 4 matching light Bs, 1 medium B, 4 light As, and 4 medium As. You may choose matching sets for a two-color block, or you may mix sets for more variety.

2. Join 1 light and 1 medium A triangles to make 1 corner unit (*Corner Unit Assembly Diagram*). Make 4 corner units.

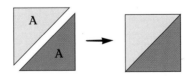

Corner Unit Assembly Diagram

3. Lay out corner units and B squares as shown in *Light Block Assembly Diagram* for light block. Join into rows; join rows to complete 1 light Shoo Fly block (*Light Block Diagram*).

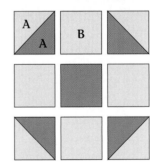

Light Block Assembly Diagram

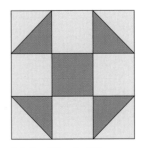

Light Block Diagram

4. Make 15 light and 15 medium Shoo Fly blocks *(Medium Block Diagram)*.

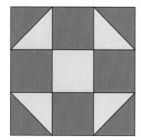

Medium Block Diagram

Quilt Assembly

1. Referring to *Quilt Top Assembly Diagram,* alternate 5 blocks and 4 sashing strips. Join to make 1 block row. Make 6 block rows.

2. Alternate block rows and horizontal sashing strips. Join to complete center.

3. Add side borders to quilt. Add top and bottom borders. *(Note:* Quilt shown in photos has no top border.)

Quilting and Finishing

1. Divide backing fabric into 3 (3-yard) lengths. Join to make backing. Seams will run horizontally.

2. Layer backing, batting, and quilt top; baste. Quilt as desired. Quilt shown was quilted in a grid.

3. Join 2¼"-wide dark print strips into 1 continuous piece for straight-grain French-fold binding. Add binding to quilt.

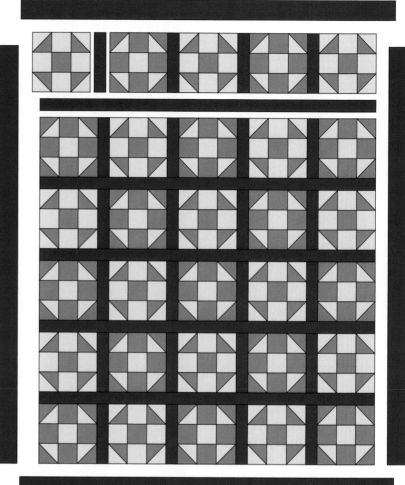

Quilt Top Assembly Diagram

Chinese Block

The Chinese Block was first published in 1938 in *The Kansas City Star*, a weekly journal for farmers and their wives. Here, the blocks are set on point, creating an interesting chain effect.

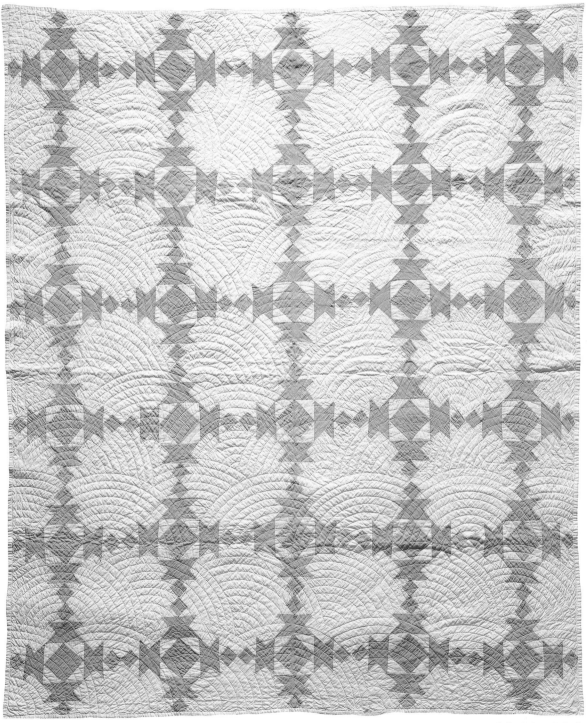

Quilt by JoAnn Schall

Finished Quilt Size
74¼" x 89"

Number of Blocks and Finished Size
30 (10½") Chinese Blocks

Materials
6 yards white for blocks, setting pieces, and binding
2½ yards peach for blocks
5¼ yards fabric for backing
Twin-size batting

Cutting
Measurements include ¼" seam allowances. Border strips are exact length needed. You may want to cut them longer to allow for piecing variations.

From white, cut:
- 7 (11"-wide) strips. Cut strips into 20 (11") setting squares.
- 3 (16"-wide) strips. Cut strips into 5 (16") squares. Cut squares in quarters diagonally to make 20 side setting triangles. You will have 2 extra.
- From remainder, cut 2 (8⅜") squares. Cut squares in half diagonally to make 4 corner setting triangles.
- 5 (3⅜"-wide) strips. Cut strips into 60 (3⅜") squares. Cut squares in half diagonally to make 120 B triangles.
- 12 (2¼"-wide) strips. Cut strips into 120 (2¼" x 4") D rectangles.
- 8 (2⅝"-wide) strips. Cut strips into 120 (2⅝") squares. Cut squares in half diagonally to make 240 E triangles.
- 9 (2¼"-wide) strips for binding.

From peach, cut:
- 3 (4"-wide) strips. Cut strips into 30 (4") A squares.
- 7 (4⅜"-wide) strips. Cut strips into 60 (4⅜") squares. Cut squares in half diagonally to make 120 C triangles.
- 8 (2⅝"-wide) strips. Cut strips into 120 (2⅝") squares. Cut squares in half diagonally to make 240 E triangles.
- 8 (2¼"-wide) strips. Cut strips into 120 (2¼") F squares.

Block Assembly
1. Referring to *Center Diagram 1,* join 1 white B triangle to 1 side of 1 A square. Join 1 white B triangle to opposite side of A square. Repeat to complete A/B block center.

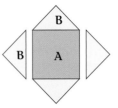

Center Diagram 1

2. Referring to *Center Diagram 2,* repeat with C triangles to complete block center.

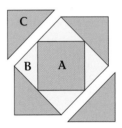

Center Diagram 2

3. Referring to *Triangle Unit Diagram,* join 1 white and 1 peach E to make 1 E unit. Make 8 E units.

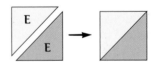

Triangle Unit Diagram

4. Referring to *Block Assembly Diagram,* lay out center, E units, 4 D rectangles, and 4 F squares. Join into strips; join strips as shown to complete 1 Chinese Block (*Block Diagram*).

5. Make 30 Chinese Blocks.

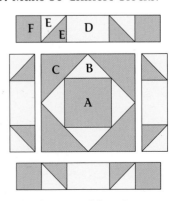

Block Assembly Diagram

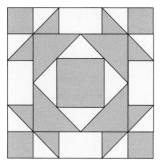

Block Diagram

Quilt Assembly

1. Lay out blocks and setting pieces as shown in *Quilt Top Assembly Diagram.*

2. Join into diagonal rows; join rows to complete quilt.

Quilting and Finishing

1. Divide backing fabric into 2 (2⅝-yard) lengths. Cut 1 piece in half lengthwise. Sew 1 narrow panel to each side of wide panel. Press seam allowances toward narrow panels.

2. Layer backing, batting, and quilt top; baste. Quilt as desired. Quilt shown is quilted in Baptist Fans. (Or see our alternate quilting pattern on page 45.)

3. Join 2¼"-wide white strips into 1 continuous piece for straight-grain French-fold binding. Add binding to quilt.

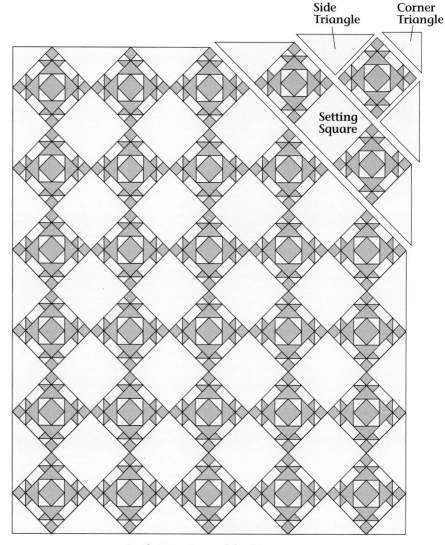

Side Triangle

Corner Triangle

Setting Square

Quilt Top Assembly Diagram

Quilt Label
Trace, scan, or photocopy this quilt label to finish your quilt.

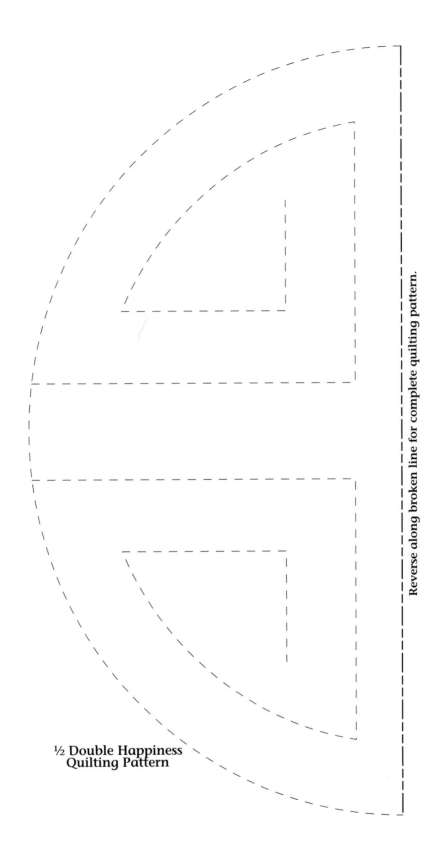

½ **Double Happiness**
Quilting Pattern

Alternate Quilting Pattern

Because there are plain setting squares in this quilt, you might opt to stitch a fancy quilting pattern in the open areas rather than doing an overall quilting pattern. The Double Happiness pattern shown on this page is an ancient Chinese symbol often seen on rugs and on decorative ceramics. It is especially appropriate when used on an item intended for a gift. It means, "May you live a long life and gather many riches."

Burgoyne Surrounded

October 17, 1777, marks the American Revolutionary War's
Battle of Saratoga, New York. American soldiers surrounded
British General Burgoyne's troops and forced them to surrender.
Legend has it that this quilt pattern was actually designed from the
battle sketches of the American commander, General Gates.

Quilt by Donna Hanson Eines

Finished Quilt Size
87" x 105"

Number of Blocks and Finished Size
20 (15") Burgoyne Surrounded Blocks

Materials
6 yards navy print
7 yards white
8¼ yards backing
Queen-size batting

Cutting
Measurements include ¼" seam allowances. Border strips are exact length needed. You may want to cut them longer to allow for piecing variations.

From navy print, cut:
- 20 (1½"-wide) strips. Piece strips to make 2 (1½" x 73½") inner top and bottom borders, 2 (1½" x 93½") inner side borders, 2 (1½" x 85½") outer top and bottom borders, and 2 (1½" x 105½") outer side borders.
- 40 (1½"-wide) strips for units 1–4, sashing posts, and pieced border.
- 21 (2½"-wide) strips for units 3–4 and pieced border.
- 5 (3½"-wide) strips for pieced border.
- 1 (5½"-wide) strip. Cut strip into 4 (2½" x 5½") K rectangles and 1 (4½" x 8") strip for Strip Set J.

From white, cut:
- 4 (15½"-wide) strips. Cut strips into 31 (3½" x 15½") inner sashing strips and 18 (2½" x 15½") outer sashing strips.
- 22 (3½"-wide) strips. Cut strips into 80 (3½" x 5½") A rectangles, and 160 (2½" x 3½") B rectangles.
- 30 (1½"-wide) strips for units 1–4, sashing posts ,and pieced border corners. Cut 1 strip into 1 (1½" x 8") section for Strip Set J.
- 22 (2½"-wide) strips for units 3–4 and pieced border.

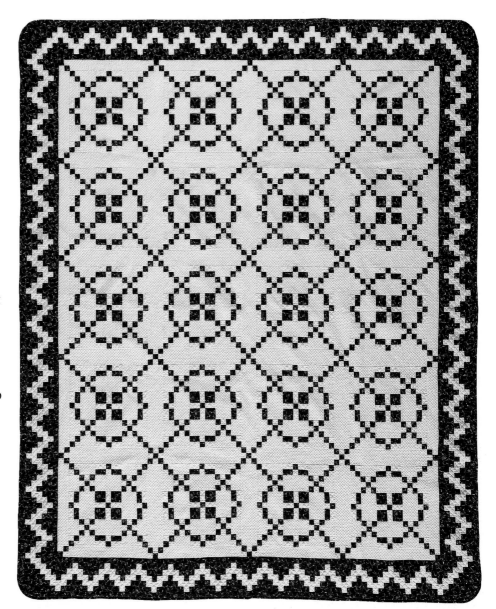

Unit Assembly

1. Referring to *Unit 1 Diagram*, join 1 navy and 1 white 1½"-wide strip to make 1 Unit 1 Strip Set. Make 7 Unit 1 strip sets. Cut strip sets into 168 (1½"-wide) segments. Join 2 segments as shown to make 1 of Unit 1. Make 84 Unit 1s.

1½" 1½"

Unit 1 Strip Set Diagram

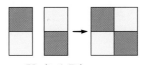

Unit 1 Diagram

2. Referring to *Strip Set C Diagram*, join 2 navy and 1 white 1½"-wide strips to make 1 Strip Set C. Make 8 Strip Sets C. Cut strip sets into 198 (1½"-wide) C segments.

1½" 1½"

Strip Set C Diagram

3. Referring to *Strip Set D Diagram*, join 2 white and 1 navy 1½"-wide strip to make 1 Strip Set D. Make 4 Strip Sets D. Cut strip sets into 106 (1½"-wide) D segments.

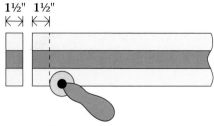

Strip Set D Diagram

4. Referring to *Unit 2 Assembly Diagram*, lay out 2 C and 1 D segments as shown. Join to make 1 of Unit 2. Make 92 Unit 2s.

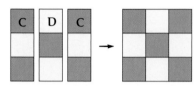

Unit 2 Assembly Diagram

5. Referring to *Outer Sashing Post Diagram*, lay out 1 C and 1 D segments as shown for outer sashing posts. Join to make 1 outer sashing post. Make 14 outer sashing posts.

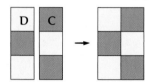

Outer Sashing Post Diagram

6. Referring to *Strip Set E Diagram*, join 2 white 2½"-wide strips and 1 navy 1½"-wide strip to make 1 Strip Set E. Make 4 Strip Sets E. Cut strip sets into 100 (1½"-wide) E segments.

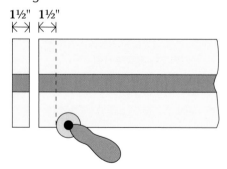

Strip Set E Diagram

7. Referring to *Strip Set F Diagram*, join 2 navy 2½"-wide strips and 1 white 1½"-wide strip to make 1 Strip Set F. Make 6 Strip Sets F. Cut strip sets into 80 (1½"-wide) F segments and 40 (2½"-wide) G segments (*Segment G Diagram*).

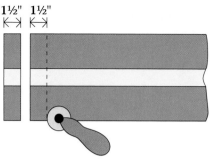

Strip Set F Diagram

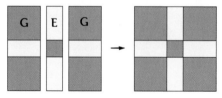

Segment G Diagram

8. Referring to *Unit 3 Diagram*, lay out 1 E and 1 F segment as shown. Join to make 1 of Unit 3. Make 80 Unit 3s.

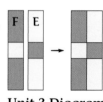

Unit 3 Diagram

9. Referring to *Unit 4 Diagram*, lay out 2 Gs and 1 E as shown. Join to make 1 of Unit 4. Make 20 Unit 4s.

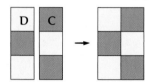

Unit 4 Diagram

10. Referring to *Strip Set H Diagram*, join 1 (1½"-wide) navy strip and 1 each navy and white 2½"-wide strips to make 1 Strip Set H. Make 9 Strip Sets H. Cut strip sets into 228 (1½"-wide) H segments.

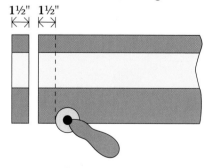

Strip Set H Diagram

11. Referring to *Strip Set I Diagram*, join 1 (2½"-wide) white strip and 1 (3½"-wide) navy strip to make 1 Strip Set I. Make 5 Strip Sets I. Cut strip sets into 116 (1½"-wide) I segments.

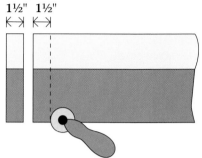

Strip Set I Diagram

12. Referring to *Border Unit Assembly Diagram*, lay out 2 Hs and 1 I segment as shown for border units. Join to make 1 border unit. Make 112 border units.

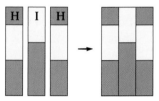

Border Unit Assembly Diagram

13. Referring to *Strip Set J Diagram*, join 1 (4½" x 8") navy strip and 1 (1½" x 8") white strip to make 1 Strip Set J. Cut strip set into 4 (1½"-wide) J segments.

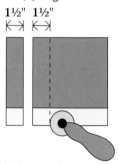

Strip Set J Diagram

14. Referring to *Border Corner Assembly Diagram*, lay out 1 each H, I, J and K segments as shown for

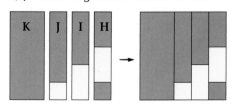

Border Corner Assembly Diagram

border corners. Join to make 1 border corner. Make 4 border corners.

Block Assembly

1. Referring to *Block Assembly Diagram,* lay out 4 each Units 1–3, 1 Unit 4, 4 As, and 8 Bs. Join into rows; join rows to complete 1 Burgoyne Surrounded block *(Block Diagram).*

2. Make 20 Burgoyne Surrounded blocks.

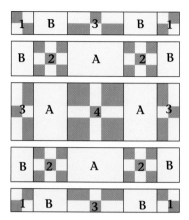

Block Assembly Diagram

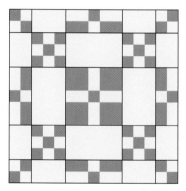

Block Diagram

Quilt Assembly

1. Referring to *Quilt Top Assembly Diagram,* lay out blocks, inner and outer sashing strips, and sashing post units. Join into rows; join rows to complete quilt center.

2. Add inner top and bottom navy borders to quilt. Add inner side borders to quilt.

3. Join 31 border units, alternating direction as shown, to make 1 side border. Repeat. Add to quilt as shown.

4. Join 25 border units, alternating direction as shown. Add 1 border corner to each end, rotating as shown. Join to top of quilt. Repeat for bottom border.

5. Add outer top and bottom borders to quilt. Add outer side borders to quilt.

Quilting and Finishing

1. Divide backing fabric into 3 (2¾-yard) lengths. Join to make backing. Seams will run horizontally.

2. Layer backing, batting, and quilt top; baste. Quilt as desired. Quilt shown is quilted in a diagonal grid.

3. For square corners: Cut 11 (2¼" x 42") strips from navy print. Join strips into 1 continuous piece for straight-grain French-fold binding. Add binding to quilt.

4. For rounded corners: Make 11 yards of 2¼"-wide bias strip from 36" navy square. Fold and press to make bias French-fold binding. Add binding to quilt. Round corners before turning binding to back.

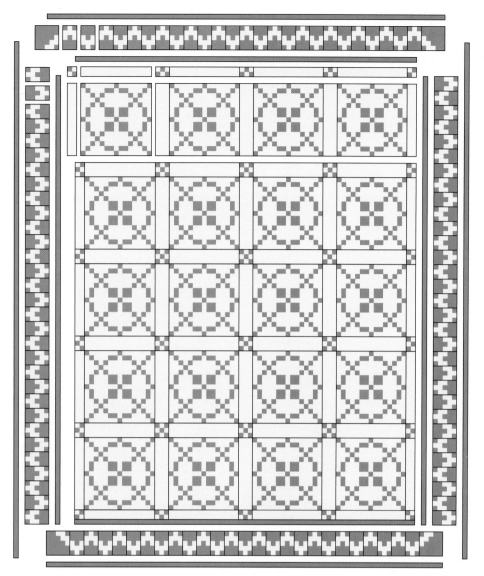

Quilt Top Assembly Diagram

Quilt from The Fosters, Pittsfield, Illinois

Honeybee

Honeybee was first published in the
Kansas City Star in 1929. The rounding
effect is created by placing a curved piece of
fabric near a straight one. This quilt
would also be fun stitched in the black
and yellow of its namesake.

Finished Quilt Size
85" x 102"

Number of Blocks and Finished Size
20 (13³⁄₈") Honeybee Blocks

Materials
3 yards solid cream for blocks and border
4 yards solid brown for blocks, border, and binding
3¼ yards brown print for blocks and sashing
2 yards solid blue for blocks and sashing squares
1 yard cream print for block corners
7½ yards fabric for backing
Queen-size batting

Cutting
Measurements include ¼" seam allowances. Pattern is on page 53.

From solid cream, cut:
- 11 (3³⁄₄"-wide) strips. Piece strips to make 2 (3³⁄₄" x 105") inner side borders and 2 (3³⁄₄" x 95") inner top and bottom borders.
- 4 (6⁷⁄₈"-wide) strips. Cut strips into 40 (4" x 6⁷⁄₈") D rectangles.
- 4 (6⁷⁄₈"-wide) strips for Strip Sets C.

From solid brown, cut:
- 11 (3³⁄₄"-wide) strips. Piece strips to make 2 (3³⁄₄" x 105") inner side borders and 2 (3³⁄₄" x 95") inner top and bottom borders.
- 160 Es.

From brown print, cut:
- 8 (2⁵⁄₈"-wide) strips for Strip Sets A and B.
- 6 (13⁷⁄₈"-wide) strips. Cut strips into 49 (4¼" x 13⁷⁄₈") sashing strips.

From solid blue, cut:
- 7 (2⁵⁄₈"-wide) strips for Strip Sets A and B.
- 4 (4¼"-wide) strips. Cut strips into 30 (4¼") sashing squares.
- 80 Es.

From cream print, cut:
- 8 (4"-wide) strips for Strip Sets C.

Block Assembly

1. Referring to *Strip Set A Diagram*, join 2 brown print and 1 solid blue strip to make Strip Set A. Make 3 Strip Sets A. Cut sets into 40 (2⁵⁄₈"-wide) A segments.

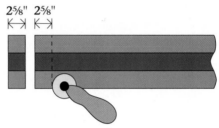

Strip Set A Diagram

2. Referring to *Strip Set B Diagram*, join 2 blue and 1 brown print strip to make Strip Set B. Make 2 Strip Sets B. Cut sets into 20 (2⁵⁄₈"-wide) B segments.

Strip Set B Diagram

3. Referring to *Nine-Patch Assembly Diagram*, lay out 2 A and 1 B segment. Join to make 1 center Nine-Patch unit. Make 20 center units.

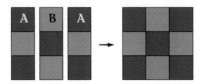

Nine-Patch Assembly Diagram

4. Referring to *Strip Set C Diagram*, join 2 cream print and 1 solid cream strip as shown to make strip

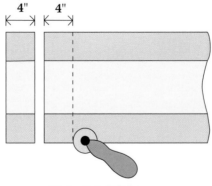

Strip Set C Diagram

Set C. Make 4 Strip Sets C. Cut sets into 40 (4"-wide) C segments.

5. Referring to *Block Assembly Diagram*, lay out 1 center unit, 2 C segments, and 2 Ds. Join into rows; join rows.

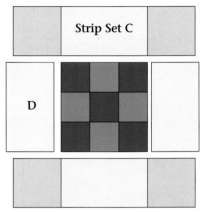

Block Assembly Diagram

6. Referring to *E Placement Pattern* on page 53 and *Block Diagram*, appliqué 4 blue and 8 brown Es as shown to complete 1 Honeybee block.

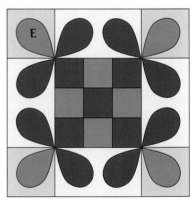

Block Diagram

7. Make 20 Honeybee Blocks.

Quilt Assembly

1. Lay out blocks, sashing, and sashing squares as shown in *Quilt Top Assembly Diagram* on page 53. Join into rows; join rows to complete quilt center.

2. Join 1 cream and 1 brown border strips along long side to make 1 border strip. Make 4 border strips.

3. With cream strip next to quilt, center each border on quilt sides and add. Miter corners.

Quilting and Finishing

1. Divide backing fabric into 3 (2½-yard) lengths. Join to make backing. Seams will run horizontally.

2. Layer backing, batting, and quilt top; baste. Quilt as desired. Quilt shown is outline-quilted in piecework, with appliqué quilted in-the-ditch. Sashing has a chain pattern, and sashing squares feature an eight pointed star pattern. (See page 54 for quilting patterns.) Borders are quilted in diagonal fill.

3. For straight corners: Cut 10 (2¼"-wide) brown strips. Join into 1 continuous piece for straight-grain French-fold binding. Add binding to quilt.

4. For rounded corners: Make 400" of 2¼"-wide bias strip from 1 (35") brown square. Fold to make bias French-fold binding. Add binding to quilt. Round corners after applying binding to front of quilt. Stitch binding to back.

Quilt Top Assembly Diagram

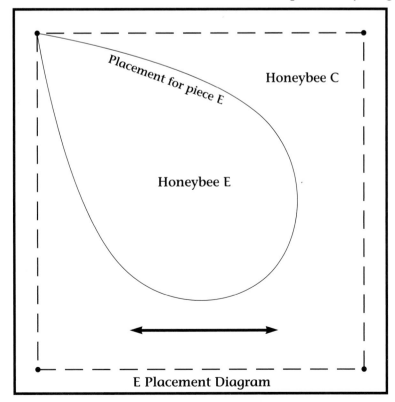

Placement for piece E

Honeybee C

Honeybee E

E Placement Diagram

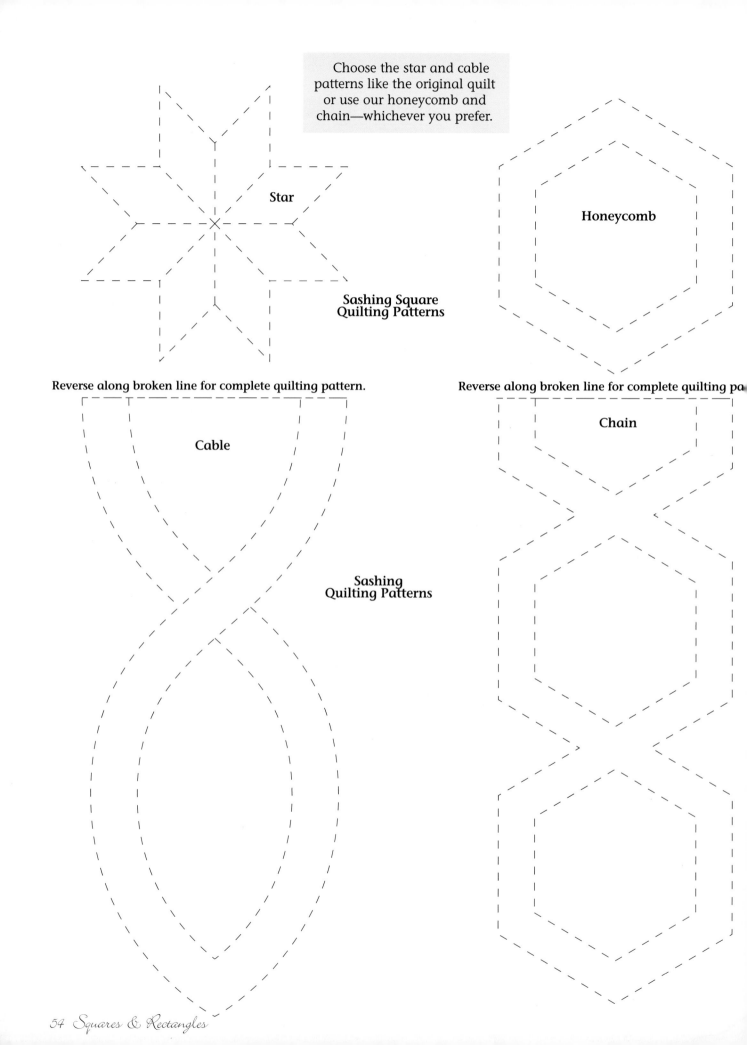

Choose the star and cable patterns like the original quilt or use our honeycomb and chain—whichever you prefer.

Star

Honeycomb

Sashing Square
Quilting Patterns

Reverse along broken line for complete quilting pattern.

Reverse along broken line for complete quilting pa

Cable

Chain

Sashing
Quilting Patterns

Puss in the Corner

Cats and quilts just seem to go together. Perhaps because the quiltmaker spends so much time working on a quilt, a cat is happy to nestle in a soft bundle that smells like its person. The pattern became popular in the 1930s as an example of this long-lived relationship.

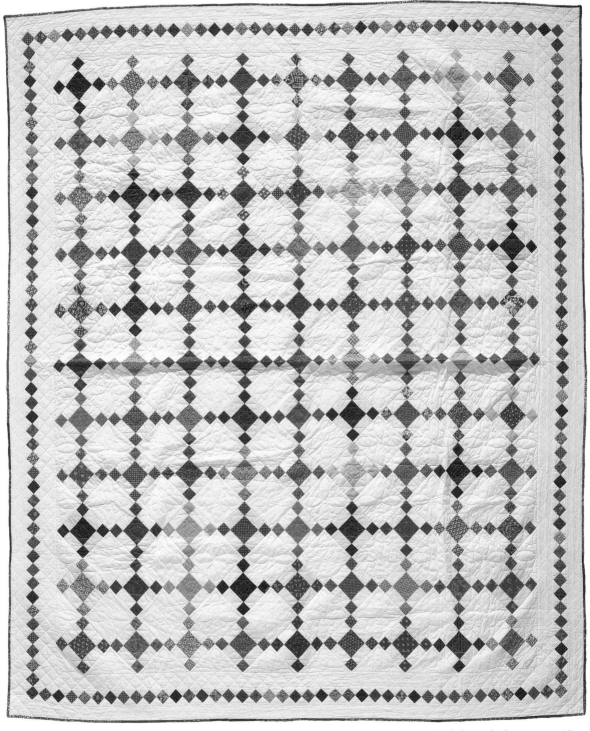

Quilt by Mabeth H. Oxenreider

Finished Quilt Size
89" x 106"

Number of Blocks and Finished Size
99 (6") Puss in the Corner Blocks

Materials
4 yards total assorted red prints for blocks and pieced border

8 yards off white for blocks and borders

8¼ yards backing

Queen-size batting

Cutting
Measurements include ¼" seam allowances.

From red prints, cut:
- 99 sets of:
  - 1 (3½") A square.
  - 4 (2") C squares.
- 172 (2") assorted C squares for pieced border.
- For straight-grain binding, cut 11 (2¼"-wide) assorted strips.
- For candy-stripe binding, cut 16 (3"-wide) assorted strips.

From off white, cut:
- 20 (2⅝"-wide) strips. Piece strips to make 2 (2⅝" x 100") side inner borders, 2 (2⅝" x 82") top and bottom inner borders, 2 (2⅝" x 108") side outer borders, and 2 (2⅝" x 92") top and bottom outer borders.
- 20 (3½"-wide) strips. Cut strips into 396 (2" x 3½") B rectangles for blocks.
- 14 (6½"-wide) strips. Cut strips into 80 (6½") setting squares.
- 3 (9¾"-wide) strips. Cut strips into 9 (9¾") squares. Cut squares in quarters diagonally to make 36 side setting triangles.
- From remainder, cut 2 (5⅛") squares. Cut squares in half diagonally to make 4 corner setting triangles.
- 8 (3⅜"-wide) strips. Cut strips into 84 (3⅜") squares. Cut squares in quarters diagonally to make 336 D triangles.
- 1 (2"-wide) strip. Cut strip into 8 (2") squares. Cut squares in half diagonally to make 16 E triangles.

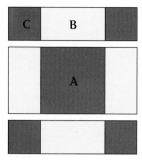

Block Assembly Diagram

Block Assembly

1. Referring to *Block Assembly Diagram,* lay out 1 set of red pieces (1 A, 4 Cs) with 4 Bs. Join into rows; join rows to complete 1 Puss in the Corner block *(Block Diagram).*

2. Make 99 Puss in the Corner blocks.

Block Diagram

Quilt Assembly

1. Lay out blocks and setting pieces as shown in *Quilt Top Assembly Diagram.* Join into diagonal rows; join rows to complete quilt center.

2. Center inner borders on each side of quilt and join. Miter corners.

3. Referring to *Border Unit Diagram,* join 1 D triangle to opposite sides of 1 C square to make 1 border unit. Make 164 border units.

Border Unit Diagram

4. Referring to *Border Assembly Diagram,* join 44 border units. Add 1 C, 1 D, and 2 Es to each end to complete 1 side border. Repeat. Add to sides of quilt.

Border Assembly Diagram

5. Join 38 border units. Add 1 C, 1 D, and 2 Es to each end to complete top border. Repeat for bottom border. Add to quilt.

6. Center outer borders on each side of quilt and join. Miter corners.

Quilting and Finishing

1. Divide backing fabric into 3 (2¾-yard) lengths. Join to make backing. Seams will run horizontally.

2. Layer backing, batting, and quilt top; baste. Quilt as desired. Quilt shown is outline-quilted in blocks and pieced border. Setting squares feature a flower pattern. Outer borders are filled with diagonal grid.

3. For straight-grain binding: Join 2¼"-wide red strips into 1 continuous piece for straight-grain French-fold binding. Add binding to quilt.

4. Candy-stripe binding: Join 3"-wide red strips, offsetting by approximately ½". Press seams to 1 side. Using rotary cutter and 60° marking on ruler, straighten 1 end as shown in *Binding Diagram 1.*

Quilt Top Assembly Diagram

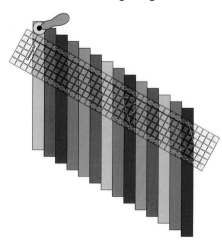

Binding Diagram 1

Cut strips 2¼"-wide. Join strips *(Binding Diagram 2)* and fold to

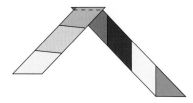

Binding Diagram 2

make candy stripe binding *(Binding Diagram 3).* Add binding to quilt.

Binding Diagram 3

Flower Quilting Pattern

Jack in the Pulpit

Although this quilt name may conjure images of a country preacher in his pulpit, it is actually named after an Appalachian plant used by Native American Indians for medicinal purposes.

Quilt by Lula Ard Reynolds

The original quilt was made with a variety of red prints. In the late 1800s and early 1900s, many red prints were not colorfast and faded to a khaki color after multiple washings. The *Quilt Top Assembly Diagram* (page 62) shows how the quilt would have looked when it was new.

Finished Quilt Size

74" x 81"

Number of Blocks and Finished Size

30 (10") Jack in the Pulpit Blocks

Materials

4 yards solid tan for sashing, borders, and binding
30 fat eighths (9" x 22") assorted red prints for blocks
2¼ yards muslin for blocks
5 yards fabric for backing
Full-size batting

Cutting

Measurements include ¼" seam allowances. Border strips are exact length needed. You may want to cut them longer to allow for piecing variations.

From tan, cut:

- 2⅜ yards. Cut yardage into 10 (3½"-wide) lengthwise strips. Trim strips to make 4 (3½" x 81½") outer side borders, 2 (3½" x 62½") top and bottom borders, 4 (3½" x 75½") vertical sashing strips and 4 (3½" x 10½") short sashing strips.
- 2 (10½"-wide) strips. Cut strips into 21 (3½" x 10½") short sashing strips. You will need a total of 25 short sashing strips.
- 9 (2¼"-wide) strips for binding.

From red prints, cut:

- 30 sets of:
  - 1 (3¾") A square.
  - 2 (1¾" x 5⅛") C strips.
  - 2 (1¾" x 7⅝") D strips.
  - 2 (3⅜") squares. Cut squares in half diagonally to make 4 E triangles.

From muslin, cut:

- 5 (3¼"-wide) strips. Cut strips into 60 (3¼") squares. Cut squares in half diagonally to make 120 B triangles.
- 16 (3⅜"-wide) strips. Cut strips into 180 (3⅜") squares. Cut squares in half diagonally to make 360 E triangles.

Quilt Top Assembly Diagram

Block Assembly

1. Choose 1 set of red pieces. Referring to *Block Assembly Diagram*, join 2 B triangles to opposite sides of 1 A square. Join 2 B triangles to remaining sides to make center.

2. Join 2 C strips to opposite sides of center. Add D strips.

3. Join 1 red and 3 muslin E triangles to make 1 corner unit. Make 4 corner units. Join to center in opposite pairs to complete 1 Jack in the Pulpit block *(Block Diagram)*.

4. Make 30 Jack in the Pulpit blocks.

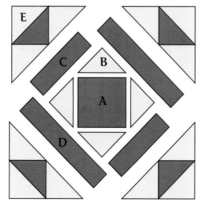

Block Assembly Diagram

Block Diagram

Quilt Assembly

1. Lay out blocks and sashing as shown in *Quilt Top Assembly Diagram.* Join blocks and short sashing strips into vertical rows. Join 5 vertical block rows with 4 vertical sashing strips.

2. Add top and bottom border strips.

3. Join 2 side border strips to make 1 border strip. Repeat. Add to sides to complete quilt.

Quilting and Finishing

1. Divide backing fabric into 2 (2½-yard) lengths. Cut 1 piece in half lengthwise. Sew 1 narrow panel to each side of wide panel. Press seam allowances toward narrow panels.

2. Layer backing, batting, and quilt top; baste. Quilt as desired. Quilt shown is outline-quilted in blocks with a center X. Borders have straight-line quilting.

3. Join tan strips into 1 continuous piece for straight-grain French-fold binding. Add binding to quilt.

In this block, the red fabric has faded to khaki.

A single piece of fabric in this block has faded to khaki.

This block was made with two red prints. One print has faded to khaki.

In this block, the red fabrics have retained their original vibrancy.

Flying Dutchman

Most antique Flying Dutchman quilts are in
mint condition. Their owners did not want to display them
in their homes after Word War II, since the
block resembles the swastika. However, the design is a
centuries-old symbol for good luck or even God.

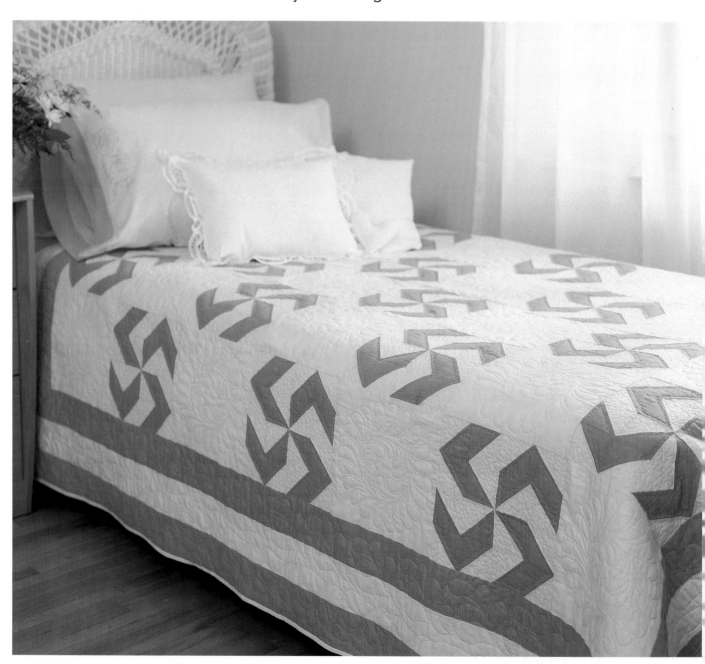

Quiltmaker unknown; purchased from Mary Koval Antiques.
Machine-quilted by New Traditions; owned by Rhonda Richards

Finished Quilt Size
72" x 81"

Number of Blocks and Finished Size
21 (9") Flying Dutchman Blocks

Materials
3½ yards pink
5 yards white
5 yards fabric for backing
Twin-size batting

Cutting
Measurements include ¼" seam allowances.

From pink, cut:
- 2⅜ yards. Cut yardage into 8 (3½"-wide) lengthwise strips for borders.
- From remainder, cut 4 (3⅛"-wide) lengthwise strips. Cut strips into 108 (3⅛"-wide) squares for half-square triangle units.
- 5 (3⅛"-wide) crosswise strips. Cut strips into 60 (3⅛") squares for half-square triangle units. You will need 168 squares total.

From white, cut:
- 2⅜ yards. Cut yardage into 4 (3½"-wide) lengthwise strips for borders.
- From remainder, cut 7 (3⅛"-wide) lengthwise strips. Cut strips into 168 (3⅛") squares for half-square triangle units.
- 6 (9½"-wide) crosswise strips. Cut strips into 21 (9½") setting squares.
- 9 (2¼"-wide) crosswise strips for binding.

Block Assembly
1. On wrong side of 1 white square, draw 1 diagonal line from corner to corner as shown in *Triangle Unit Assembly Diagram*. Place 1 white and 1

Triangle Unit Assembly Diagram

pink square together, right sides facing. Stitch ¼" on both sides of drawn line. Cut apart on drawn line. Press open to make 2 units. Make 16 half-square triangle units.

2. Lay out 4 half-square triangle units as shown in *Corner Unit*

Quilt Top Assembly Diagram

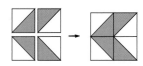

Corner Unit Assembly Diagram

Assembly Diagram. Join to make 1 corner unit. Make 4 corner units.

3. Referring to *Block Assembly Diagram*, lay out 4 corner units. Join to make 1 Flying Dutchman block (*Block Diagram*).

4. Make 21 blocks.

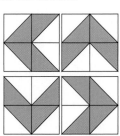

Block Assembly Diagram

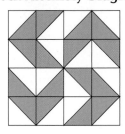

Block Diagram

Quilt Assembly
1. Lay out blocks and setting squares as shown in *Quilt Top Assembly Diagram*. Join into rows; join rows to complete quilt center.

2. Join 2 pink and 1 white strip to make 1 border strip. Make 4 border strips.

3. Center 1 border strip on each side of quilt and join. Miter corners.

Quilting and Finishing
1. Divide backing fabric into 2 (2½-yard) lengths. Cut 1 piece in half lengthwise. Sew 1 narrow panel to each side of wide panel. Press seam allowances toward narrow panels.

2. Layer backing, batting, and quilt top; baste. Quilt as desired. Quilt shown is outline-quilted in waves in pink areas of blocks, with stippling in white background. Setting squares have feathered wreath patterns, and border strips feature a vine and leaf pattern.

3. Join white strips into 1 continuous piece for straight-grain French-fold binding. Add binding to quilt.

Chapter 2

Diamonds & Stars

Star patterns from basic to challenging are among the most common, yet eyecatching, of quilt designs.

- If you're a beginner, *Clay's Choice* on page 80 or *Ohio Star* on page 96 are easy to cut and to assemble.

- If you're an experienced quilter, try one of the quilts with multiple diamonds, such as *Carpenter's Wheel* on page 68, *Rolling Star* on page 106, or *Dove at the Window* on page 110.

- Several quilts in this chapter require set-in seams. That is, the block cannot be assembled with continuous straight seams. The pieces must be set into the openings between previously joined pieces. Refer to pages 354–355 for step-by-step photos and diagrams.

- Diamonds can be rotary-cut or cut with templates. See page 355 for detailed rotary-cutting tips and a how-to photo. The instructions in this chapter include diagrams to remind you how to position the ruler.

All of the quilts in this chapter can be rotary cut. Choose your favorite design, and start your own stellar quilt!

Often a quilt pattern may be known by several different names. For instance, Carpenter's Wheel is sometimes called Dutch Rose, Broken Star, Diadem Star, Double Star, Lone Star of Paradise, Twinkling Stars, Star Within a Star, Sunflower, and Star of Bethlehem.

Finished Quilt Size
81" x 108"

Number of Blocks and Finished Size
12 (17") Carpenter's Wheel Blocks

Materials
2¼ yards medium blue for blocks
1⅝ yards light blue for blocks
4 yards muslin for blocks and sashing
4 yards dark blue for sashing, borders, and binding
7½ yards fabric for backing
Queen-size batting

Cutting
Measurements include ¼" seam allowances. Border strips are exact length needed. You may want to cut them longer to allow for piecing variations. If you prefer using templates over rotary-cutting diamonds, patterns are on page 71. Or use the templates to check the accuracy of your cutting.

From medium blue, cut:
• 4 (3"-wide) strips. Cut strips into 48 (3") A squares.
• 24 (2¼"-wide) strips. Referring to *Cutting Diamonds Diagram* and

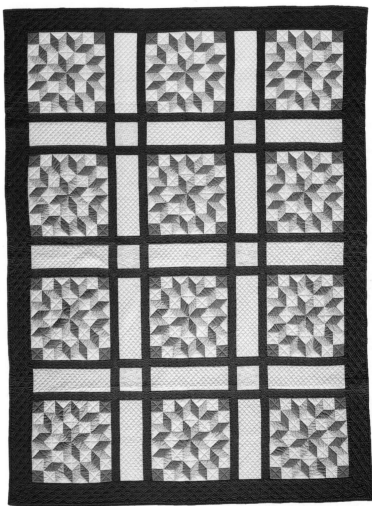

Quilt by Betty Ekern Suiter

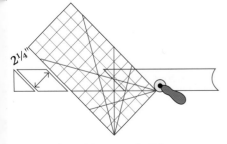

Cutting Diamonds Diagram

using 45° marker on ruler, trim 1 end of strip. Cut 192 (2¼"-wide) B diamonds.

From light blue, cut:
• 24 (2¼"-wide) strips. Referring to *Cutting Diamonds Diagram* and using 45° marker on ruler, trim 1 end of strip. Cut 192 (2¼"-wide) B diamonds.

From muslin, cut:
• 15 (3"-wide) strips. Cut strips into 192 (3") A squares.
• 3 (4¾"-wide) strips. Cut strips into 24 (4¾") squares. Cut squares in quarters diagonally to make 96 C triangles.
• 10 (6½"-wide) strips. Cut strips into 17 (6½" x 17½") sashing strips and 6 (6½") sashing squares.

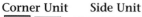

...ark blue, cut:

- ...(2½"-wide) strips. Join in pairs ...nd trim to 2½" x 71½" to make 6 horizontal sashing strips.
- 10 (2½"-wide) strips. Cut strips into 16 (2½" x 17½") sashing strips and 12 (2½" x 6½") sashing strips.
- 10 (5½"-wide) strips. Piece strips to make 2 (5½" x 71½") top and bottom borders and 2 (5½" x 108½") side borders.
- 10 (2¼"-wide) strips for binding.

Block Assembly

Refer to *Block Assembly Diagram* throughout.

Block Assembly Diagram

1. To allow for set-in seams, stitch only on seam lines as indicated on templates. Do not sew to the edge; leave seam allowances loose for ease in joining sections.

2. To make center star, join 1 light blue and 1 medium blue B diamond to make 1 quadrant. Make 4 quadrants. Join to make LeMoyne Star.

3. To make side units, join 1 light blue and 1 medium blue B diamond. Set in 1 muslin A square. Add 2 C triangles as shown to complete 1 side unit. Repeat to make 4 side units.

4. To make corner units, join 1 light blue and 1 medium blue B diamonds. Set in 1 muslin A square. Repeat. Join as shown. Set in 1 muslin and 1 medium blue A squares as shown to make 1 corner unit. Repeat to make 4 corner units.

5. Lay out star, 4 side units, and 4 corner units as shown. Set in side units. Set in corner units to com-

plete 1 Carpenter's Wheel block *(Block Diagram)*.

6. Make 12 Carpenter's Wheel blocks.

Block Diagram

Sashing Unit

Block Row

Quilt Top Assembly Diagram

Quilt Assembly

Refer to *Quilt Top Assembly Diagram* throughout.

1. Join 1 (2½" x 17½") dark blue strip to each long side of 1 (6½" x 17½") muslin sashing strip to make 1 sashing unit. Make 8 sashing units.

2. Alternate 3 blocks and 2 sashing units. Join to make 1 block row. Make 4 block rows.

3. Join 2 (2½" x 6½") dark blue strips to opposite sides of 1 (6½") muslin sashing square to make 1 sashing square unit. Make 6 square units.

4. Alternate 3 (6½" x 17½") sashing strips and 2 square units. Join to make 1 sashing strip.

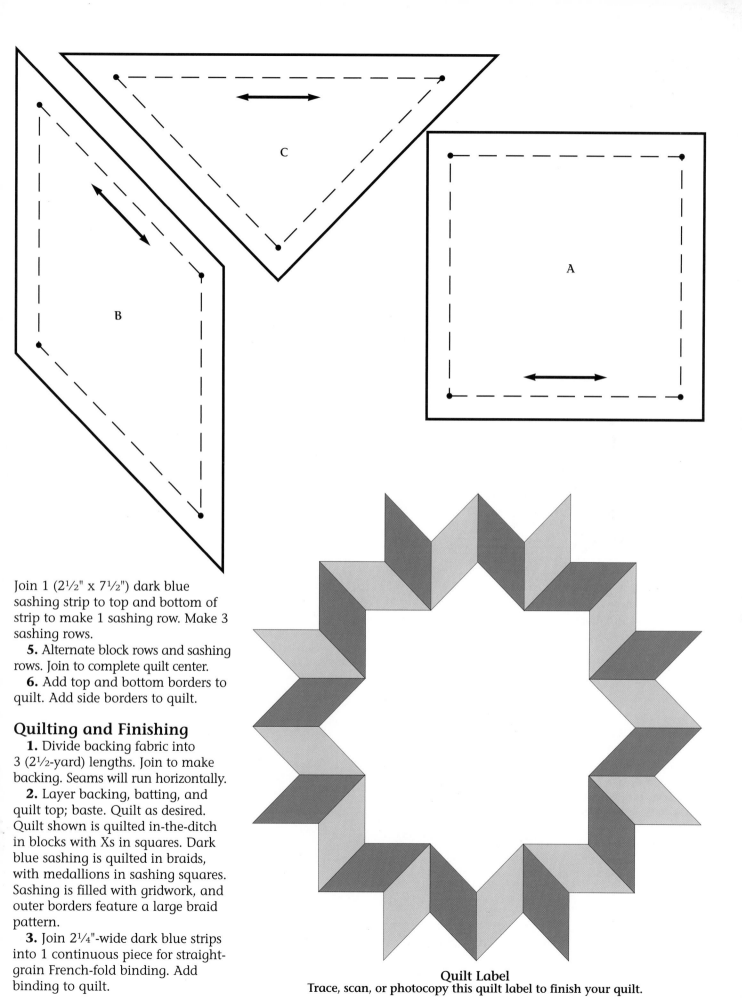

Join 1 (2½" x 7½") dark blue sashing strip to top and bottom of strip to make 1 sashing row. Make 3 sashing rows.

5. Alternate block rows and sashing rows. Join to complete quilt center.

6. Add top and bottom borders to quilt. Add side borders to quilt.

Quilting and Finishing

1. Divide backing fabric into 3 (2½-yard) lengths. Join to make backing. Seams will run horizontally.

2. Layer backing, batting, and quilt top; baste. Quilt as desired. Quilt shown is quilted in-the-ditch in blocks with Xs in squares. Dark blue sashing is quilted in braids, with medallions in sashing squares. Sashing is filled with gridwork, and outer borders feature a large braid pattern.

3. Join 2¼"-wide dark blue strips into 1 continuous piece for straight-grain French-fold binding. Add binding to quilt.

Quilt Label
Trace, scan, or photocopy this quilt label to finish your quilt.

Hands All Around

Quilting bees were occasions for people to come together
to perform many essential tasks. While the women quilted,
the men might gather hay or raise a barn. The group workday often
ended with a rollicking square dance. From this social activity came
several quilt names, including Hands All Around.

Quilt by Lorene Payne

Finished Quilt Size
78" x 96½"

Number of Blocks and Finished Size
20 (14") Hands All Around Blocks

Materials
2¾ yards dark brown print for blocks
2 yards cream for blocks
5 yards rust for blocks, sashing, and border
2 yards light print for block centers, sashing squares, and binding
6 yards fabric for backing
Queen-size batting

Cutting
Measurements include ¼" seam allowances. Border strips are exact length needed. You may want to cut them longer to allow for piecing variations. Patterns are on pages 74–75.

From dark brown print, cut:
• 40 (2¼"-wide) strips. Trim 1 end of strip at 45° angle, using marking on ruler. Referring to *Cutting Diamonds Diagram,* cut strips into 320 (2¼"-wide) A diamonds. (Check your cutting accuracy by placing a cut piece on Template A.)

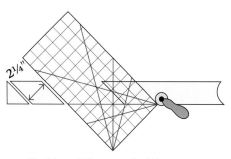

Cutting Diamonds Diagram

From cream, cut:
• 5 (4¾"-wide) strips. Cut strips into 40 (4¾") squares. Cut squares in quarters diagonally to make 160 B triangles.
• 13 (3"-wide) strips. Cut strips into 160 (3") C squares.

From rust, cut:
• 9 (4½"-wide) strips. Piece strips to make 2 (4½" x 89") side borders and 2 (4½" x 78½") top and bottom borders.
• 16 (4½"-wide) strips. Cut strips into 31 (4½" x 15") sashing strips.
• 80 Ds.

From light print, cut:
• 2 (4½"-wide) strips. Cut strips into 12 (4½") sashing squares.
• 20 Es.
• 10 (2¼"-wide) strips for binding.

Block Assembly
Refer to *Block Assembly Diagram* throughout.

1. Join 4 A diamonds to make 1 half star. Set in 2 B triangles and 1 C square as shown to make 1 corner unit. Make 4 corner units.

2. Join 1 D to each side of 1 E to make center.

3. Lay out center, corner units, and 4 C squares. Join, setting in seams, to complete 1 Hands All Around block (*Block Diagram*).

4. Make 20 Hands All Around blocks.

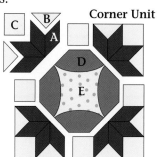

Block Assembly Diagram

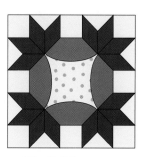

Block Diagram

Quilt Assembly

Refer to *Quilt Top Assembly Diagram* throughout.

1. Alternate 4 blocks and 3 sashing strips. Join to make 1 block row. Make 5 block rows.

2. Alternate 4 sashing strips and 3 sashing squares. Join to make 1 sashing row. Make 4 sashing rows.

3. Alternate block rows and sashing rows. Join to complete quilt center.

4. Add side borders to quilt. Add top and bottom borders.

Quilting and Finishing

1. Divide backing fabric into 2 (3-yard) lengths. Cut 1 piece in half lengthwise. Sew 1 narrow panel to each side of wide panel. Press seam allowances toward narrow panels.

Block Row
Sashing Row

Quilt Top Assembly Diagram

2. Layer backing, batting, and quilt top; baste. Quilt as desired. Quilt shown is outline-quilted in blocks. Sashing and borders feature a diamond pattern.

3. Join 2¼"-wide light print strips into 1 continuous piece for straight-grain French-fold binding. Add binding to quilt.

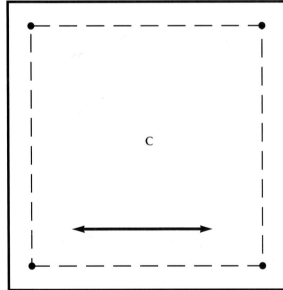

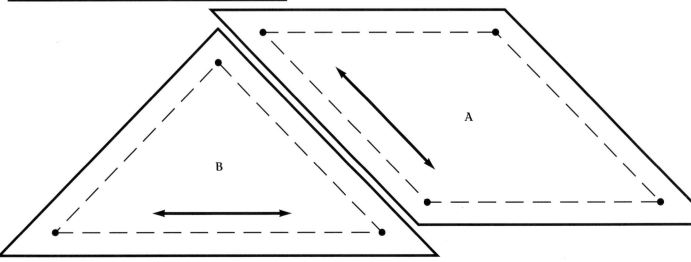

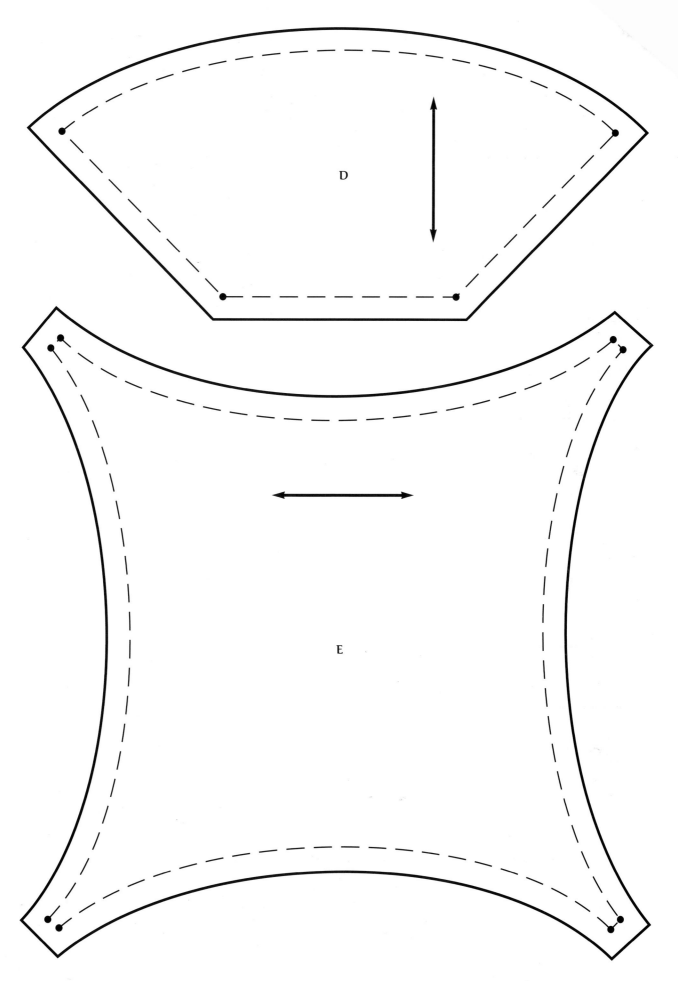

D

E

Feathered Star

This pattern is named Feathered Star because each
point of the block is "feathered" with smaller triangles.
The pattern probably originated in northern England; but by the
late 19th and early 20th centuries, it was enjoying widespread
popularity among American quilters.

Quilt by Patricia Knapp, owned by Linda Edington

Finished Quilt Size
43¼" x 43¼"

Number of Blocks and Finished Size
4 (14") Feathered Star Blocks

Materials
1¼ yards large black floral print for block centers, border, and binding
1 fat quarter (18" x 22") small black floral print for blocks
1¼ yards teal print for blocks and border
¼ yard rose print for border
1½ yard light brown print for background and border
2½ yards fabric for backing
Crib-size batting

Cutting
Measurements include ¼" seam allowances. Border strips are exact length needed. You may want to cut them longer to allow for piecing variations. Patterns are on page 79.

From large black floral print, cut:
- 5 (3½"-wide) strips. Trim and piece strips to make 2 (3½" x 37¾") outer side borders and 2 (3½" x 43¾") outer top and bottom borders.
- 1 (4½"-wide) strip. Cut strip into 4 (4½") A squares. You may center square on a floral motif if desired.
- 5 (2¼"-wide) strips for binding.

From small black floral print, cut:
- 3 (1½" x 22") strips. Cut strips into 32 (1½") C squares.
- 6 (1⅞" x 22") strips. Cut strips into 64 (1⅞") squares for D units.

From teal print, cut:
- 4 (2½"-wide) strips. Cut strips into 16 Bs and 16 Bs reversed.
- 2 (1½"-wide) strips. Trim 1 end of strip at 45° angle, using marking on ruler. Referring to *Cutting Diamonds Diagram,* cut strips into 32 (1½"-wide) E diamonds.
- 7 (1⅞"-wide) strips. Cut strips into 74 (1⅞") squares for border units.
- 8 (1"-wide) strips for inner borders.

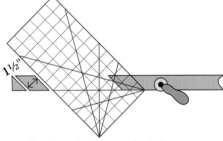

Cutting Diamonds Diagram

From rose print, cut:
- 4 (¾"-wide) strips for inner borders.
- 1 (1¾"-wide) strip. Cut strip into 13 (1¾") squares for sashing squares and inner border corners.

From light brown print, cut:
- 9 (1⅞"-wide) strips. Cut strips into 170 (1⅞") squares. Cut 32 squares in half diagonally to make 64 D triangles. Hold 138 squares for D units and border units.
- 2 (4⅝"-wide) strips. Cut strips into 16 (4⅝") F squares.
- 1 (7¼"-wide) strip. Cut strips into 4 (7¼") squares. Cut squares in quarters diagonally to make 16 G triangles.

- 6 (1¾"-wide) strips. Cut strips into 12 (1¾" x 14½") sashing strips.
- 4 (1"-wide) strips. Trim strips to make 2 (1" x 36¾") top and bottom borders and 2 (1" x 37¾") side borders.

Block Assembly
Refer to *Block Assembly Diagram* throughout.

1. Referring to *Triangle-Square Diagram,* draw a diagonal line from corner to corner on back of 16 light brown 1⅞" squares. Place 1 light

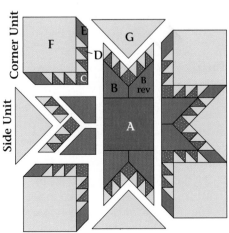

Block Assembly Diagram

brown and 1 small black floral square together, right sides facing. Stitch ¼" from line on both sides. Cut apart and press open to make 2 D units. Make 32 D units.

Triangle-Square Diagram

2. To make corner units, join 2 D units, 1 light brown D triangle, and 1 E into a strip, referring to diagram for unit orientation. Repeat. Add 1 C square to second strip. Join strips to 1 F as shown to make 1 corner unit. Make 4 corner units.

3. To make side units, join 2 D units and 1 light brown D triangle as shown. Repeat. Add 1 C square to second strip. Join strips to 1 G triangle as shown, leaving outer seam allowances loose. Add 1 B and 1 B reversed as shown to make 1 side unit. Make 4 side units.

4. Lay out side units, corner units, and 1 A square. Join into rows; join rows. Complete triangle seams to complete 1 Feathered Star block *(Block Diagram).*

5. Make 4 Feathered Star blocks.

Quilt Top Assembly Diagram

Block Diagram

Quilt Assembly
Refer to *Quilt Top Assembly Diagram* throughout.

1. Lay out blocks with sashing strips and sashing squares. Join into rows; join rows to complete center.

2. Join 2 teal and 1 rose strips. Trim to 32¼" long to make inner border strip. Make 4 inner border strips. Join 1 strip to opposite sides

of center. Add 1 rose square to opposite ends of remaining strips. Add to top and bottom of quilt.

3. Draw a diagonal line from corner to corner on back of 74 light brown 1⅞" squares. Place 1 light brown and 1 teal squares together, right sides facing. Stitch ¼" from line on both sides. Cut apart and press open to make 2 border D units. Make 148 border units.

4. Join 36 border units as shown to make pieced side border. Repeat. Add to sides of quilt, adjusting seams to fit as needed.

5. Join 38 border units to make pieced top border. Repeat for bottom border. Add to quilt, adjusting seams to fit as needed.

6. Add light brown top and bottom borders to quilt. Add light brown side borders.

7. Add black floral outer side borders to quilt. Add black floral top and bottom borders.

Quilting and Finishing
1. Divide backing fabric into 2 (1¼-yard) lengths. Cut 1 piece in half lengthwise. Sew 1 narrow panel to 1 side of wide panel. Press seam allowances toward narrow panel. Remaining panel is extra and may be used to make a hanging sleeve.

2. Layer backing, batting, and quilt top; baste. Quilt as desired. Quilt shown is quilted in-the-ditch in block pieces and pieced borders. Block backgrounds have a pinwheel pattern, and outer border has a diamond pattern. (See patterns on templates F and G, opposite page.)

3. Join 2¼"-wide black floral strips into 1 continuous piece for straight-grain French-fold binding. Add binding to quilt.

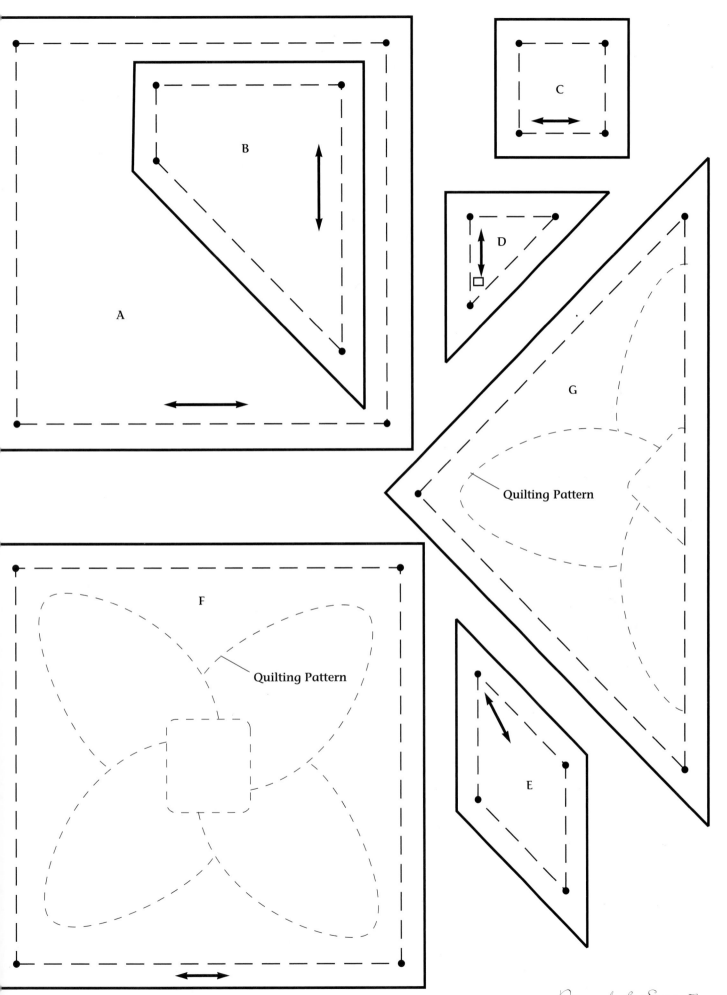

A

B

C

D

E

F

Quilting Pattern

G

Quilting Pattern

Clay's Choice

This quilt block was probably named for Henry Clay,
a 19th-century patriot and politician who founded the
Whig party. Other names for the pattern include
Clay's Star, Clay's Favorite, Henry of the West, and Harry's Star.

Quilt by Jean Briggs

Finished Quilt Size
75" x 90"

Number of Blocks and Finished Size
20 (12") Clay's Choice Blocks

Materials
2¼ yards light navy print
4½ yards dark navy print
1½ yards solid red
5½ yards fabric for backing
Full-size batting

Cutting
Measurements include ¼" seam allowances. Border strips are exact length needed. You may want to cut them longer to allow for piecing variations.

From light navy print, cut:
- 8 (1½"-wide) strips. Piece to make 2 (1½" x 78½") side borders and 2 (1½" x 63½") top and bottom borders.
- 8 (3½"-wide) strips. Cut strips into 80 (3½") A squares.
- From remainder, cut 4 (2½") border corner squares.
- 8 (3⅞"-wide) strips. Cut strips into 80 (3⅞") squares for B triangles.

From dark navy print, cut:
- 22 (3½"-wide) strips. Piece to make 5 (3½" x 72½") vertical sashing strips, 2 (3½" x 63½") inner top and bottom borders, 2 (3½" x 84½") outer side borders and 2 (3½" x 69½") outer top and bottom borders.
- 6 (3½"-wide) strips. Cut strips into 16 (3½" x 12½") sashing strips.
- From remainder, cut 4 (1½") border corner squares.
- 8 (3⅞"-wide) strips. Cut strips into 80 (3⅞") squares for B triangles.
- 9 (2¼"-wide) strips for binding.

From solid red, cut:
- 8 (2½"-wide) strips. Piece to make 2 (2½" x 80½") side borders and 2 (2½" x 65½") top and bottom borders.
- 8 (3½"-wide) strips. Cut strips into 80 (3½") A squares and 4 (3½") border corner squares.

Block Assembly
1. Referring to *Triangle-Square Diagram*, draw a diagonal line from corner to corner on back of light navy 3⅞" squares. Place 1 light navy and 1 dark navy squares together, right sides facing. Stitch ¼" from line on both sides. Cut apart and press open to make 2 B units. Make 160 B units.

2. Referring to *Block Assembly Diagram*, lay out 8 B units, 4 red A squares, and 4 light navy A squares. Join into quadrants as

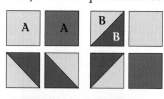

Triangle-Square Diagram

Block Assembly Diagram

Quilt Top Assembly Diagram

Block Diagram

shown. Join quadrants to make 1 Clay's Choice block *(Block Diagram)*.

3. Make 20 Clay's Choice blocks.

Quilt Assembly

1. Lay out blocks and sashing strips as shown in *Quilt Top Assembly Diagram.* Join blocks and short sashing strips into vertical rows. Join rows with vertical sashing strips to complete quilt center.

2. Add top and bottom dark navy borders to quilt.

3. Add light navy side borders to quilt. Add dark navy squares to ends of remaining light navy border strips. Add to top and bottom of quilt.

4. Add red side borders to quilt. Add light navy squares to ends of remaining red border strips. Add to top and bottom of quilt.

5. Add dark navy side borders to quilt. Add red squares to ends of remaining dark navy border strips. Add to top and bottom of quilt.

Quilting and Finishing

1. Divide backing fabric into 2 (2¾-yard) lengths. Cut 1 piece in half lengthwise. Sew 1 narrow panel to each side of wide panel.

Press seam allowances toward narrow panels.

2. Layer backing, batting, and quilt top; baste. Quilt as desired. Quilt shown is outline-quilted in diamonds, with flowers in red squares. Block corner squares are quilted with a cathedral windows pattern. Borders and sashing have a chain pattern. (Quilting patterns are shown on this page.)

3. Join 2¼"-wide dark navy strips into 1 continuous piece for straight-grain French-fold binding. Add binding to quilt.

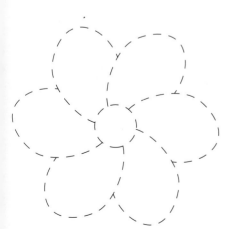

Flower Quilting Pattern

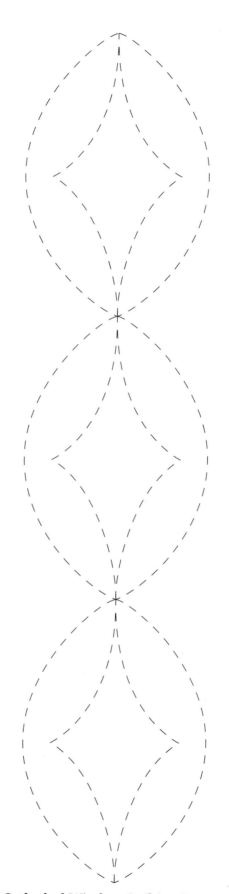

Cathedral Window Quilting Pattern

Chain Quilting Pattern

Mexican Star

Mexican Star commemorates the Mexican War of 1846–1848, which resulted from the U.S. annexation of Texas in 1845. When the treaty was signed in 1848, the U.S. gained all Mexican territory north of the Rio Grande River from Texas to the Pacific Ocean.

Finished Quilt Size
72½" x 87"

Number of Blocks and Finished Size
30 (14½") Mexican Star Blocks

Materials
2¾ yards total assorted red prints (or 30 fat eighths*)
30 (2½"-wide) strips assorted blue prints (or 10 fat eighths*)
3½ yards total assorted light prints (or 30 fat eighths*)
⅝ yards blue for binding
5½ yards fabric for backing
Full-size batting
*Fat eighth = 9" x 22"

Cutting
Measurements include ¼" seam allowances. Pattern is on page 86.

From assorted red prints, cut:
• 30 sets of 5 (2½") E squares.
• 30 sets of 4 (2½" x 8") A strips.

From each strip of blue print, cut:
• 4 Cs and 4 Cs reversed.

From assorted light prints, cut:
• 30 sets of 4 (2½") E squares.
• 30 sets of 4 (3¾") squares. Cut squares in half diagonally to make 30 sets of 8 B triangles.
• 30 (7¼") squares. Cut squares in quarters diagonally to make 30 sets of 4 D triangles.

From blue, cut:
• 9 (2¼"-wide) strips for binding.

Block Assembly
1. Referring to *Nine-Patch Assembly Diagram*, lay out 5 red and 4 light E squares. Join to make center Nine-Patch.

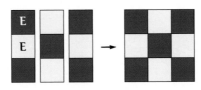

Nine-Patch Assembly Diagram

2. Referring to *Corner Unit Assembly Diagram*, join 1 B to 1 C. Repeat with 1 B and 1 C reversed. Place on each side of 1 A strip and join to make corner unit. Make 4 corner units.

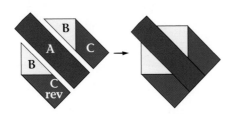

Corner Unit Assembly Diagram

3. Referring to *Block Assembly Diagram*, lay out center, corner units, and D triangles. Join as shown. Trim block to 15" x 15" to complete 1 Mexican Star block *(Block Diagram)*.
4. Make 30 Mexican Star blocks.

Quilt Assembly
1. Referring to *Quilt Top Assembly Diagram*, lay out blocks in 6 horizontal rows of 5 blocks each.
2. Join into rows; join rows to complete quilt.

Block Assembly Diagram

Block Diagram

Quilting and Finishing
1. Divide backing fabric into 2 (2¾-yard) lengths. Cut 1 piece in half lengthwise. Sew 1 narrow panel to each side of wide panel. Press seam allowances toward narrow panels.
2. Layer backing, batting, and quilt top; baste. Quilt as desired. Quilt shown is outline-quilted, with stars in light areas between blocks.
3. Join blue strips into 1 continuous piece for straight-grain French-fold binding. Add binding to quilt.

Quilt Top Assembly Diagram

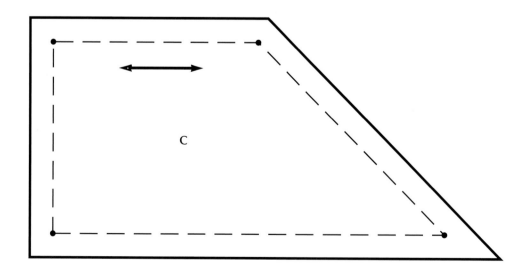

C

Quilt by Milly Splitstone

Using a variety of fabrics keeps the eye moving across this quilt.

Delectable Mountains

The name of this quilt pattern comes from John Bunyan's *The Pilgrim's Progress*, a religious allegory published in 1678. Along with the Bible, this was one of the few books considered appropriate for young women in Colonial society to read. Because the Delectable Mountains in the story represent a place of great beauty, it seems appropriate that quilters should give the name to a beautiful quilt pattern.

Quilt by Mildred Winnick Estrin

Finished Quilt Size
96" x 111"

Number of Blocks and Finished Size
30 (12") Delectable Mountains Blocks

Materials
7 yards solid brown for blocks, sashing, and borders

4¼ yards brown print for blocks, sashing squares and prairie points

4 yards muslin for blocks and prairie points.

8¼ yards fabric for backing

King-size batting

Cutting
Measurements include ¼" seam allowances.

From solid brown, cut:
- 3¼ yards. Cut yardage into 4 (9½" x 117") lengthwise border strips.
- 24 (3½"-wide) strips. Cut strips into 71 (3½" x 12½") sashing strips.
- 2 (2⅝"-wide) strips. Cut strips into 30 (2⅝") A squares.
- 3 (3⅜"-wide) strips. Cut strips into 30 (3⅜") squares. Cut squares in quarters diagonally to make 120 B triangles.
- 5 (3"-wide) strips. Cut strips into 60 (3") squares. Cut squares in half diagonally to make 120 C triangles.

From brown print, cut:
- 23 (2⅜"-wide) strips. Cut strips into 360 (2⅜") squares for F border units.
- 9 (5⅜"-wide) strips. Cut strips into 60 (5⅜") squares. Cut squares in half diagonally to make 120 D triangles.
- 4 (3½"-wide) strips. Cut strips into 42 (3½") sashing squares.
- 8 (3"-wide) strips. Cut strips into 104 (3") squares for prairie points.

From muslin, cut:
- 8 (2⅝"-wide) strips. Cut strips into 120 (2⅝") A squares.
- 3 (3⅜"-wide) strips. Cut strips into 30 (3⅜") squares. Cut squares in quarters diagonally to make 120 B triangles.
- 23 (2⅜"-wide) strips. Cut strips

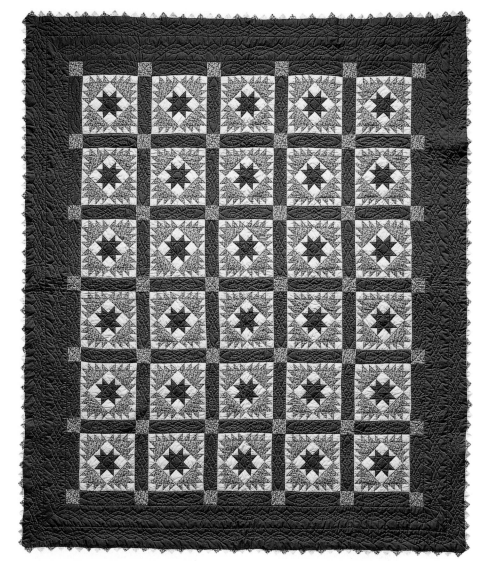

into 360 (2⅜") squares for F border units.
- 6 (2"-wide) strips. Cut strips into 120 (2") E squares.
- 8 (3"-wide) strips. Cut strips into 100 (3") squares for prairie points.

Block Assembly
1. Referring to *Point Assembly Diagram*, join 1 muslin and 1 solid brown B triangles to make triangle. Add 1 C triangle to make point unit. Make 4 point units.

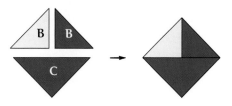

Point Assembly Diagram

2. Referring to *Star Assembly Diagram*, lay out point units, 4 muslin As, and 1 solid brown A. Join into rows; join rows to complete star. Add 1 D triangle to each side to complete block center.

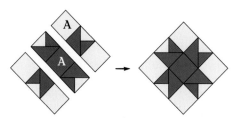

Star Assembly Diagram

3. Referring to *Triangle-Square Diagram*, draw a diagonal line from corner to corner on back of muslin 2⅜" squares. Place 1 muslin and 1 brown print squares together, right sides facing. Stitch ¼" from line on both sides. Cut apart and press

Triangle-Square Diagram

open to make 2 F border units. Make 24 border units.

4. Referring to *Block Assembly Diagram,* lay out block center, border units, and 4 E corner squares. Join into units; join units to complete 1 Delectable Mountains block *(Block Diagram).*

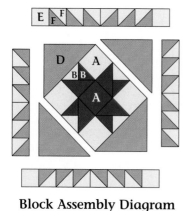

Block Assembly Diagram

5. Make 30 Delectable Mountains blocks.

Block Diagram

Quilt Assembly

1. Referring to *Quilt Top Assembly Diagram,* alternate 6 sashing squares and 5 sashing strips. Join to make 1 sashing row. Make 7 sashing rows.

2. Alternate 6 sashing strips and 5 blocks. Join to make 1 block row. Make 6 block rows.

3. Alternate sashing rows and block rows. Join to complete center.

4. Center 1 border strip on each side of quilt and add. Miter corners.

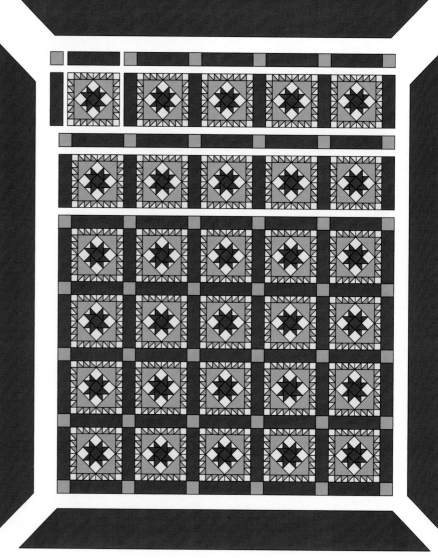

Quilt Top Assembly Diagram

Quilting and Finishing

1. Divide backing fabric into 3 (2¾-yard) lengths. Join to make backing. Seams will run horizontally.

2. Layer backing, batting, and quilt top; baste. Quilt as desired. Quilt shown is outline-quilted, with a cable pattern in sashing and border. Quilting pattern is on page 91.

3. For prairie point edging, fold 3" squares (104 brown print, 100 muslin) diagonally in half *(Prairie Point Diagram 1),* then half again

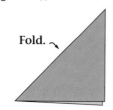

Prairie Point Diagram 1

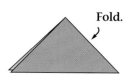

Prairie Point Diagram 2

(Prairie Point Diagram 2). Place on quilt, adjust spacing as shown in *Prairie Point Diagram 3,* and baste in

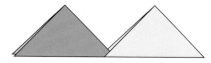

Prairie Point Diagram 3

place, alternating brown print and muslin points. There are 47 points on top and bottom, and 55 points on each side. Folding backing out of the way, stitch prairie points in

place through top and batting
(Prairie Point Diagram 4). Trim

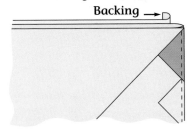

Prairie Point Diagram 4

batting even with quilt top. Trim
backing 1" larger on all sides. Fold
prairie points out, then fold backing
under and whipstitch in place
(Prairie Point Diagram 5).

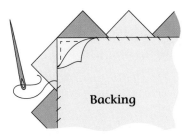

Prairie Point Diagram 5

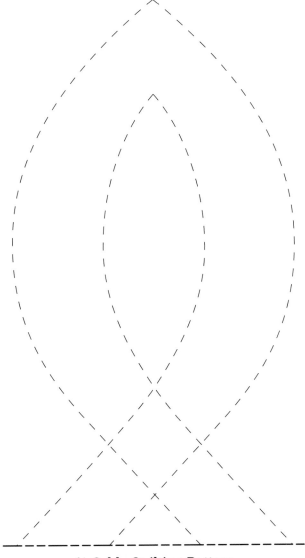

½ Cable Quilting Pattern
Reverse along this line for complete pattern.

Four Winds

The shape of the Four Winds closely resembles markings on old maps. The idea is that the four large diamonds represent the winds from North, South, East, and West. Other names for this pattern include Star and Crescent and Star of the Four Winds.

Finished Quilt Size
73" x 88"

Number of Blocks and Finished Size
20 (15") Four Winds Blocks

Materials
7 yards white for blocks, borders, and binding
3 yards blue for appliqué
5½ yards fabric for backing
Full-size batting

Cutting
Measurements include ¼" seam allowances. Border strips are exact length needed. You may want to cut them longer to allow for piecing variations. Patterns are on pages 94–95.

From white, cut:
• 10 (15½"-wide) strips. Cut strips into 20 (15½") squares for blocks.
• 8 (2"-wide) strips. Piece to make 2 (2" x 75½") inner side borders and 2 (2" x 63½") inner top and bottom borders.
• 8 (5½"-wide) strips. Piece to make 2 (5½" x 78½") outer side borders and 2 (5½" x 73½") outer top and bottom borders.
• 9 (2¼"-wide) strips for binding.

From blue, cut:
• 80 As.
• 80 Bs.
• 94 Cs.

Quilt owned by Mary Lu Ellis

Block Assembly
1. Referring to *Folding Diagram*, fold 1 (15½") square into quarters and press to make guidelines.
2. Place 4 As and 4 Bs as shown in *Block Diagram* and appliqué to make 1 Four Winds block.
3. Make 20 Four Winds blocks.

Folding Diagram

Block Diagram

Quilt Assembly

1. Referring to *Quilt Top Assembly Diagram*, lay out blocks in 5 horizontal rows of 4 blocks each. Join into rows; join rows to complete quilt center.

2. Add inner side borders to quilt. Add inner top and bottom borders.

3. Appliqué 26 Cs on inner edge of 1 outer side border strip. Repeat for second side border. Join to sides of quilt.

4. Appliqué 21 Cs on inner edge of outer top border strip. Repeat for bottom border. Add to quilt.

Quilting and Finishing

1. Divide backing fabric into 2 (2¾-yard) lengths. Cut 1 piece in half lengthwise. Sew 1 narrow panel to each side of wide panel. Press seam allowances toward narrow panels.

2. Layer backing, batting, and quilt top; baste. Quilt as desired. Quilt shown is outline-quilted around blue, with diamond grid quilting fill. White areas have a feathered wreath pattern filled with diamond grid.

3. Join white strips into 1 continuous piece for straight-grain French-fold binding. Add binding to quilt.

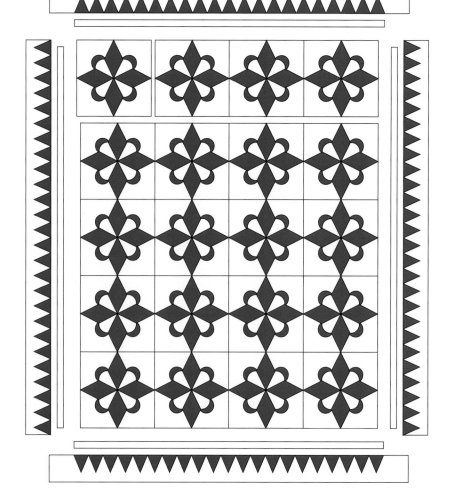

Quilt Top Assembly Diagram

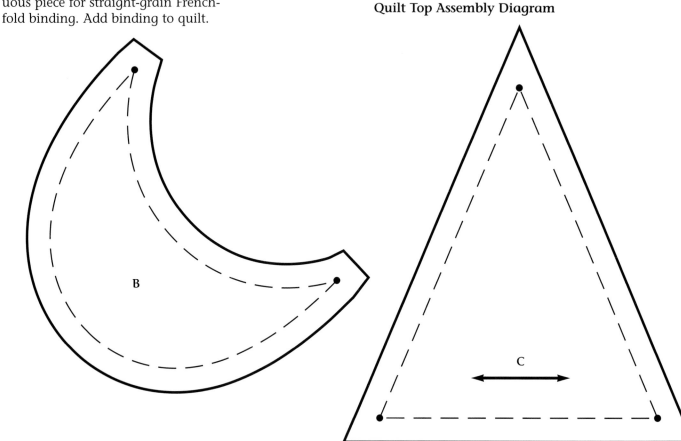

B

C

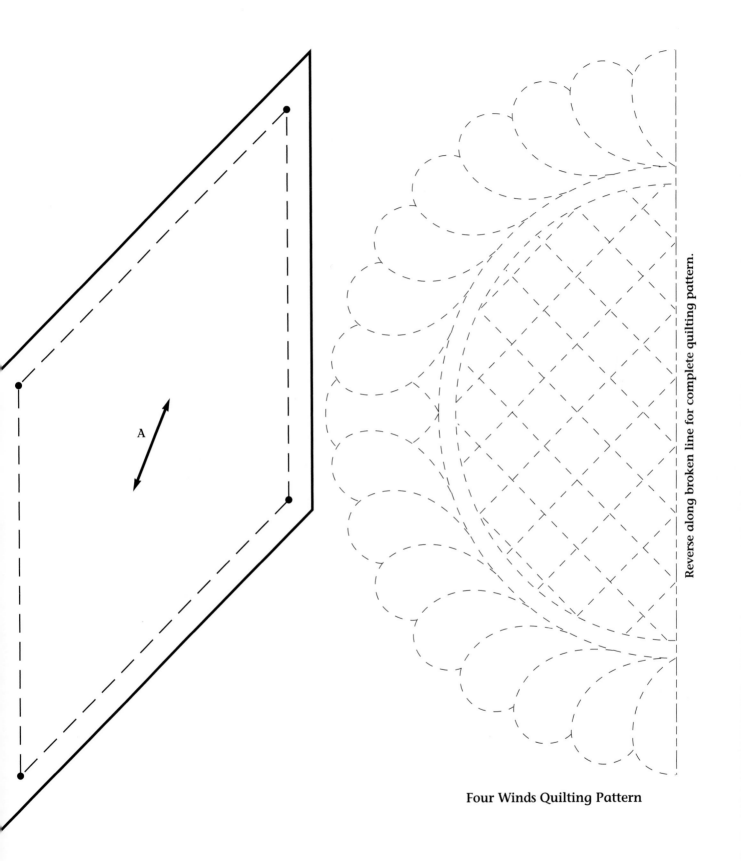

A

Reverse along broken line for complete quilting pattern.

Four Winds Quilting Pattern

Ohio Star

Ohio Star is one of the oldest patchwork patterns.
Examples have been found on English quilts prior to
American colonization. Settlers moving along the Ohio River
into the Northwest Territory called the pattern Ohio Star
in honor of the shining hope the new land brought them.

Finished Quilt Size
92" x 92"

Number of Blocks and Finished Size
36 (12") Ohio Star Blocks

Materials
36 (5" x 16") strips assorted blue prints for blocks
4 yards white for blocks
4 yards blue print for sashing and binding
8¼ yards fabric for backing
King-size batting

Cutting
Measurements include ¼" seam allowances. Sashing strips are exact length needed. You may want to cut them longer to allow for piecing variations. Patterns are on page 98.

From each blue print, cut:
- 1 (4½") A square.
- 2 (5¼") squares. Cut squares in quarters diagonally to make 8 B triangles.

From white, cut:
- 11 (5¼"-wide) strips. Cut strips into 72 (5¼") squares. Cut squares in quarters diagonally to make 288 B triangles.
- 16 (4½"-wide) strips. Cut strips into 144 (4½") A squares.

From blue print, cut:
- 2⅝ yards. Cut yardage into 5 (4½"-wide) lengthwise strips. Trim strips to make 5 (4½" x 92½") horizontal sashing strips.
- From remainder, cut 20 (4½"-wide) widthwise strips (approximately 17½"). Cut strips into 20 (4½" x 12½") sashing strips.
- 4 (4½"-wide) strips. Cut strips into

Quilt by Kate Louck

10 (4½" x 12½") sashing strips. You will need a total of 30 sashing strips.
- 10 (2¼"-wide) strips for binding.

Block Assembly
1. Choose 1 blue set. Join 2 blue and 2 white B triangles to make 1 point unit (*Point Unit Diagram*). Make 4 point units.

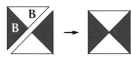

Point Unit Diagram

2. Referring to *Block Assembly Diagram*, lay out point units with 1 matching blue A square and 4 white A squares. Join into rows; join

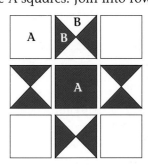

Block Assembly Diagram

rows to complete 1 Ohio Star block
(*Block Diagram*).

3. Make 36 Ohio Star blocks.

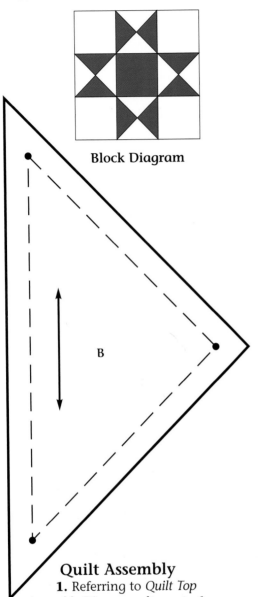

Block Diagram

Quilt Top Assembly Diagram

Quilt Assembly

1. Referring to *Quilt Top Assembly Diagram,* alternate 6 blocks with 5 sashing strips. Join to make 1 block row. Make 6 block rows.

2. Join block rows with long sashing strips to complete quilt.

Quilting and Finishing

1. Divide backing fabric into 3 (2¾-yard) lengths. Join to make backing. Seams will run horizontally.

2. Layer backing, batting, and quilt top; baste. Quilt as desired. Quilt shown is outline-quilted in blocks, with Xs in white areas.

3. Join 2¼"-wide blue print strips into 1 continuous piece for straight-grain French-fold binding. Add binding to quilt.

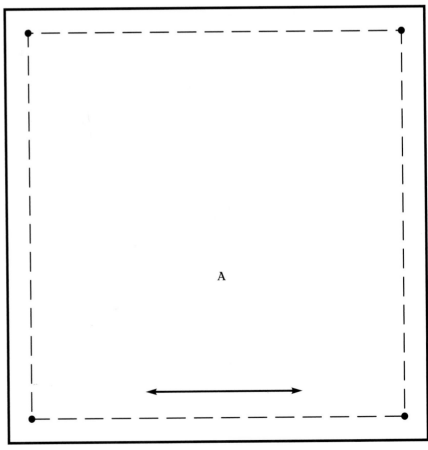

Goose Tracks

Dyes used in the 1800s were made from natural materials and often faded. This quilt began in the popular red and green color scheme. What looks like blue fabric was likely overdyed with yellow to make green. Where the yellow dye has faded, the fabric now looks teal. Reds frequently turned into khaki.

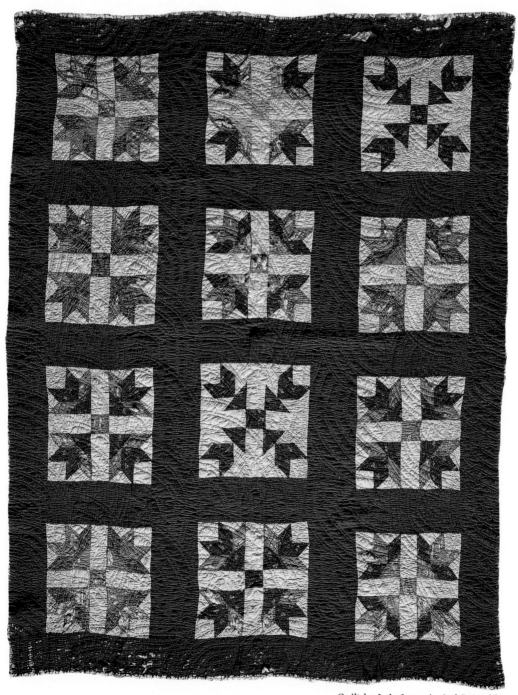

Quilt by Lula Lavonia Ard Reynolds

Finished Quilt Size
61" x 79½"

Number of Blocks and Finished Size
12 (13") Goose Tracks Blocks

Materials
3 yards solid teal for sashing, border, and binding
1½ yards white for blocks
1½ yards teal print for blocks
1 yard brown print for blocks
5 yards fabric for backing
Twin-size batting

Cutting
Measurements include ¼" seam allowances. Border strips are exact length needed. You may want to cut them longer to allow for piecing variations. Patterns are on pages 101–102.

From solid teal, cut:
- 14 (6"-wide) strips. Piece as needed and trim to make 2 (6" x 80") outer side borders, 2 (6" x 50½") outer top and bottom borders, 2 (6" x 69") vertical sashing strips, and 9 (6" x 13½") short sashing strips.
- 8 (2¼"-wide) strips for binding.

From white, cut:
- 4 (3¼"-wide) strips. Cut strips into 48 (3¼") A squares.
- 3 (4"-wide) strips. Cut strips into 24 (4") squares. Cut squares in quarters diagonally to make 96 C triangles.
- 8 (2½"-wide) strips. Cut strips into 48 (2½" x 6") E strips.

From teal print, cut:
- 14 (1⅞"-wide) strips. Cut strips into 48 Bs and 48 Bs reversed.
- 3 (3⅝"-wide) strips. Cut strips into 24 (3⅝") squares. Cut squares in half diagonally to make 48 D triangles.
- From remainder, cut 12 (2½") F squares.

From brown print, cut:
- 14 (1⅞"-wide) strips. Cut strips into 48 Bs and 48 Bs reversed.

Block Assembly

1. Referring to *Block Assembly Diagram,* join 1 teal B and 1 brown print B reversed. Set in C triangle. Repeat to make another unit as shown. Join, then set in 1 A square. Add 1 D triangle to make 1 quadrant. Make 4 quadrants.

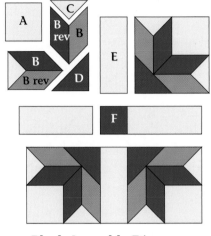

Block Assembly Diagram

2. Lay out quadrants with 4 E strips and 1 F square. Join into rows; join rows to complete 1 Goose Tracks block *(Block Diagram).*

3. Make 12 Goose Tracks blocks.

Block Diagram

Quilt Assembly

1. Referring to *Quilt Top Assembly Diagram,* alternate 4 blocks with 3 short sashing strips. Join to make 1 vertical block row. Make 3 vertical block rows.

2. Alternate block rows with sashing strips. Join to complete quilt center.

3. Add top and bottom borders to quilt. Add side borders to quilt.

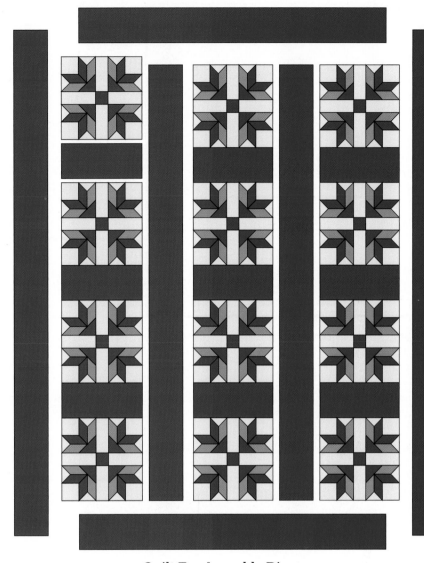

Quilt Top Assembly Diagram

Quilting and Finishing

1. Divide backing fabric into 2 (2½-yard) lengths. Cut 1 length into 1 (30"-wide) lengthwise panel. Sew 30"-wide panel to 1 side of wide panel. Press seam allowance toward narrow panel. Remaining panel is extra and may be used to make a hanging sleeve.

2. Layer backing, batting, and quilt top; baste. Quilt as desired. Quilt shown is quilted in Baptist Fans.

3. Join 2¼"-wide solid teal strips into 1 continuous piece for straight-grain French-fold binding. Add binding to quilt.

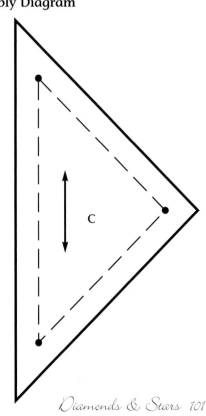

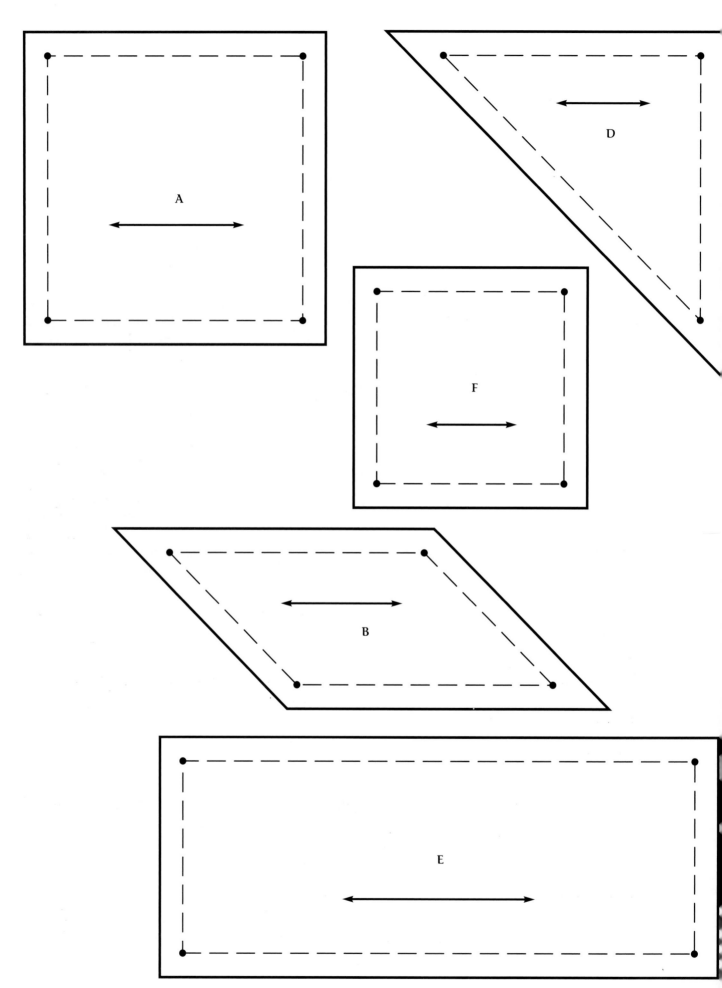

LeMoyne Star

The LeMoyne Star is likely named for the French-Canadian explorer, Pierre LeMoyne. Many American cities now bear his name. He and his brother, Jean-Baptiste LeMoyne, shaped the culture of many cities along the Southern coast.

Quilt by Judith Thompson

Star Blocks

Materials

4 yards solid blue for blocks, borders
  and binding
½ yard yellow print for borders
3½ yards total assorted prints for
  blocks
3½ yards fabric for backing
Twin-size batting

Cutting

Measurements include ¼" seam
allowances. Border strips are exact
length needed. You may want to cut
them longer to allow for piecing
variations. Pattern is on page 105.

From solid blue, cut:

• 7 (6½"-wide) strips. Piece strips to
  make 2 (6½" x 64½") side borders
  and 2 (6½" x 58½") top and
  bottom borders.
• 8 (2¼"-wide) strips for binding.
• 17 (2¼"-wide) strips. Cut strips
  into 280 (2¼") B squares.
• 7 (3¾"-wide) strips. Cut strips into
  70 (3¾") squares. Cut squares in
  quarters diagonally to make 280
  C triangles.

From yellow print, cut:

• 6 (2½"-wide) strips. Piece strips to
  make 2 (2½" x 60½") side borders
  and 2 (2½" x 46½") top and
  bottom borders.

From assorted prints, cut:

• 560 A diamonds. Use template on
  page 105, or cut scraps into 1¾"-
  wide strips. Referring to *Cutting
  Diagram* and using 45° mark on
  ruler, cut strips in 1¾" increments
  to make diamonds.

Block Assembly

1. For each star, select 8 diamonds,
4 triangles, and 4 squares.

2. Following instructions on page
355, make 4 of Unit 1 using
diamonds and triangles.

3. Continue following instructions
on page 355 to make 1 LeMoyne
Star block.

4. Make 70 LeMoyne Star blocks.

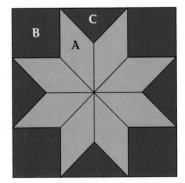

Block Diagram

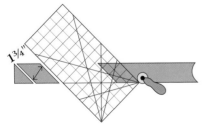

Cutting Diagram

Quilt Assembly

1. Lay out blocks in 10 horizontal rows of 7 blocks each. Join into rows; join rows to complete quilt center.

2. Add yellow side borders to quilt. Add top and bottom borders.

3. Add blue side borders to quilt. Add top and bottom borders.

Quilting and Finishing

1. Divide backing fabric into 2 (1¾-yard) lengths. Cut 1 piece in half lengthwise. Sew 1 narrow panel to each side of wide panel. Press seam allowances toward narrow panels. Seams will run horizontally.

2. Layer backing, batting, and quilt top; baste. Quilt as desired. Quilt shown is quilted in diagonal latticework, with scalloped border patterns.

3. Join 2¼"-wide blue strips into 1 continuous piece for straight-grain French-fold binding. Add binding to quilt.

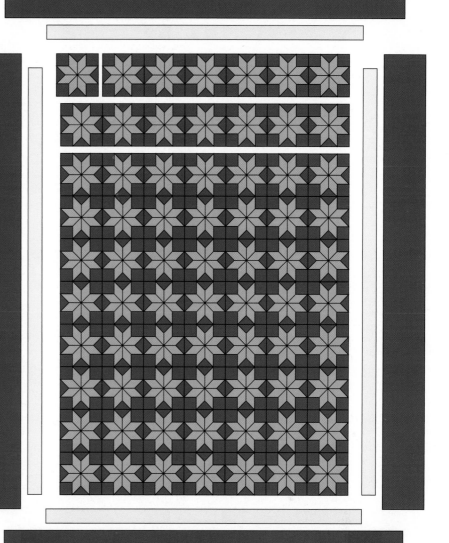

Quilt Top Assembly Diagram

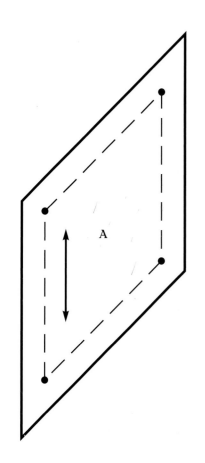

A

Rolling Star

This quilt pattern was first published in *Capper's Weekly* in 1927. While the block center is a basic LeMoyne Star, it is surrounded by set-in diamonds. The blocks must, therefore, be set in to one another, making this a particularly challenging quilt.

Quilt by Mable Azbill Webb; owned by Bradford L. Webb

Finished Quilt Size
96½" x 114½"

Number of Blocks and Finished Size
20 (18") Rolling Star Blocks

Materials
5 yards blue print for blocks and border
5½ yards rust print for blocks and border
5 yards peach print for blocks, border, and binding
8⅝ yards fabric for backing
King-size batting

Cutting
Measurements include ¼" seam allowances. Pattern is on page 109.

From blue print, cut:
- 3¼ yards. Cut yardage into 4 (4½"-wide) lengthwise strips for inner border strips.
- 2 (12"-wide) widthwise strips from remainder. Cut strips into 2 (12") squares. Cut squares in quarters diagonally to make 8 side setting triangles. You will have 2 extra.
- From remainder, cut 1 (6¼") square. Cut square in half diagonally to make 2 corner setting triangles.
- 160 As. Use template on page 109, or cut fabric into 3⅛"-wide strips. Referring to *Cutting Diagram* and using 45° mark on ruler, cut strips in 3⅛"-wide increments to make diamonds.

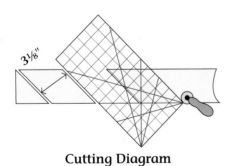

Cutting Diagram

From rust print, cut:
- 3¼ yards. Cut yardage into 4 (6½"-wide) lengthwise strips for middle border strips.
- From remainder, cut 27 (4¼"-wide) widthwise strips. Cut strips into 81 (4¼") B squares.

- 9 (4¼"-wide) strips. Cut strips into 79 (4¼") B squares. You will need 160 total.
- 3 (8"-wide) strips. Cut strips into 12 (8") setting squares.

From peach print, cut:
- 3¼ yards. Cut yardage into 4 (2½"-wide) lengthwise strips for outer border strips.
- 1 (12"-wide) widthwise strip from remainder. Cut strip into 2 (12") squares. Cut squares in quarters diagonally to make 8 side setting triangles.
- From remainder, cut 1 (6¼") square. Cut square in half diagonally to make 2 corner setting triangles.
- 160 As. Use template on page 109, or cut fabric into 3⅛"-wide strips. Referring to *Cutting Diagram* and using 45° mark on ruler, cut strips in 3⅛"-wide increments to make diamonds.
- 12 (2¼"-wide) strips for binding.

Block Assembly
Do not sew into seam allowances.
1. Lay out pieces as shown in *Block Assembly Diagram* for 1 block. Join 1 blue and 1 peach A diamond. Set in 1 B square to make 1 star quadrant. Make 4 star quadrants.

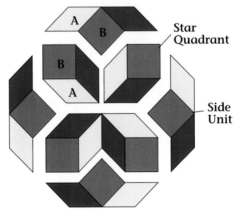

Block Assembly Diagram

2. Join 4 star quadrants.
3. Join 1 blue and 1 peach A diamond to 1 B squares as shown to make side unit. Make 4 side units.
4. Set in side units to complete 1 Rolling Star block (*Block Diagram*).
5. Make 20 Rolling Star blocks.

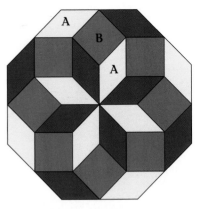

Block Diagram

Quilt Assembly
1. Referring to *Quilt Top Assembly Diagram,* join 4 blocks horizontally to make 1 block row. Make 5 block rows.
2. Add top corner triangles. Set in top row side setting triangles.
3. Set in 3 setting squares and 2 side setting triangles.
4. Set in second row. Continue setting rows; complete quilt top by adding bottom corner setting triangles.
5. Join in order 1 blue, 1 rust, and 1 peach strips to make 1 border strip. Make 4 border strips.
6. Center 1 border strip on each side of quilt, blue edge to inside, and add. Miter corners.

Quilting and Finishing
1. Divide backing fabric into 3 (2⅞-yard) lengths. Join to make backing. Seams will run horizontally.
2. Layer backing, batting, and quilt top; baste. Quilt as desired. Quilt shown is outline-quilted in blocks, with stars in setting squares. Borders feature a chain pattern.
3. Join 2¼"-wide peach strips into 1 continuous piece for straight-grain French-fold binding. Add binding to quilt.

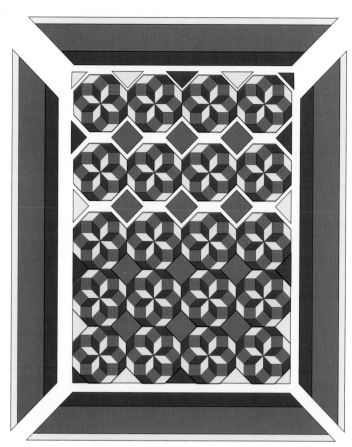

Quilt Top Assembly Diagram

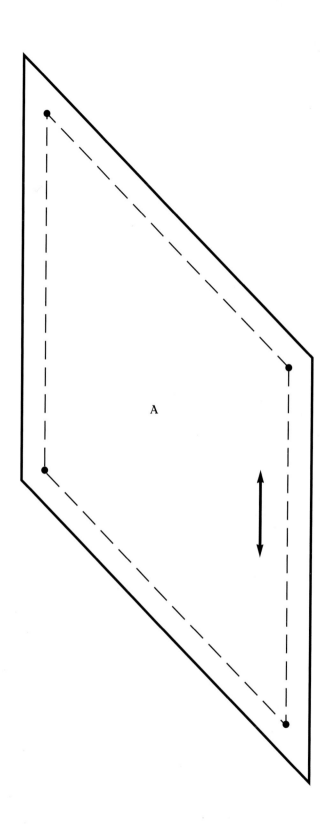

A

Dove at the Window

According to family history, Araminta Jane Marr
made this quilt in 1856, when she was only 18 years old.
Although the fabrics are worn, the quilt is still lovely.
The pattern was later published
in *Mrs. Danner's Quilts, Book 1,* in 1934.

Quilt made by Araminta Jane Marr,
owned by Betty J. Simpson

Finished Quilt Size
80" x 90"

Number of Blocks and Finished Size
36 (10") Dove at the Window Blocks

Materials
5½ yards muslin
1½ yards red print
2¼ yards light brown print
3 yards dark brown print for blocks and binding
7½ yards fabric for backing
Full-size batting

Cutting
Measurements include ¼" seam allowances. Patterns are on page 113.

From muslin, cut:
- 9 (10½"-wide) strips. Cut strips into 36 (10½") setting blocks.
- 12 (4¼"-wide) strips. Cut strips into 108 (4¼") squares. Cut squares in quarters diagonally to make 432 B triangles.
- 10 (2⅝"-wide) strips. Cut strips into 144 (2⅝") D squares.

From red print, cut:
- 4 (3½"-wide) strips. Cut strips into 36 (3½") A squares.
- 10 (2⅝"-wide) strips. Cut strips into 144 (2⅝") D squares for setting blocks.

From light brown print, cut:
- 288 Cs. Or cut fabric into 2"-wide strips. Using the 45° mark on ruler and referring to *Cutting Diagram*, cut strips in 2" increments to make diamonds. Lay pieces over template to check your accuracy.

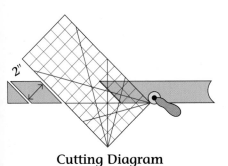

Cutting Diagram

From dark brown print, cut:
- 288 Cs. Or cut fabric into 2"-wide strips. Using the 45° mark on ruler and referring to *Cutting Diagram*, cut strips in 2" increments to make diamonds. Lay pieces over template to check your accuracy.
- 9 (2¼"-wide) strips for binding.

Block Assembly
1. Referring to *Center Assembly Diagram*, join 2 B triangles to opposite sides of 1 A square. Repeat to complete center.

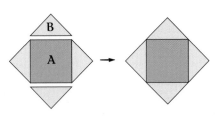

Center Assembly Diagram

2. Referring to *Corner Unit Assembly Diagram*, join 2 dark brown and 2 light brown C diamonds as shown. Set in 2 B triangles. Set in 1 D square to make 1 corner unit. Make 4 corner units.

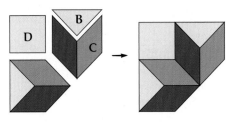

Corner Unit Assembly Diagram

3. Lay out corner units and center as shown in *Block Assembly Diagram* on page 112. Join, setting in side seams, to make 1 Dove at the Window block (*Block Diagram*).

4. Make 36 Dove at the Window blocks.

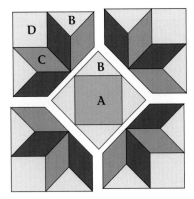

Block Assembly Diagram

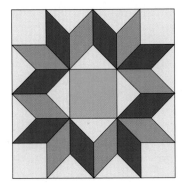

Block Diagram

5. Referring to *Diagonal Seams Diagram*, place 1 red D square atop 1 corner of 1 setting block. Stitch diagonally from corner to corner. Trim excess fabric ¼" from stitching line. Press open to reveal triangle. Repeat on each corner to make 1 setting block. Make 36 setting blocks.

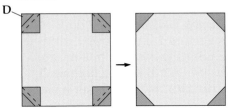

Diagonal Seams Diagram

Quilt Assembly

1. Lay out blocks and setting blocks as shown in *Quilt Top Assembly Diagram.*

2. Join into rows; join rows to complete quilt.

Quilting and Finishing

1. Divide backing fabric into 3 (2½-yard) lengths. Cut 1 piece in half lengthwise. Sew 1 narrow panel between wide panels. Press seam allowances toward narrow panel.

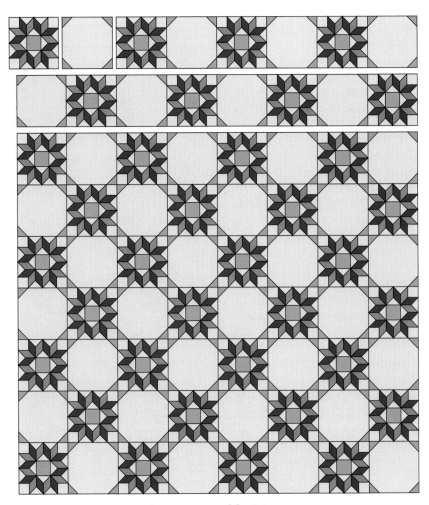

Quilt Top Assembly Diagram

Remaining panel is extra and may be used to make a hanging sleeve. Seams will run horizontally.

2. Layer backing, batting, and quilt top; baste. Quilt as desired. Quilt shown is outline-quilted in blocks, with diamond grid fill in setting blocks. Use dove quilting pattern from page 113 in setting blocks, if desired.

3. Join 2¼"-wide dark brown print strips into 1 continuous piece for straight-grain French-fold binding. Add binding to quilt.

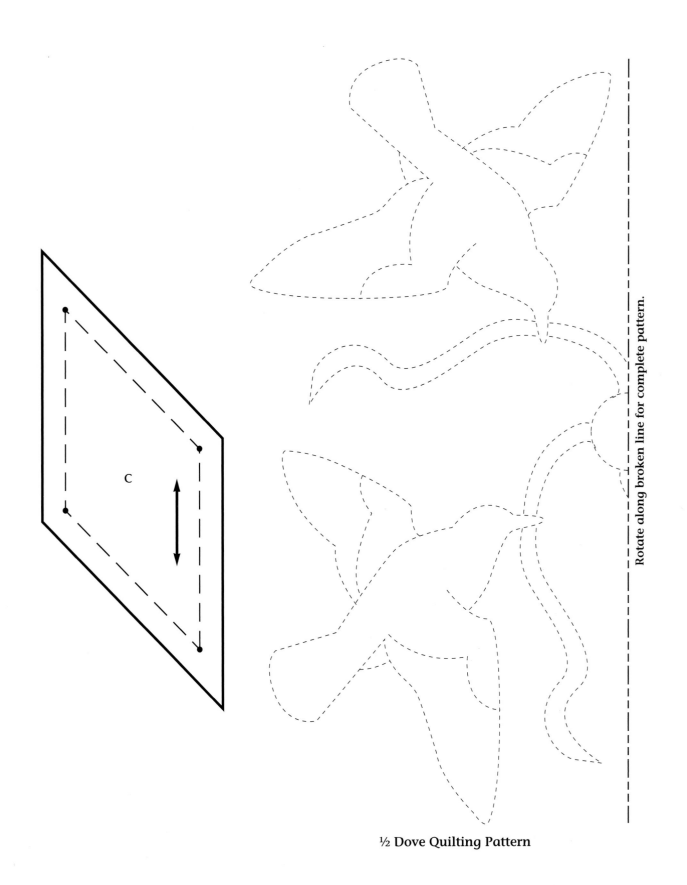

C

Rotate along broken line for complete pattern.

½ Dove Quilting Pattern

Martha Washington

This pattern honoring our First Lady appeared in the
Farmer's Wife in 1926. Colonial-style home furnishings,
along with a renewed interest in quiltmaking,
were gaining in popularity.

Quilt by Bessie Case, owned by Kelly Davis

Finished Quilt Size
75" x 86"

Number of Blocks and Finished Size
42 (8") Martha Washington Blocks

Materials
6¾ yards muslin for blocks, setting pieces, and pieced border
1½ yards solid blue for borders
42 (9" x 11") pieces assorted prints for blocks
¾ yard solid pink for binding
5 yards fabric for backing
Full-size batting

Cutting
Measurements include ¼" seam allowances. Patterns are on page 117.

From muslin, cut:
• 4 (3¼"-wide) strips. Cut strips into 42 (3¼") squares. Cut squares in quarters diagonally to make 168 A triangles.
• 6 (2⅞"-wide) strips. Cut strips into 84 (2⅞") squares. Cut squares in half diagonally to make 168 B triangles.
• 11 (4½"-wide) strips. Cut strips into 168 (2½" x 4½") C rectangles.
• 11 (2½"-wide) strips. Cut strips into 168 (2½") D squares.
• 8 (8½"-wide) strips. Cut strips into 30 (8½") setting squares.
• 2 (12¾"-wide) strips. Cut strips into 6 (12¾") squares. Cut squares in quarters diagonally to make 24 side setting triangles. You will have 2 extra.
• 1 (6¾"-wide) strip. Cut strip into 2 (6¾") squares. Cut squares in half diagonally to make 4 corner setting triangles.
• 7 (2¾"-wide) strips. Using template, cut 206 Es for pieced border.

From solid blue, cut:
• 9 (2¼"-wide) strips. Piece to make 2 (2¼" x 90") side borders and 2 (2¼" x 80") top and bottom borders.
• 7 (2¾"-wide) strips. Using template E, cut strips into 214 Es for pieced border.

From each piece of assorted prints, cut:
• 1 (3¼") square. Cut square in quarters diagonally to make 4 A triangles.
• 8 (2½") D squares.

From solid pink, cut:
• 9 (2¼"-wide) strips for binding.

Block Assembly
1. Choose 1 set of print pieces. Referring to *Block Assembly Diagram*, join 1 muslin and 1 print A triangle to make 1 pieced triangle. Add 1 B triangle to make 1 square unit. Make 4 square units. Join as shown to make pinwheel center.

2. Referring to *Diagonal Seams Diagram*, place 1 print D square atop 1 end of 1 C rectangle. Stitch

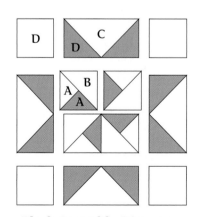

Block Assembly Diagram

diagonally from corner to corner. Trim excess fabric ¼" from stitching. Press open to reveal triangle.

Diagonal Seams Diagrams

Repeat on opposite end to make 1 Goose Chase unit. Make 4 Goose Chase units.

3. Referring to *Block Assembly Diagram,* lay out pinwheel center, Goose Chase units, and 4 muslin D squares. Join into rows; join rows to complete 1 Martha Washington Star block *(Block Diagram).*

4. Make 42 Martha Washington Star blocks.

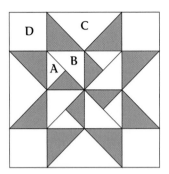

Block Diagram

Quilt Assembly

1. Lay out blocks and setting pieces as shown in *Quilt Top Assembly Diagram.* Join into diagonal rows; join rows to complete quilt center.

2. Center 1 blue border on each side of quilt and add. Miter corners.

3. Join 55 muslin and 56 blue Es to make 1 side border. Repeat. Add side borders to quilt, adjusting seams as needed.

4. Join 48 muslin and 49 blue Es to make top border. Add 1 E to each end as shown for corners. Repeat for bottom border. Add borders to quilt, adjusting seams as needed.

Quilting and Finishing

1. Divide backing fabric into 2 (2½-yard) lengths. Cut 1 piece in half lengthwise. Sew 1 narrow panel to each side of wide panel. Press seam allowances toward narrow panels.

2. Layer backing, batting, and quilt top; baste. Quilt as desired. Quilt shown is outline-quilted in blocks and pieced border. Setting squares have feathered wreaths and are filled with gridwork.

3. Join pink strips into 1 continuous piece for straight-grain French-fold binding. Add binding to quilt.

Quilt Top Assembly Diagram

Quilt Label
Trace, scan, or photocopy this quilt label to finish your quilt.

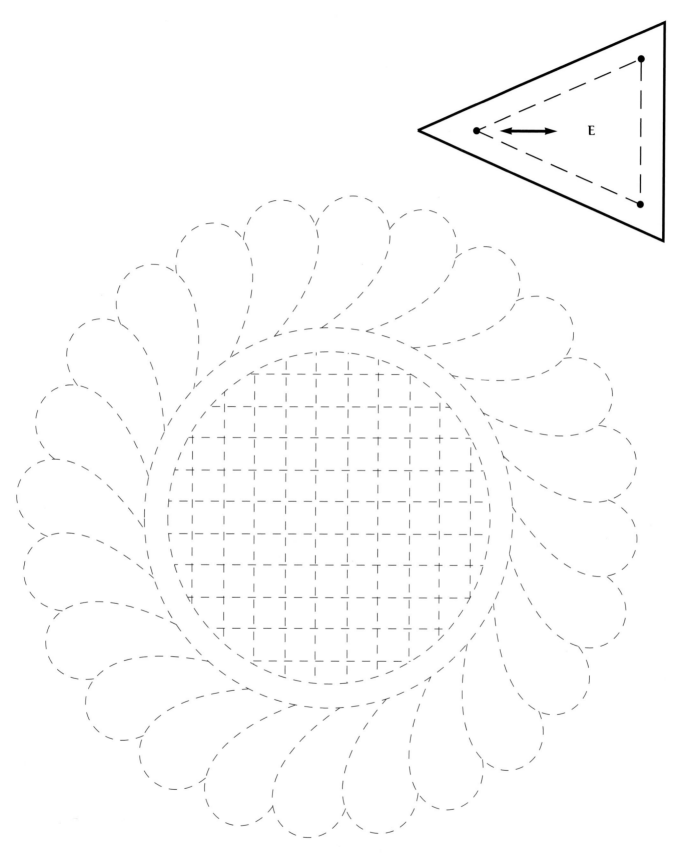

Wreath Quilting Pattern

E

Chapter 3

Circles & Curves

Once thought of as something only a seasoned quiltmaker should tackle, curved seams are easy with modern quiltmaking techniques.

- You can sew curved seams easily on your sewing machine. See the step-by-step photos on page 356 for tips on achieving perfect curves.

- Paper foundation piecing makes achieving sharp points along curved seams more accessible on patterns like *Cottage Tulips* on page 120, *Pickle Dish* on page 133, and *Baby Bunting* on page 141.

- If you've never tried curved seams before, consider making *Drunkard's Path* on page 125, *Windmill* on page 138, or *Love Ring* on page 129. Although they have small curves, there are no sharp points to precision-piece.

- All of the quilts in this chapter require templates, which can be made from template plastic, freezer paper, non-fusible stabilizer, paper, or cardboard.

Step up to the next level of quiltmaking by stitching your own curved seam quilt.

Cottage Tulips

This quilt is a faithful reproduction of an 1800s quilt that Doris Dunlap saw at a quilt show. Red and green was a common color scheme for 19th-century quilts. Although the pattern has been around a while, it was first published in the *Kansas City Star* in 1931.

Quilt by Doris Angell Dunlap; owned by Benjamin and Jennifer Dunlap

Finished Quilt Size

78" x 102½"

Number of Blocks and Finished Size

12 (20") Cottage Tulips Blocks

Materials

3½ yards solid red for blocks and borders
4 yards solid green for blocks and borders
3 yards muslin for blocks
3 yards light brown print for background and setting squares
7½ yards fabric for backing
Queen-size batting

Cutting

Measurements include ¼" seam allowances. Patterns are on page 122-124.

From red, cut:

- 12 As.
- 12 (2"-wide) strips. Cut strips into 96 (2" x 5") D pieces for paper piecing.
- 2 (20½"-wide) strips. Cut strips into 31 (2" x 20½") strips for sashing units.
- 5 (2"-wide) strips for sashing square assembly.

From green, cut:

- 24 (1½"-wide) strips. Cut strips into 192 (1½" x 5") C pieces for paper piecing.
- 3 (20½"-wide) strips. Cut strips into 62 (2" x 20½") strips for sashing units.
- 10 (2¼"-wide) strips for binding.

From muslin, cut:

- 96 Bs.
- 10 (3½"-wide) strips. Cut strips into 192 (2" x 3½") E pieces for paper piecing.

From light brown print, cut:

- 48 Fs for background.
- 4 (2"-wide) strips for sashing square assembly.

Block Assembly

1. Copy or trace *C/D/E Paper Piecing Pattern* on page 124. You will need 96 copies.

2. Place 1 red D on wrong side of

paper pattern, aligned over #1 area; pin. Place 1 E piece, right sides facing, along seam line between 1 and 2, leaving seam allowance, so that muslin will cover area #2 after stitching. Stitch from right side of pattern along line. Trim seam allowance if needed and flip E over to cover area #2; finger-press in place. Repeat with second E in area #3. Continue with green Cs for areas 4 and 5. When complete, trim unit along outer line. Make 8 C/D/E units. Remove paper.

C/D/E Unit Diagram

3. Referring to *Block Assembly Diagram*, join 1 C/D/E unit to 1 B unit, leaving bottom seam allowance loose. Make 8 units.

4. Join 1 B from above units to 1 scallop of A. Repeat on adjacent

scallop with second unit. Set in seam between units. Continue until circle is complete.

5. Join 1 F to each quarter of circle, centering as shown. Set in side seams to complete 1 Cottage Tulips block *(Block Diagram)*.

6. Make 12 Cottage Tulips blocks.

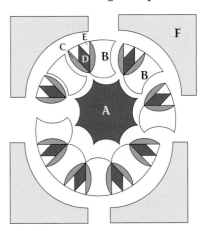

Block Assembly Diagram

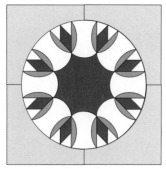

Block Diagram

Sashing Assembly

1. Referring to *Sashing Strip Diagram*, join 2 green and 1 red 2" x 20½" strip to make 1 sashing strip. Make 31 sashing strips.

Sashing Strip Diagram

2. Referring to *Strip Set A Diagram*, join 2 red and 1 light brown print 2"-wide strips to make 1 Strip Set A. Make 2 strip sets A. Cut strip sets into 40 (2"-wide) A segments.

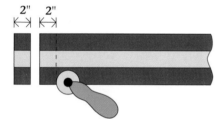

Strip Set A Diagram

3. Referring to *Strip Set B Diagram*, join 2 light brown and 1 red 2"-wide strips to make 1 strip set B. Cut strip set into 20 (2"-wide) B segments.

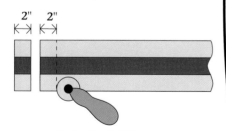

Strip Set B Diagram

4. Referring to *Sashing Square Assembly Diagram*, lay out 2 A and 1 B segment. Join to make 1 sashing square. Make 20 sashing squares.

Quilt Top Assembly Diagram

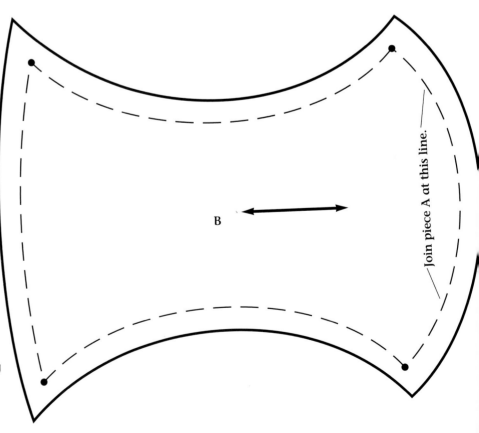

B

Join piece A at this line.

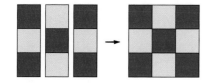

Sashing Square Assembly Diagram

Quilt Assembly

1. Lay out blocks, sashing strips, and sashing squares as shown in *Quilt Top Assembly Diagram*.

2. Join 4 sashing squares and 3 sashing strips as shown to make 1 sashing strip row. Make 5 sashing strip rows.

3. Join 4 sashing strips and 3 blocks as shown to make 1 block row. Make 4 block rows.

4. Join rows to complete quilt top.

Quilting and Finishing

1. Divide backing fabric into 3 (2½-yard) lengths. Join to make backing. Seams will run horizontally.

2. Layer backing, batting, and quilt top; baste. Quilt as desired. Quilt shown has a tulip design in A pieces, and a feathered circle around piecework. All other pieces are outline-quilted.

3. Join 2¼"-wide green strips into 1 continuous piece for straight-grain French-fold binding. Add binding to quilt.

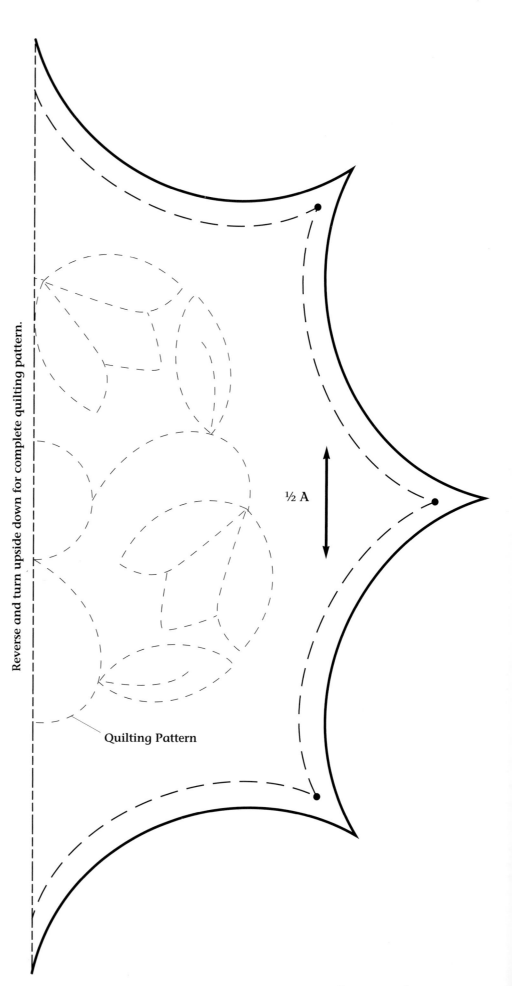

Reverse and turn upside down for complete quilting pattern.

½ A

Quilting Pattern

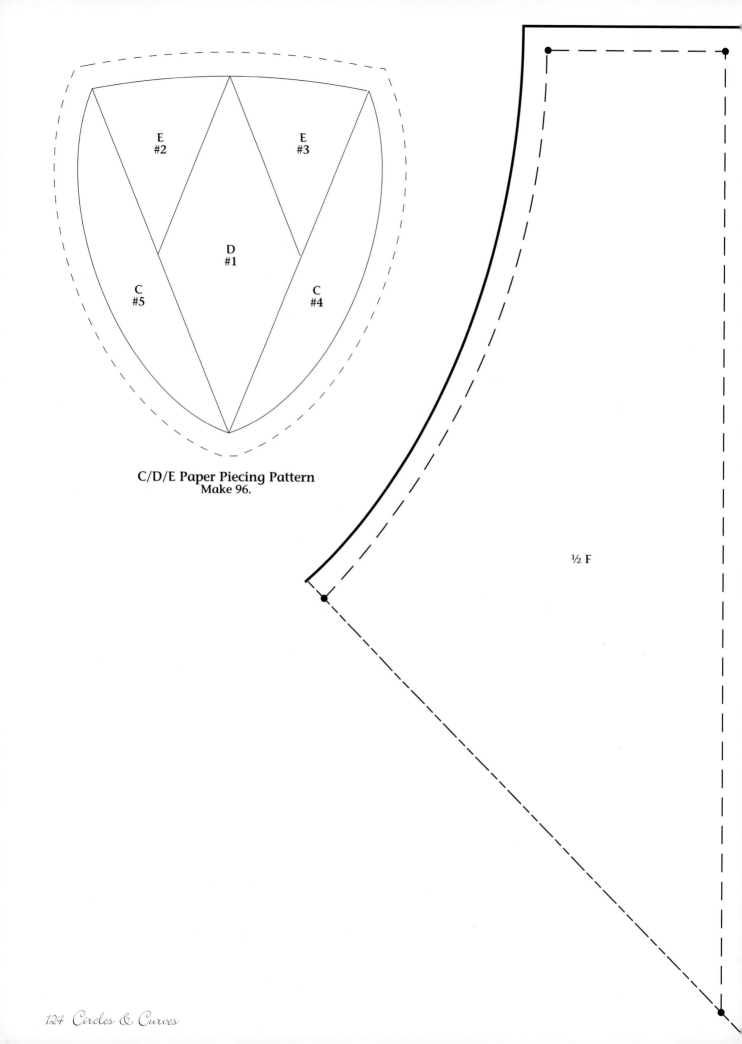

C/D/E Paper Piecing Pattern
Make 96.

E
#2

E
#3

D
#1

C
#5

C
#4

½ F

Drunkard's Path

Drunkard's Path became a popular pattern during the
Women's Temperance Movement of the 1920s,
which discouraged alcohol consumption. Drunkard's Path
is only one of several designs that can be made using
the same curved unit in different arrangements.

Quilt by Malvina Shelton; owned by Carol M. Tipton

Finished Quilt Size

Twin: 64" x 78"
Full/Queen: 78" x 92"
King: 92" x 106"

Number of Blocks and Finished Size

Twin: 20 (14") Drunkard's Path Blocks
Full/Queen: 30 (14") Blocks
King: 42 (14") Blocks

Materials

Twin Size:
4¼ yards green
3¾ yards cream
5 yards fabric for backing
Twin-size batting

Cutting

Measurements include ¼" seam allowances. You may want to cut borders longer to allow for piecing variations. Patterns are on pages 127–128.

From green, cut:
• 160 As.
• 160 Bs.
• 8 (2½"-wide) strips. Piece to make 2 (2½" x 74½") outer side borders and 2 (2½" x 64½") outer top and bottom borders.
• 8 (2¼"-wide) strips for binding.

From cream, cut:
• 160 As.
• 160 Bs.
• 8 (2½"-wide) strips. Piece to make 2 (2½" x 70½") inner side borders and 2 (2½" x 60½") inner top and bottom borders.

Block Assembly

1. Referring to *Unit A Diagram*, join 1 cream B to 1 green A to make 1 Unit A. Make 160 Unit As.

2. Referring to *Unit B Diagram*, join 1 green B to 1 cream A to make 1 Unit B. Make 160 Unit Bs.

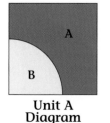

Unit A Diagram

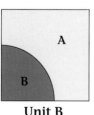

Unit B Diagram

This quilt shows half blocks going down the left side. For easier assembly, our directions call for whole blocks. Follow the instructions and the *Quilt Top Assembly Diagram* to make your quilt.

3. Lay out 8 each of Units A and B as shown in *Drunkard's Path Block Diagram*. Join into rows; join rows to make 1 Drunkard's Path block.

4. Make 20 Drunkard's Path blocks.

Unit A   Unit B
↓   ↓

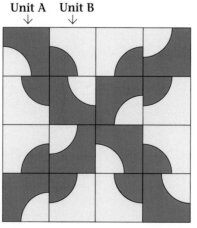

Drunkard's Path Block Diagram

Quilt Assembly

1. Referring to *Quilt Top Assembly Diagram*, lay out blocks in 5 horizontal rows of 4 blocks each. Join into rows; join rows to complete quilt center.

2. Add inner side borders to quilt. Add top and bottom borders.

3. Add outer side borders to quilt. Add top and bottom borders.

Quilting and Finishing

1. Divide backing fabric into 2 (2½-yard) lengths. Cut 1 length into 1 (30"-wide) lengthwise panel. Sew 30"-wide panel to 1 side of wide panel. Press seam allowance toward narrow panel. Remaining panel is extra and may be used to make a hanging sleeve.

2. Layer backing, batting, and quilt top; baste. Quilt as desired. Quilt shown is quilted in a 1" diagonal grid.

3. Join green strips into 1 continuous piece for straight-grain French-fold binding. Add binding to quilt.

Materials
Full/Queen Size:
5¾ yards green
5¼ yards cream
5½ yards fabric for backing
Full/queen-size batting

Cutting
Measurements include ¼" seam allowances. You may want to cut borders longer to allow for piecing variations. Patterns are on pages 127-128.

From green, cut:
• 240 As.
• 240 Bs.
• 9 (2½"-wide) strips. Piece to make 2 (2½" x 88½") outer side borders and 2 (2½" x 78½") outer top and bottom borders.
• 10 (2¼"-wide) strips for binding.

From cream, cut:
• 240 As.
• 240 Bs.
• 9 (2½"-wide) strips. Piece to make 2 (2½" x 84½") inner side borders and 2 (2½" x 74½") inner top and bottom borders.

Block Assembly
1. Referring to *Unit A Diagram*, join 1 cream B to 1 green A to make 1 Unit A. Make 240 Unit As.

2. Referring to *Unit B Diagram*, join 1 green B to 1 cream A to make 1 Unit B. Make 240 Unit Bs.

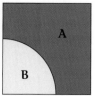

Unit A Diagram

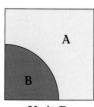

Unit B Diagram

3. Lay out 8 each of Units A and B as shown in *Drunkard's Path Block Diagram*. Join into rows; join rows to

Quilt Top Assembly Diagram

Unit A   Unit B

Drunkard's Path Block Diagram

make 1 Drunkard's Path block.

4. Make 30 Drunkard's Path blocks.

Quilt Assembly
1. Lay out blocks in 5 horizontal rows of 6 blocks each.

Join into rows; join rows to complete quilt center.

2. Add inner side borders to quilt. Add top and bottom borders.

3. Add outer side borders to quilt. Add top and bottom borders.

B

Quilting and Finishing

1. Divide backing fabric into 2 (2¾-yard) lengths. Cut 1 piece in half lengthwise. Sew 1 narrow panel to each side of wide panel. Press seam allowances toward narrow panels.

2. Layer backing, batting, and quilt top; baste. Quilt as desired. Quilt shown is quilted in a 1" diagonal grid.

3. Join green strips into 1 continuous piece for straight-grain French-fold binding. Add binding to quilt.

Materials

King Size:
7¾ yards green
7 yards cream
8¼ yards fabric for backing
King-size batting

From green, cut:
• 336 As.
• 336 Bs.
• 11 (2½"-wide) strips; piece to make 2 (2½" x 102½") outer side borders and 2 (2½" x 92½") outer top and bottom borders.
• 11 (2¼"-wide) strips for binding.

From cream, cut:
• 336 As.
• 336 Bs.
• 10 (2½"-wide) strips; piece to make 2 (2½" x 98½") inner side borders and 2 (2½" x 88½") inner top and bottom borders.

Block Assembly

1. Referring to *Unit A Diagram*, join 1 cream B to 1 green A to make 1 Unit A. Make 336 Unit As.

2. Referring to *Unit B Diagram*, join 1 green B to 1 cream A to make 1 Unit B. Make 336 Unit Bs.

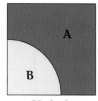

Unit A
Diagram

Unit B
Diagram

3. Lay out 8 each of Units A and B as shown in *Drunkard's Path Block Diagram*. Join into rows; join rows to make 1 Drunkard's Path block.

4. Make 42 Drunkard's Path blocks.

Unit A   Unit B

Drunkard's Path Block Diagram

Quilt Assembly

1. Lay out blocks in 6 horizontal rows of 7 blocks each. Join into rows; join rows to complete quilt center.

2. Add inner side borders to quilt. Add top and bottom borders.

3. Add outer side borders to quilt. Add top and bottom borders.

Quilting and Finishing

1. Divide backing fabric into 3 (2¾-yard) lengths. Join along sides to make backing. Seams will run horizontally.

2. Layer backing, batting, and quilt top; baste. Quilt as desired. Quilt shown is quilted in a 1" diagonal grid.

3. Join 2¼"-wide green strips into 1 continuous piece for straight-grain French-fold binding. Add binding to quilt.

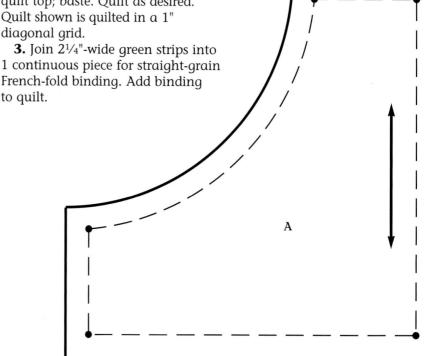

A

Love Ring

This design is another variation of the Drunkard's Path block. It is also known by other names, such as Nonesuch, the Jigsaw Puzzle, and Ozark Puzzle. This quiltmaker added an interesting twist by using the blocks to make a winding border.

Quilt by Lottie M. Hearn

Finished Quilt Size
81" x 108"

Number of Blocks and Finished Size
35 (12") Love Ring Blocks

Materials
3½ yards white
5½ yards burgundy
2 yards blue
3 yards pink print
7½ yards fabric for backing
Queen-size batting

Cutting
Measurements include ¼" seam allowances. Instructions yield results slightly different from photo for greater ease in math. Patterns are on page 132.

From white, cut:
• 360 As.

From burgundy, cut:
• 10 (3½"-wide) strips. Piece to make 2 (3½" x 102½") side borders and 2 (3½" x 81½") top and bottom borders.
• 11 (2¼"-wide) strips for binding.
• 280 As.
• 251 Bs.

From blue, cut:
• 5 (2"-wide) strips. Piece strips to make 2 (2" x 84½") inner side borders.
• 4 (3½"-wide) strips. Piece strips to make 2 (3½" x 63½") inner top and bottom borders.
• 249 Bs.

From pink print, cut:
• 140 As.
• 280 Bs.

Block Assembly
1. Referring to *Block Assembly Diagram*, join 1 blue B to 1 pink print A to make 1 inner unit. Make 4 inner units.

Inner Unit

2. Join 1 pink print B to 1 burgundy A to make 1 side unit. Make 8 side units.

SideUnit

3. Join 1 burgundy B to 1 white A to make 1 corner unit. Make 4 corner units.

Corner Unit

4. Lay out units as shown in *Block Assembly Diagram*. Join into rows; join rows to complete 1 Love Ring block *(Block Diagram)*.

5. Make 35 Love Ring blocks.

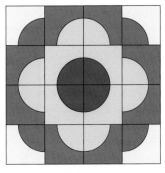

Block Assembly Diagram

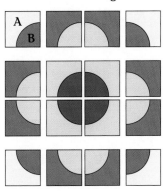

Block Diagram

Quilt Assembly
1. Referring to *Quilt Top Assembly Diagram*, lay out blocks in 7 horizontal rows of 5 blocks each. Join into rows; join rows to complete quilt center.

2. Add blue inner side borders to quilt. Add top and bottom borders.

3. Join 1 blue B to 1 white A to make 1 blue border unit. Make 109 blue border units.

Blue Border Unit

4. Join 1 burgundy B to 1 white A to make 1 burgundy border unit. Make 111 burgundy border units.

Burgundy Border Unit

5. Refer carefully to *Quilt Top Assembly Diagram*. To make side border, join 60 blocks into 2 rows of 30 blocks each as shown. Adjust seams as needed to fit side of quilt. Add to quilt. Repeat.

6. To make top border, join 50 blocks into 2 rows of 25 blocks each as shown. Adjust as needed and join to top. Repeat for bottom.

7. Add burgundy side borders to quilt. Add top and bottom borders.

Quilting and Finishing
1. Divide backing fabric into 3 (2½-yard) lengths. Join to make backing. Seams will run horizontally.

2. Layer backing, batting, and quilt top; baste. Quilt as desired. Quilt shown is outline-quilted in blocks, with stars in white areas. Pieced borders have a spray pattern, with diagonal stripes in solid borders.

3. Join 2¼"-wide burgundy strips into 1 continuous piece for straight-grain French-fold binding. Add binding to quilt.

Quilt Label
Trace, scan, or photocopy this quilt
label to finish your quilt.

Quilt Top Assembly Diagram

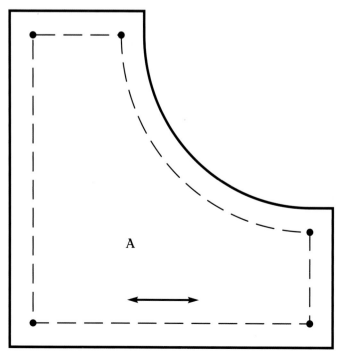

A

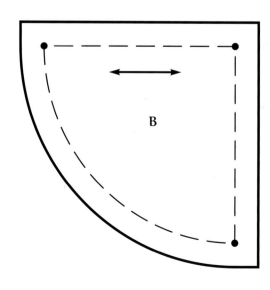

B

Pickle Dish

In the late 1800s, Pickle Dish was a favorite among quilters who enjoyed working with pieced curves. The color scheme was usually in red and white, as in this example. It was meant to recall the shimmer of light on cranberry-colored cut-glass serving dishes, hence the name Pickle Dish.

Quilt from Hannah Antiques, Birmingham, Alabama

Finished Quilt Size

66" x 72"

Number of Blocks and Finished Size

9 (21") Pickle Dish Blocks

Materials

5½ yards red
9 yards white
4 yards fabric for backing
Twin-size batting

Cutting

Measurements include ¼" seam allowances. Border strips are exact length needed. You may want to cut them longer to allow for piecing variations. Patterns are on pages 136–137.

From red, cut:

• 8 (2"-wide) strips. Piece strips to make 2 (2" x 63½") top and bottom borders and 2 (2" x 66½") side borders.
• 648 Cs [or cut 648 (1½" x 2") pieces for paper piecing].
• 648 Es [or cut 648 (1½" x 2") pieces for paper piecing].
• 72 Gs.
• 72 Gs reversed.

From white, cut:

• 4 (3½"-wide) strips. Piece strips to make 2 (3½" x 66½") top and bottom borders.
• 8 (2¼"-wide) strips for binding.
• 36 As.
• 36 Bs.
• 576 Ds [or cut 576 (1½" x 3") pieces for paper piecing].
• 144 Fs [or cut 144 (1½" x 3") pieces for paper piecing].
• 72 Hs.

Block Assembly

1. Referring to *Block Assembly Diagram*, join 1 C, 1 D, and 1 E in order shown to make 1 D unit. Make 8 D units. Join units to make 1 arc. Make 8 arcs. (For paper piecing, make 576 copies of *Paper Piecing Pattern C/D/E* on page 136. Paper-piece 64 units for each block.)

2. Join 1 E and 1 F to 1 end of 1 arc. Join 1 C and 1 F to opposite end of arc. Repeat for all arcs.

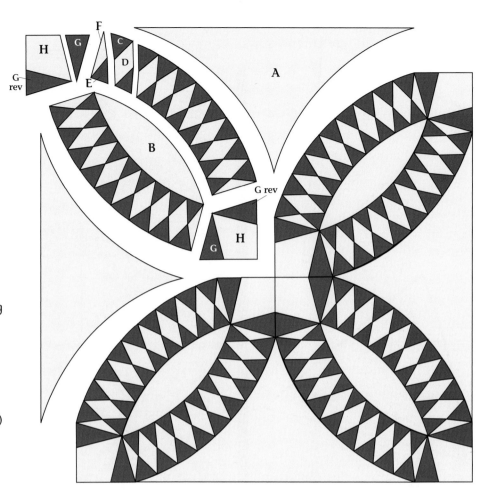

Block Assembly Diagram

(For paper piecing, make 144 copies each of *Paper Piecing Pattern E/F and C/F* on page 136. Paper-piece 16 units for each block.)

3. Join 1 B to inner edge of 1 arc. Join second arc to opposite side of B.

4. Join 1 G and 1 G reversed to sides of 1 H to make 1 end unit. Make 8 end units.

5. Join 1 H unit to each end of 1 arc unit, setting in seams. Repeat for all arc units.

6. Join 2 arc units along H and G. Set in A for half block. Repeat. Join block halves along Hs and Gs. Set in As to complete 1 Pickle Dish block.

7. Make 9 Pickle Dish blocks.

Quilt Assembly

1. Referring to *Quilt Top Assembly Diagram*, lay out 3 horizontal rows of 3 blocks each. Join into rows; join rows to complete quilt center.

2. Add red top and bottom borders to quilt. Add red side borders.

3. Add white top and bottom borders to quilt.

Quilting and Finishing

1. Divide backing fabric into 2 (2-yard) lengths. Cut 1 piece in half lengthwise. Sew 1 narrow panel to each side of wide panel. Press seam allowances toward narrow panels.

2. Layer backing, batting, and quilt top; baste. Quilt as desired. Quilt shown is outline-quilted in piecing with grid fill in large areas.

3. Join 2¼"-wide white strips into 1 continuous piece for straight-grain French-fold binding. Add binding to quilt.

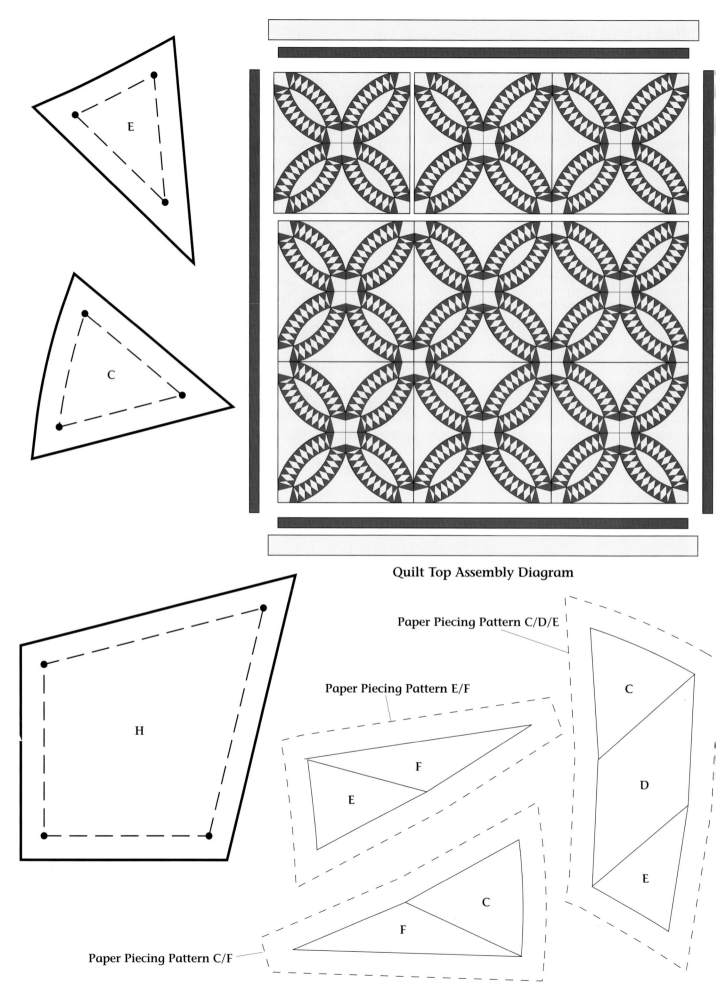

Quilt Top Assembly Diagram

E

C

H

Paper Piecing Pattern C/D/E

Paper Piecing Pattern E/F

F

E

C

D

E

C

F

Paper Piecing Pattern C/F

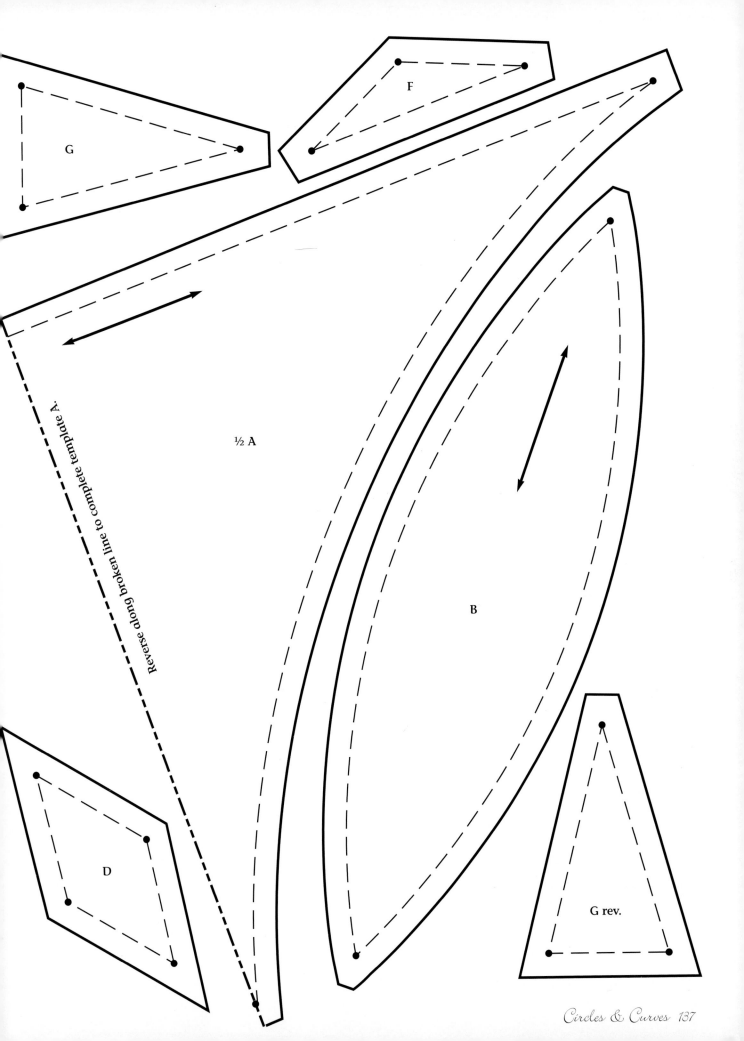

G

F

½ A

Reverse along broken line to complete template A.

B

D

G rev.

Windmill

Pioneers east of the Mississippi
knew this pattern as Mill Wheel.
But as settlers moved westward,
the whirling blades of windmills
became more familiar to them
than water mills left behind.

Finished Quilt Size
65½" x 82½"

Number of Blocks and Finished Size
63 (8½") Windmill Blocks

Materials
4 yards pink print
4 yards white
5 yards fabric for backing
Twin-size batting

Cutting
Measurements include ¼" seam allowances. Patterns are on page 140.

From pink print, cut:
• 2½ yards. Cut yardage into 4 (3½"-wide) lengthwise strips for borders. Use remainder for block pieces.
• 63 As.
• 126 Bs.

From white, cut:
• 8 (2¼"-wide) strips for binding.
• 63 As.
• 126 Bs.

Block Assembly
1. Referring to *Block Assembly Diagram*, join 2 pink Bs to 1 white A. Make 63 white halves.

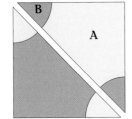

Block Assembly Diagram

2. Join 2 white Bs to 1 pink A. Make 63 pink halves.

3. Join 1 white and 1 pink half to make 1 Windmill block *(Block Diagram)*. Make 63 Windmill blocks.

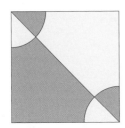

Block Diagram

Quilt by Lucille Whitaker; owned by Patricia Bundy

Quilt Assembly
1. Referring to *Row 1 Assembly Diagram*, join 7 blocks, rotating as shown. Make 5 of Row 1.

2. Referring to *Row 2 Assembly Diagram*, join 7 blocks, rotating as shown. Make 4 of Row 1.

2. Referring to quilt photo, join into rows; join rows to complete quilt center.

3. Center 1 border strip on each side of quilt and join. Miter corners.

Quilting and Finishing
1. Divide backing fabric into 2 (2½-yard) lengths. Cut 1 piece in half lengthwise. Sew 1 narrow panel to each side of wide panel. Press seam allowances toward narrow panels.

2. Layer backing, batting, and quilt top; baste. Quilt as desired. Quilt shown is quilted in Baptist fans.

3. Join 2¼"-wide white strips into 1 continuous piece for straight-grain French-fold binding. Add binding to quilt.

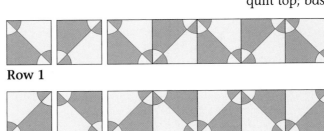

Row 1

Row 2

Row Assembly Diagram

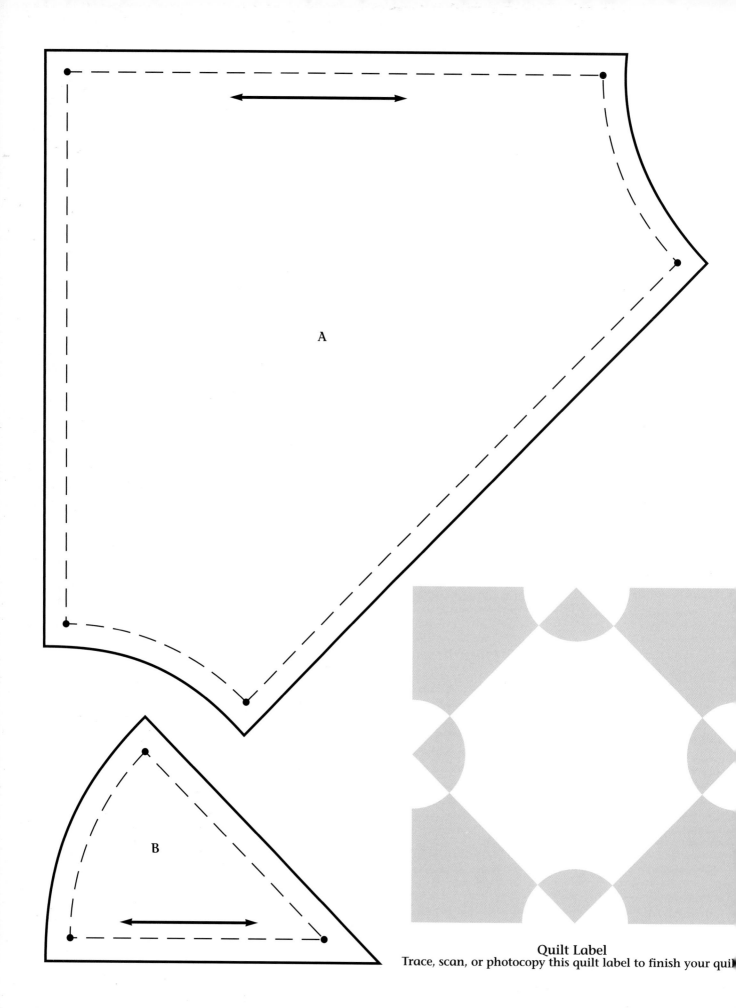

A

B

Quilt Label
Trace, scan, or photocopy this quilt label to finish your quil

Baby Bunting

This dainty pattern appeared in the Ladies Art Company catalog #493 in 1928. The design is also know by such names as The Wanderer, Broken Saw, and Chinese Fans.

Finished Quilt Size
72" x 94½"

Number of Blocks and Finished Size
12 (18") Baby Bunting Blocks

Materials
8¾ yards solid pink
8 yards solid white
5½ yards backing
Full-size batting

Cutting
Measurements include ¼" seam allowances. Patterns are on page 143.

From pink, cut:
- 192 As.
- 39 (3"-wide) strips. Cut strips into 768 (2" x 3") Bs for paper piecing.
- 35 (1½"-wide) strips. Cut strips into 384 (1½" x 3½") Ds for paper piecing.
- 16 (5"-wide) strips. Cut strips into 31 (5" x 18½") sashing strips.
- 9 (2¼"-wide) strips for binding.

From white, cut:
- 96 (1½"-wide) strips. Cut strips into 960 (1½" x 4") Cs for paper piecing.
- 192 Es.
- 3 (5"-wide) strips. Cut strips into 20 (5") sashing squares.

Block Assembly
1. Trace or photocopy 192 Arc Paper-Piecing Patterns from page 143. To paper piece arc unit, begin at one end of arc and place 1 pink D on wrong side of pattern, covering area 1. Align 1 C along seam line between areas 1 and 2, leaving seam allowance, so that when stitched and flipped over, it will cover area 2. Stitch; trim seam allowance if needed. Open out and finger press. Continue with Bs, Cs, and D (area 11) in same manner to complete 1 arc. Add 1 pink A to arc as shown. Join arc to 1 E to make 1 arc unit. Make 16 arc units.

2. Lay out arc units as shown in *Block Assembly Diagram.* Join into rows; join rows to complete 1 Baby Bunting block *(Block Diagram).*

3. Make 12 Baby Bunting blocks.

Quilt from The Patchwork Place, Franklin, Tennessee

Arc Unit

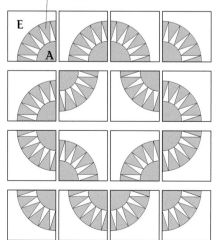

Block Assembly Diagram

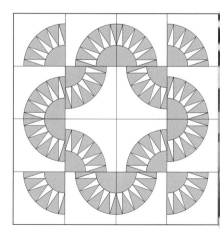

Block Diagram

Quilt Assembly

1. Referring to *Quilt Top Assembly Diagram,* lay out blocks, sashing strips, and sashing squares.

2. Join 4 sashing squares and 3 sashing strips to make 1 sashing row. Make 5 sashing rows.

3. Join 4 sashing strips and 3 blocks to make 1 block row. Make 4 block rows.

4. Join rows to complete quilt top.

Quilting and Finishing

1. Divide backing fabric into 2 (2¾-yard) lengths. Cut 1 piece in half lengthwise. Sew 1 narrow panel to each side of wide panel. Press seam allowances toward narrow panels.

2. Layer backing, batting, and quilt top; baste. Quilt as desired.

Quilt shown is outline-quilted with cable designs in sashing.

3. Join 2¼"-wide pink strips into 1 continuous piece for straight-grain French-fold binding. Add binding to quilt.

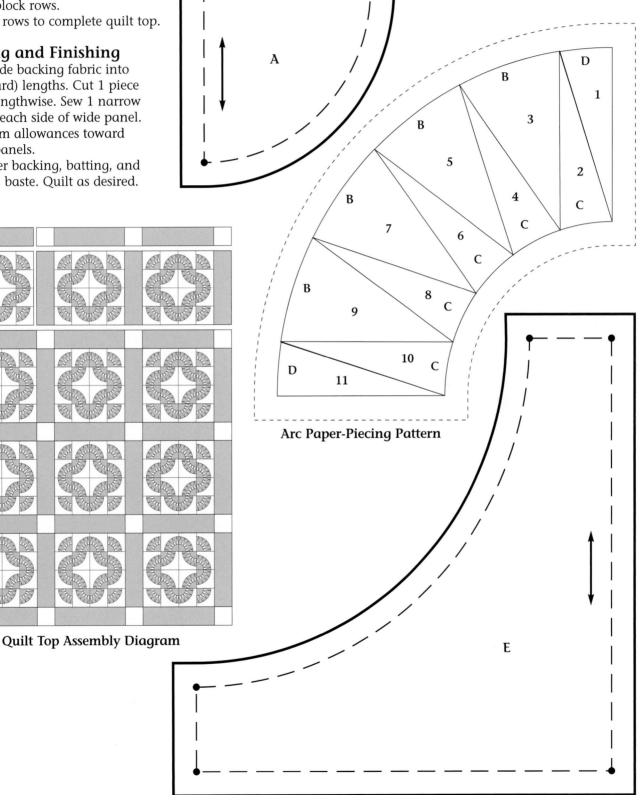

Arc Paper-Piecing Pattern

Quilt Top Assembly Diagram

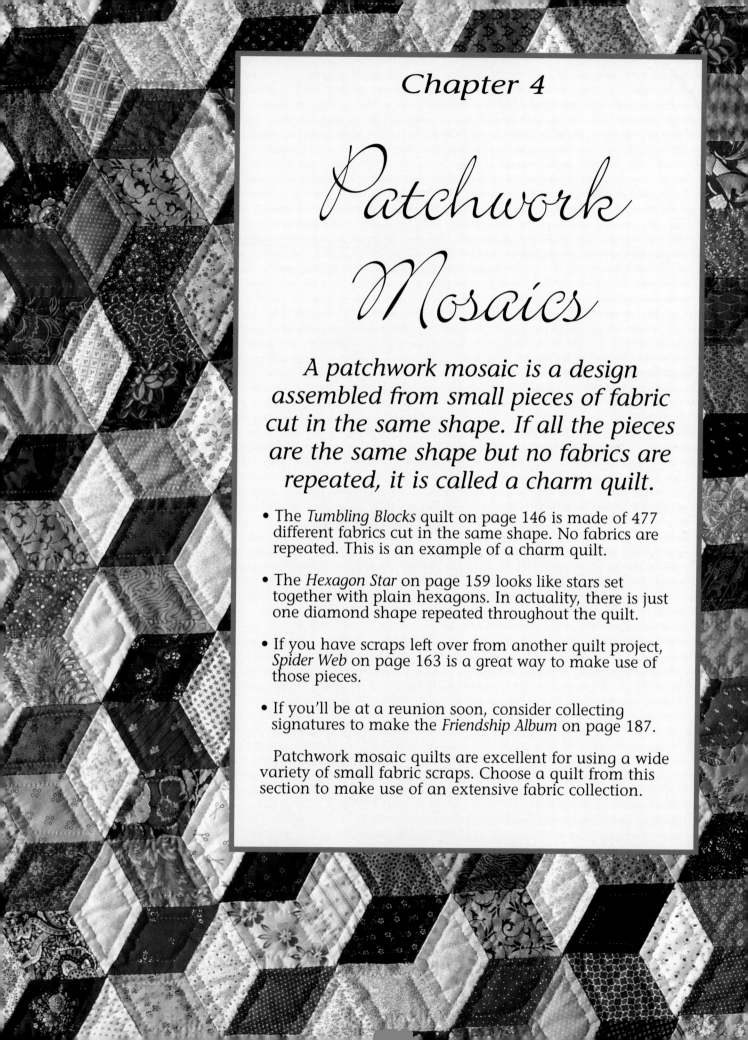

Chapter 4

Patchwork Mosaics

A patchwork mosaic is a design assembled from small pieces of fabric cut in the same shape. If all the pieces are the same shape but no fabrics are repeated, it is called a charm quilt.

- The *Tumbling Blocks* quilt on page 146 is made of 477 different fabrics cut in the same shape. No fabrics are repeated. This is an example of a charm quilt.

- The *Hexagon Star* on page 159 looks like stars set together with plain hexagons. In actuality, there is just one diamond shape repeated throughout the quilt.

- If you have scraps left over from another quilt project, *Spider Web* on page 163 is a great way to make use of those pieces.

- If you'll be at a reunion soon, consider collecting signatures to make the *Friendship Album* on page 187.

Patchwork mosaic quilts are excellent for using a wide variety of small fabric scraps. Choose a quilt from this section to make use of an extensive fabric collection.

Tumbling Blocks

Other names for this pattern include Baby Blocks, Building Blocks, Steps to the Altar, Pandora's Box, and Golden Cubes. In 1882, at age 10, President Calvin Coolidge pieced a Tumbling Blocks quilt. And as a boy, President Dwight D. Eisenhower, along with his brothers, helped his mother make Tumbling Blocks. You can see these quilts on display at the Presidents' respective homeplaces.

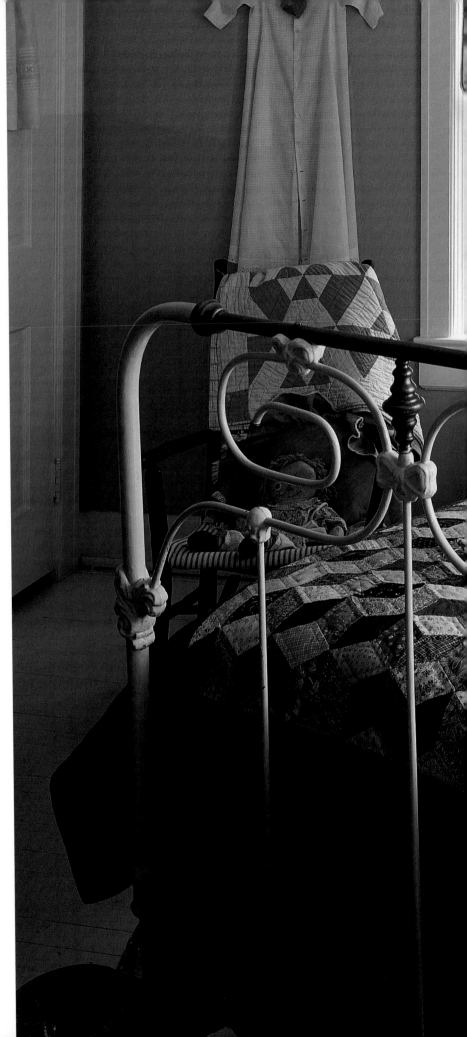

Quilt by Cindy Blackberg

Finished Quilt Size
54" x 76³⁄₈"

Number of Blocks and Finished Size:
136 Tumbling Blocks

Materials
1½ yards total assorted dark prints
1½ yards total assorted medium prints
1½ yards total assorted light prints
2¼ yards border print
2¼ yards blue print
⅝ yard coordinating print for binding
3¼ yards fabric for backing
Twin-size batting

Cutting
Measurements include ¼" seam allowances. Patterns are on page 149.

From dark prints, cut:
• 153 As.

From medium prints, cut:
• 153 As.

From light prints, cut:
• 136 As.
• 16 Bs.
• 17 Cs.
• 1 D and 1 D reversed.

From border print, cut:
• 4 (2" x 81") lengthwise strips for inner borders, centered on desired design.
• 4 (3½" x 81") lengthwise strips for outer borders, centered on desired design.

From blue print, cut:
• 4 (5½" x 81") lengthwise strips for middle borders.

From coordinating print, cut:
• 7 (2¼"-wide) strips for binding.

Block Assembly
1. Referring to *Block Diagram*, lay out 3 As: 1 light on top, 1 medium on left, 1 dark on right. Join to make 1 Tumbling Block. Make 136 blocks.

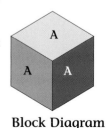

Block Diagram

2. Referring to *Top Half Block Diagram*, lay out 1 light C, 1 medium A on left, and 1 dark A on right. Join to make 1 top half block. Make 8 top half blocks.

3. Referring to *Left Side Half Block Diagram*, join 1 B and 1 dark A to make 1 left side unit. Make 8 left side units.

4. Referring to *Right Side Half Block Diagram*, join 1 B and 1 medium A to make 1 right side unit. Make 8 right side units.

Top Half Block Diagram

Left Side Half Block Diagram

Right Side Half Block Diagram

5. Referring to *Right Corner Unit Diagram*, join 1 D and 1 medium A to make right corner unit.

6. Referring to *Left Corner Unit Diagram*, join 1 D reversed and 1 dark A to make left corner unit.

Right Corner Unit Diagram

Left Corner Unit Diagram

Quilt Assembly
1. Referring to *Quilt Top Assembly Diagram*, join left corner unit, 8 top half blocks, and right corner unit to make top row (Row 1).

2. Join 9 Tumbling blocks to make Row 2. Make 8 of Row 2.

3. Join 1 left side unit, 8 Tumbling blocks and 1 right side unit to make Row 3. Make 8 of Row 3.

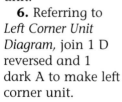

4. For 1 of Row 3, set in Cs along bottom to make Row 4 (bottom row).

5. Lay out Row 1. Alternate Rows 2 and 3. Lay out Row 4. Join rows to complete quilt center.

6. Center 1 (2"-wide) border print strip on each side of quilt top and join. Miter corners.

7. Center 1 (5½"-wide) blue border strip on each side of quilt top and join. Miter corners.

8. Center 1 (3½"-wide) border print strip on each side of quilt top and join. Miter corners.

Quilting and Finishing

1. Divide backing fabric into 2 (1⅝-yard) lengths. Cut 1 piece in half lengthwise. Sew 1 narrow panel to each side of wide panel. Press seam allowances toward narrow panels. Seams will run horizontally.

2. Layer backing, batting, and quilt top; baste. Quilt as desired. Quilt shown is outline-quilted in patchwork with cable designs in borders.

3. Join print strips into 1 continuous piece for straight-grain French-fold binding. Add binding to quilt.

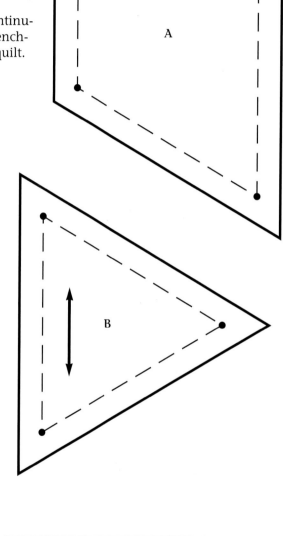

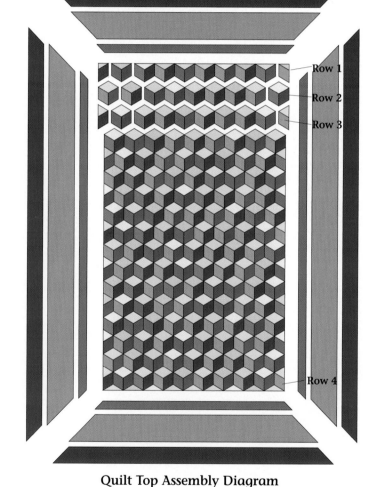

Quilt Top Assembly Diagram

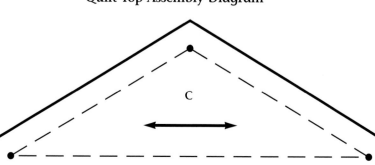

Joseph's Coat

This pattern dates back to 1933. The idea was to use as many different fabrics as possible in order to pay homage to the coat of many colors that Jacob gave his favorite son Joseph in the book of Genesis.

Finished Quilt Size
68" x 82½"

Number of Blocks and Finished Size
49 (11"-diameter) Joseph's Coat Blocks

Editor's Note:
Our staff ranks this quilt as very challenging—it is not a pattern for the beginning quilter. There are no straight seams in the entire quilt. For the greatest accuracy, we recommend hand piecing.

Materials
6 yards total assorted prints
8 yards pink
5 yards fabric for backing
Twin-size batting

Cutting
Measurements include ¼" seam allowances. Patterns are on page 152.

From prints, cut:
• 637 As.

From pink, cut:
• 406 Bs.
• 1 (36") square for bias binding. Cut 400" of 2¼"-wide bias strip. Fold and press to make bias binding.

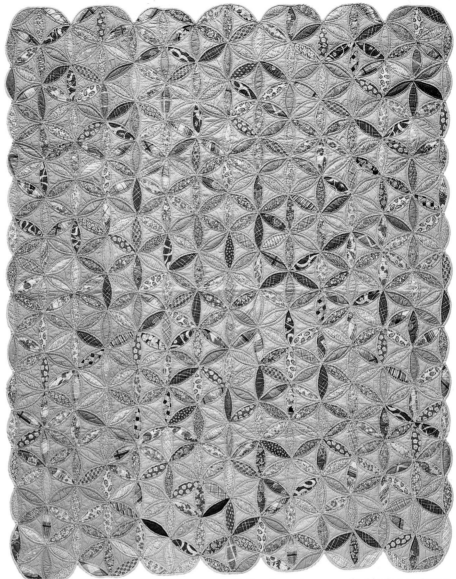

Quiltmaker unknown; quilted by Lorene Payne

Block Assembly
1. Referring to *A/B Unit Diagram*, join 2 As to 1 B as shown to make 1 unit. Make 6 units.

A/B Unit Diagram

2. Join units as shown in *Block Assembly Diagram* to make 1 Joseph's Coat block. Make 49 Joseph's Coat blocks (*Block Diagram*).

Block Assembly Diagram **Block Diagram**

3. Referring to *Bottom Left Corner Unit Diagram*, join 2 As to 1 B to make 1 unit. Make 3 units. Join

units and add 1 B as shown to make 1 bottom left corner unit.

Bottom Left Corner Unit Diagram

Repeat for *Bottom Right Corner Unit.*

Bottom Right Corner Unit Diagram

4. Referring to *Side Unit Diagram*, join 1 A and 1 B to make 1 side unit. Make 12 side units.

Side Unit Diagram

5. Referring to *Top and Bottom Unit Diagram*, join 2 As to 1 B to make 1 unit. Join 1 A and 1 B to make 1 side unit. Make 3 side units. Join 1 unit and 3 side units to make 1 top/bottom unit. Make 5 top/bottom units.

Top and Bottom Unit Diagram

Quilt Assembly

1. Lay out all units and remaining pink Bs as shown in *Quilt Top Assembly Diagram.*

2. Join units in vertical rows; join rows to complete quilt.

Quilting and Finishing

1. Divide backing fabric into 2 (2½-yard) lengths. Cut 1 piece in half lengthwise. Sew 1 narrow panel to each side of wide panel. Press seam allowances toward narrow panels.

2. Layer backing, batting, and quilt top; baste. Quilt as desired. Quilt shown is outline-quilted.

3. Add bias binding to quilt.

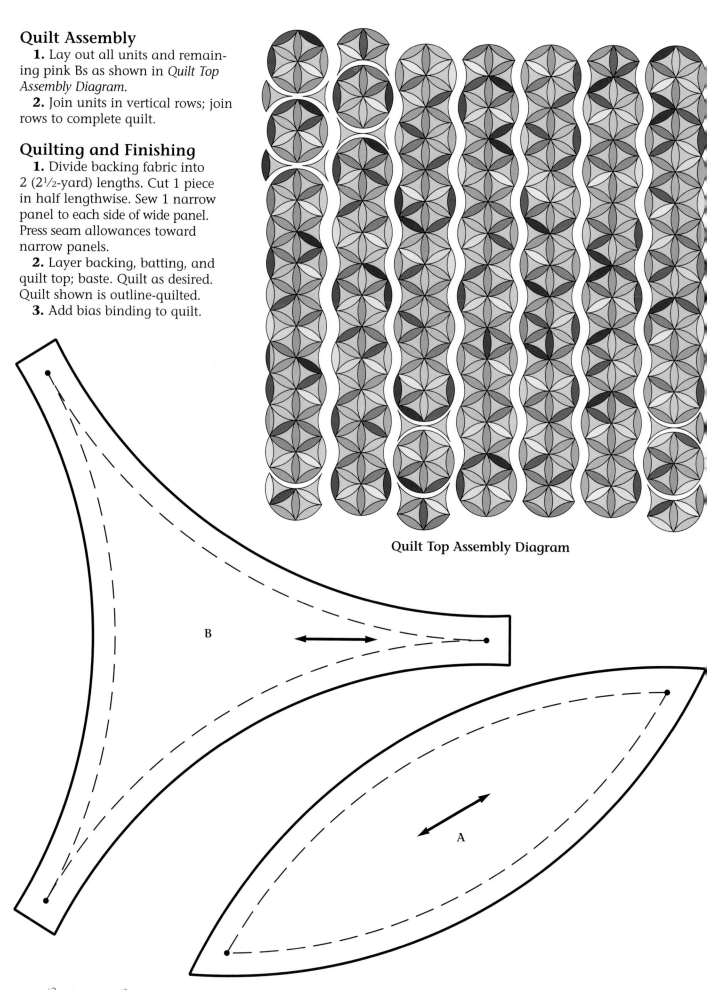

Quilt Top Assembly Diagram

B

A

Mosaic

This simple pattern, made entirely from right-angle triangles,
would have been a perfect choice to train
young hands in patchwork. It is also a good choice
for the beginning quilter, or for any quilter who wants
a simple design that results in a striking quilt.

Quilt by Rita Grierson

Editor's Note:

Our staff ranks this quilt as very easy—it is ideal for the beginning quilter. In addition to the quilt shown in the photograph, we have offered you two other options: one for a bed quilt, and one for a wall hanging. Some other ideas:

- You can make the quilt even larger by adding borders. For more on adapting the quilt size, see page 349.
- Use the white triangles for signature blocks (see pages 352 and 353).
- Add borders and then prairie points (see page 365).

Finished Quilt Size

Lap Quilt Size: 59½" x 59½"
Full/Queen Size: 87½" x 94½"
Wall Hanging Size: 28" x 28"

Number of Blocks and Finished Size

3½" x 3½" Mosaic Blocks
  289 for Lap
  675 for Full/Queen
  64 for Wall Hanging

Materials
Lap Quilt:
1¼ yards total assorted peach prints
1¼ yards total assorted blue prints
2¼ yards muslin
3½ yards fabric for backing
½ yard fabric for binding
Twin-size batting

Cutting

Measurements include ¼" seam allowances.

From peach prints, cut:
- 73 (4⅜") squares. Cut squares in half diagonally to make 146 triangles (one is extra).

From blue prints, cut:
- 72 (4⅜) squares. Cut squares in half diagonally to make 146 triangles (one is extra).

From muslin, cut:
- 17 (4⅜"-wide) strips. Cut strips into 145 (4⅜") squares. Cut squares in half diagonally to make 290 triangles.

From binding fabric, cut:
- 7 (2¼"-wide) strips for binding.

Block Assembly

1. Join 1 colored and 1 muslin triangle along long edge to make 1 triangle-square *(Block Diagram)*.

2. Make 289 blocks. You will need 145 muslin/peach blocks and 144 muslin/blue blocks.

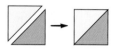

Block Diagram

Quilt Assembly

1. Referring to *Lap Quilt Top Assembly Diagram*, join blocks into 17 horizontal rows of 17 blocks each, alternating peach and blue blocks.

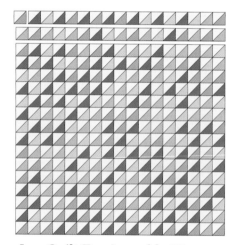

Lap Quilt Top Assembly Diagram

2. Join rows to complete quilt top.

Quilting and Finishing

1. Divide backing fabric into 2 (1¾-yard) lengths. Cut 1 length into 1 (25"-wide) lengthwise panel. Sew this panel to 1 side of wide panel. Press seam allowances toward narrow panel. Remaining panel is extra and may be used to make a hanging sleeve.

2. Layer backing, batting, and quilt top; baste. Quilt as desired. Quilt shown is outline-quilted in light triangles.

3. Join binding strips into 1 continuous piece for straight-grain French-fold binding. Add binding to quilt.

Materials
Full/Queen Quilt:
5 yards light solid
5 yards total assorted dark prints
7½ yards fabric for backing
¾ yard fabric for binding
Queen-size batting

Cutting

Measurements include ¼" seam allowances.

From light solid, cut:
- 38 (4⅜"-wide) strips. Cut strips into 338 (4⅜") squares. Cut squares in half diagonally to make 676 triangles (one is extra).

From dark prints, cut:
- 338 (4⅜") squares. Cut squares in half diagonally to make 676 triangles (one is extra).

From binding fabric, cut:
- 10 (2¼"-wide) strips for binding.

Block Assembly

1. Join 1 light triangle and 1 dark triangle along long edge to make 1 triangle-square *(Block Diagram)*.

Block Diagram

2. Make 675 blocks.

Quilt Assembly

1. Referring to *Full/Queen Quilt Top Assembly Diagram*, join blocks into 27 horizontal rows of 25 blocks each.

2. Join rows to complete quilt top.

Quilting and Finishing

1. Divide backing fabric into 3 (2½-yard) lengths. Cut 1 piece in half lengthwise. Sew 1 narrow panel between wide panels. Press seam allowances toward narrow panel. Seams will run horizontally.

2. Layer backing, batting, and quilt top; baste. Quilt as desired. Quilt shown is outline-quilted in light triangles.

Full/Queen Quilt Top Assembly Diagram

Quilt Assembly

1. Referring to *Wall Hanging Assembly Diagram*, lay out units in 8 rows of 8 blocks each, alternating red and green blocks.

2. Join into rows; join rows to complete quilt top.

Wall Hanging Assembly Diagram

Quilting and Finishing

1. Layer backing, batting, and quilt top; baste. Quilt as desired. Quilt shown is outline-quilted in light triangles.

2. Join 2¼"-wide binding strips into 1 continuous piece for straight-grain French-fold binding. Add binding to quilt.

3. Join binding strips into 1 continuous piece for *straight-grain French-fold binding*. Add binding to quilt.

Materials
Wall hanging:
⅜ yard red print
⅜ yard green print
⅝ yard white
1 yard fabric for backing
⅜ yard fabric for binding
1 (29" x 29") piece batting

Cutting
Measurements include ¼" seam allowances.

From red print, cut:
• 2 (4⅜"-wide) strips. Cut strips into 16 (4⅜") squares. Cut squares in half diagonally to make 32 triangles.

From green print, cut:
• 2 (4⅜"-wide) strips. Cut strips into 16 (4⅜") squares. Cut squares in half diagonally to make 32 triangles.

From white, cut:
• 4 (4⅜"-wide) strips. Cut strips into 32 (4⅜") squares. Cut squares in half diagonally to make 64 triangles.

From binding fabric, cut:
• 4 (2¼"-wide) strips for binding.

Block Assembly

1. Join 1 colored and 1 muslin triangle along long edge to make 1 triangle-square *(Block Diagram)*.

Block Diagram

2. Make 64 blocks. You will need 32 white/red blocks and 32 white/green blocks.

Kansas Dugout

During the westward migration of the mid-19th century,
the Kansas dugout, a crude type of dwelling
dug from the side of a hill and covered with a sod roof,
became home for many settlers.
The humble dugout inspired this traditional quilt.

Quilt by Mary E. Ramey

Finished Quilt Size
78½" x 89¼"

Number of Blocks and Finished Size
168 (5⅜") Kansas Dugout Blocks

Materials
5 yards total assorted prints
2⅝ yards white
2⅝ yards border print
2⅝ yards light print
¾ yard print for binding
5¼ yards fabric for backing
Full-size batting

Cutting
Measurements include ¼" seam allowances. Pattern is on page 158.

From assorted prints, cut:
• 672 As in matching sets of 2.

From white, cut:
• 10 (2¼"-wide) strips. Cut strips into 168 (2¼") B squares.
• 24 (2¾"-wide) strips. Cut strips into 336 (2¾") squares. Cut squares in half diagonally to make 672 C triangles.

From border print, cut:
• 4 (4½"-wide) lengthwise strips, centered on design, for outer border.

From light print, cut:
• 4 (3½"-wide) lengthwise strips for outer border.

From print, cut:
• 9 (2¼"-wide) strips for binding.

Block Assembly
1. Referring to *Block Assembly Diagram 1*, join long side of 1 A to 1 B, leaving seam allowances loose. Join matching A to opposite side of B. Repeat with second set of As. Set in

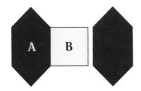

Block Assembly Diagram 1

seams between As *(Block Assembly Diagram 2)*.
2. Add 1 C triangle to each corner

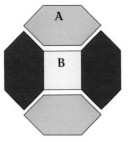

Block Assembly Diagram 2

to complete 1 Kansas Dugout block *(Block Diagram)*.

3. Make 168 Kansas Dugout blocks.

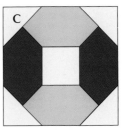

Block Diagram

Quilt Assembly

1. Referring to *Quilt Top Assembly Diagram,* lay out blocks in 14 horizontal rows of 12 blocks each. Join into rows; join rows to complete quilt center.

2. Join 1 border print strip and 1 light print strip to make 1 border strip. Make 4 border strips.

3. Center 1 border strip on each side of quilt, border print side to inside. Add to quilt, mitering corners.

Quilting and Finishing

1. Divide backing fabric into 2 (2⅝-yard) lengths. Cut 1 piece in half lengthwise. Sew 1 narrow panel to each side of wide panel. Press seam allowances toward narrow panels.

2. Layer backing, batting, and quilt top; baste. Quilt as desired. Quilt shown is outline-quilted.

3. Join 2¼"-wide print strips into 1 continuous piece for straight-grain French-fold binding. Add binding to quilt.

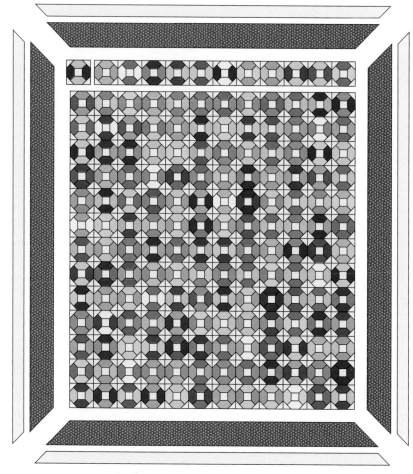

Quilt Top Assembly Diagram

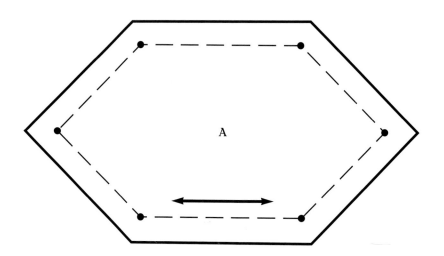

A

Hexagon Star

Although this block pattern is made up completely of diamonds, when blocks are joined together, they make a hexagonal, or six-sided shape. The cream spaces between the stars also form hexagons.

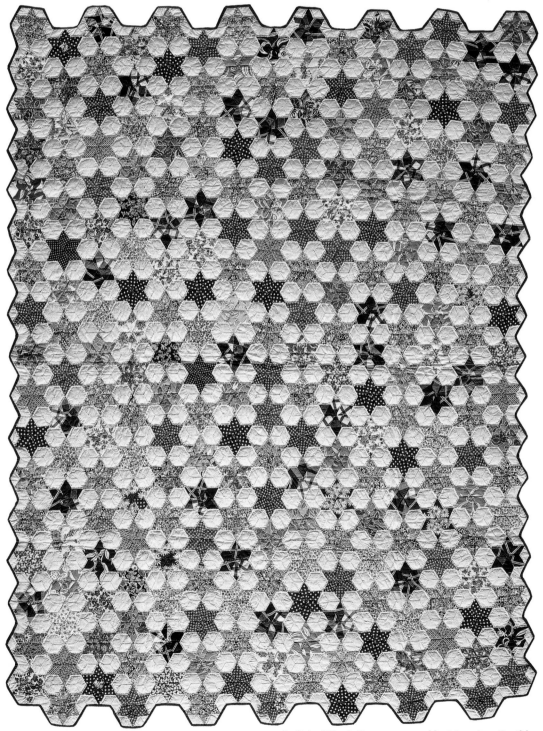

Quilt by Winnie Pearson; owned by Mary Ann Keathley

Finished Quilt Size

74¾" x 98½"

Number of Blocks and Finished Size

255 (6½" x 5⅝") Hexagon Star Blocks

Materials

7½ yards total assorted prints (or 255 [4" x 10"] scraps)
7½ yards white
6 yards fabric for backing
1 yard blue for binding
Queen-size batting

Cutting

Measurements include ¼" seam allowances. Pattern is on page 162.

From prints, cut:

- 255 sets of 6 As. If working with strips, cut strips 1⅞" wide. Referring to *Cutting Diagram*, cut strips at a 60° angle in 1⅞" increments to make 6 matching diamonds. Check your cutting accuracy against the template on page 162.

From white, cut:

- 1,530 As. Or cut yardage into 1⅞"-wide strips. Referring to *Cutting Diagram*, cut strips at a 60° angle in 1⅞" increments to make 1,530 diamonds. Check your cutting accuracy against the template on page 162.

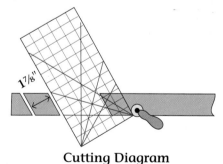

Cutting Diagram

From blue, cut:

- 1 (36") square for bias binding.

Block Assembly

1. Join 2 print As as shown in *Block Assembly Diagram*. Set in 1 white A to make 1 point unit. Make 3 point units. Join point units along print As.

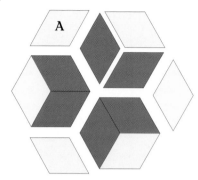

Block Assembly Diagram

2. Set in 3 white As to complete 1 Hexagon Star block *(Block Diagram)*.
3. Make 255 Hexagon Star blocks.

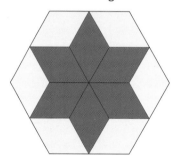

Block Diagram

Quilt Assembly

1. Referring to *Quilt Top Assembly Diagram*, lay out blocks in 15 vertical rows of 17 blocks each. Refer to *Row Assembly Diagram* as a guide.

Row Assembly Diagram

2. Join into rows as shown in *Quilt Top Assembly Diagram.* Set rows together to complete quilt.

Quilting and Finishing

1. Divide backing fabric into 2 (3-yard) lengths. Cut 1 piece in half lengthwise. Sew 1 narrow panel to each side of wide panel. Press seam allowances toward narrow panels.

2. Layer backing, batting, and quilt top; baste. Quilt as desired. Quilt shown is outline-quilted in white areas and quilted in-the-ditch in star seams.

3. Make 450" of 2¼"-wide bias strip from square. Fold and press to make French-fold bias binding. Add binding to quilt.

Quilt Top Assembly Diagram

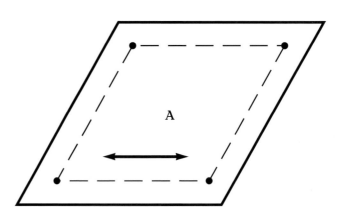

Spider Web

We think of paper or string piecing as a modern technique, but thrifty quilters have sewn small scraps of fabric onto old newspapers for generations. Not surprisingly, the technique was popular during the Depression. Small fabric bits combine beautifully to make this Spider Web pattern.

Quilt by Maurine Lee; owned by Carol M. Tipton

Finished Quilt Size
64" x 80"

Number of Blocks and Finished Size
20 (16") Spider Web Blocks

Materials
6 yards assorted scraps
2½ yards red
5 yards fabric for backing
⅝ yard muslin for binding
Twin-size batting
Foundation material (paper, tear-
   away stabilizer, or thin muslin)

Cutting
Measurements include ¼" seam
allowances. Cut assorted scraps into
random-width strips. Patterns are
on page 166.

From foundation material, cut:
• 160 As.

From red, cut:
• 80 Bs.
• 80 Bs reversed.

From muslin, cut:
• 8 (2¼"-wide) strips for binding.

Block Assembly
1. Place 1 strip right side up,
covering area past seam allowance,
on 1 foundation A and pin. Place
second scrap strip right side down
atop first strip, aligning raw edges.
Stitch in place *(Diagram A)*.

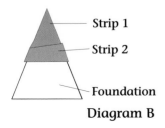

Diagram A

2. Flip second strip open and
press *(Diagram B)*.
3. Place next strip right side down

Strip 1
Strip 2
Foundation

Diagram B

over previous piece. Stitch in place
(Diagram C).

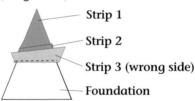

Strip 1
Strip 2
Strip 3 (wrong side)
Foundation

Diagram C

4. Flip third strip open and press
(Diagram D).

Strip 1
Strip 2
Strip 3
Foundation

Diagram D

5. Continue until foundation is
covered *(Diagram E)*. Trim to outside
line of A *(Diagram F)*. If using paper

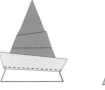

Diagram E   **Diagram F**

or other removable foundation,
remove after block is pieced.

6. String piece 8 As. Referring to
Block Assembly Diagram, lay out with
4 Bs and 4 Bs reversed. Join As to
Bs. Join to complete 1 Spider Web
block *(Block Diagram)*.

7. Make 20 Spider Web blocks.

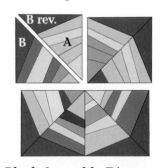

Block Assembly Diagram

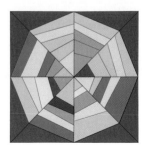

BlockDiagram

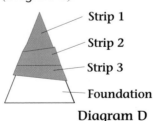

Quilt Top Assembly Diagram

Quilt Assembly

1. Referring to *Quilt Top Assembly Diagram,* lay out blocks in 5 horizontal rows of 4 blocks each.

2. Join into rows; join rows to complete quilt.

Quilting and Finishing

1. Divide backing fabric into 2 (2½-yard) lengths. Cut 1 piece in half lengthwise. Sew 1 narrow panel to each side of wide panel. Press seam allowances toward narrow panels.

2. Layer backing, batting, and quilt top; baste. Quilt as desired. Quilt shown is outline-quilted.

3. Join 2¼"-wide light strips into 1 continuous piece for straight-grain French-fold binding. Add binding to quilt.

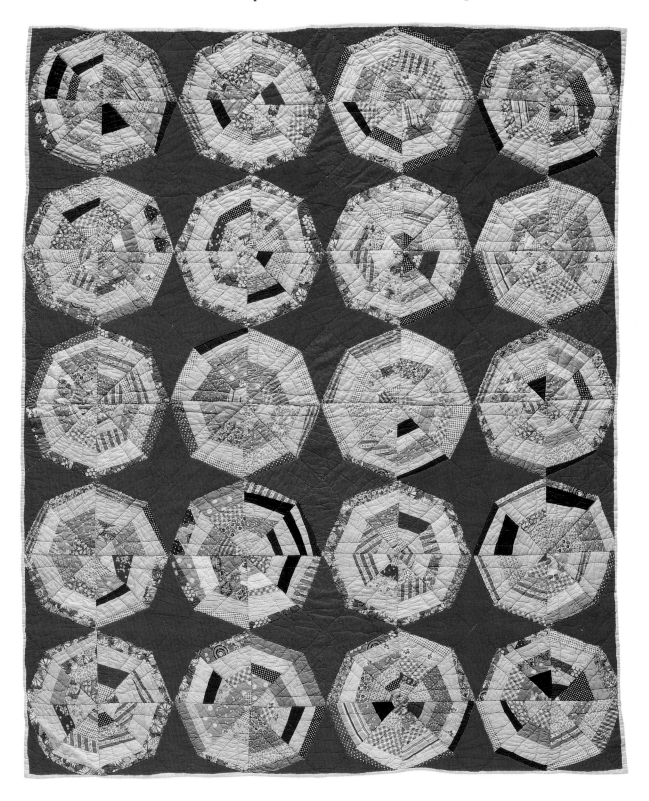

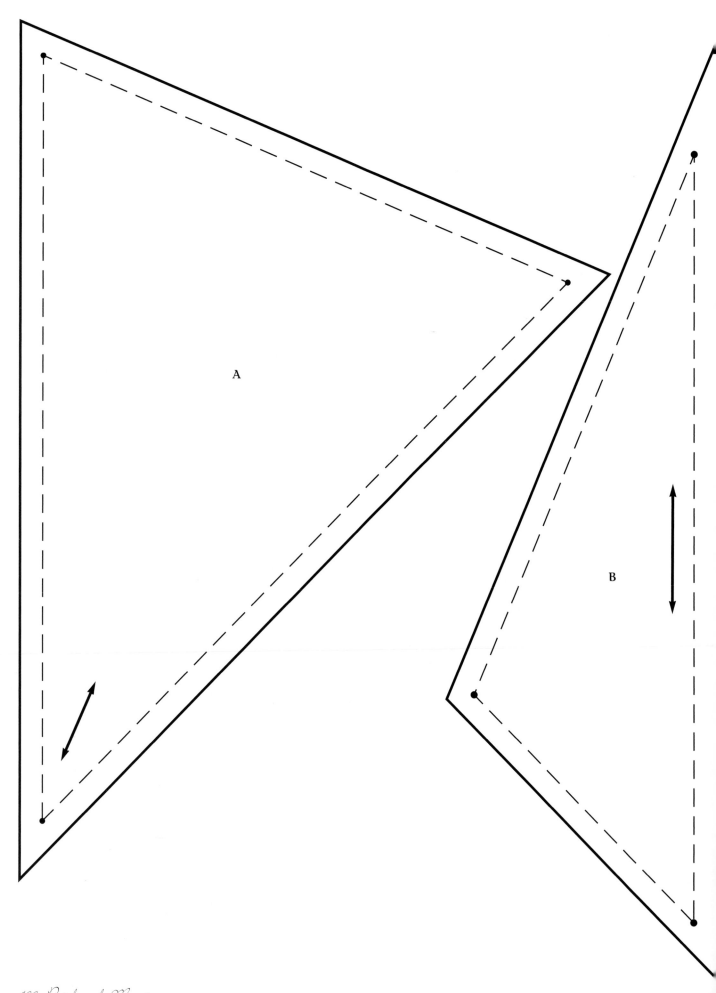

A

B

Twist

Although this design may look complex, it is actually made up of just two different blocks put together in an alternate set. Other names for this pattern include Twisted Rope and Plaited Block.

Quilt by Annie Phillips

Finished Quilt Size

82" x 99"

Number of Blocks and Finished Size

63 (6") Bright Hopes Blocks (Block 1)
80 (6") Snowball Blocks (Block 2)

Materials

4 yards black print
2½ yards red print
4 yards white
7½ yards fabric for backing
Queen-size batting

Cutting

Measurements include ¼" seam allowances. Border strips are exact length needed. You may want to cut them longer to allow for piecing variations.

From black print, cut:

- 14 (2½"-wide) strips. Cut strips into 126 (2½" x 4½") A rectangles.
- 9 (2½"-wide) strips. Cut strips into 142 (2½") D squares.
- 9 (5½"-wide) strips. Piece strips to make 2 (5½" x 89½") side borders and 2 (5½" x 82½") top and bottom borders.
- 10 (2¼"-wide) strips for binding.

From red print, cut:

- 14 (2½"-wide) strips. Cut strips into 126 (2½" x 4½") A rectangles.
- 9 (2½"-wide) strips. Cut strips into 142 (2½") D squares.
- 9 (2½"-wide) strips. Piece strips to make 2 (2½" x 85½") side borders and 2 (2½" x 72½") top and bottom borders.

From white, cut:

- 4 (2½"-wide) strips. Cut strips into 63 (2½") B squares.
- 14 (6½"-wide) strips. Cut strips into 80 (6½") C squares.
- 2 (9¾"-wide) strips. Cut strips into 8 (9¾") squares. Cut squares in quarters diagonally to make 32 side setting triangles.
- 1 (5⅛"-wide) strip. Cut strip into 2 (5⅛") squares. Cut squares in half diagonally to make 4 corner setting triangles.

Block Assembly

1. Referring to *Block 1 Assembly Diagram*, use partial seams to join 1 red A to top of 1 B. Join 1 black A to right side, 1 red A to bottom, and 1 black A to left side. Complete seam on top to complete 1 of Block 1. Make 63 of Block 1 (*Block 1 Diagram*).

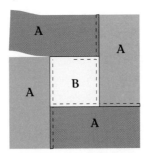

**Block 1 Assembly Diagram
(back of block)**

Block 1 Diagram

2. Referring to *Block 2 Assembly Diagram*, use diagonal seams to place 1 black D atop 1 corner of 1 C. Stitch diagonally from corner to corner. Trim excess fabric ¼" from stitching. Press open to reveal triangle. Repeat with black Ds on 4 corners to complete 1 of Block 2. Make 24 of Block 2.

Block 2 Assembly Diagram

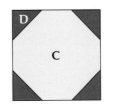

Block 2 Diagram

3. Referring to *Block 3 Diagram*, use diagonal seams method as in Step 2, using 4 red Ds.

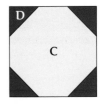

Block 3 Diagram

4. Referring to *Block 4 Diagram*, use diagonal seams method as in Step 2, using 3 black Ds. Leave remaining corner unpieced. Make 14 of Block 4.

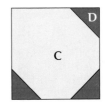

Block 4 Diagram

5. Referring to *Block 5 Diagram*, use diagonal seams method as in Step 4, using 3 red Ds.

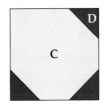

Block 5 Diagram

6. Referring to *Block 6 Diagram*, use diagonal seams to add 2 black Ds to 1 C. Make 2 of Block 6.

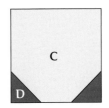

Block 6 Diagram

7. Referring to *Block 7 Diagram*, use diagonal seams to add red Ds to 1 C. Make 2 of Block 7.

Block 7 Diagram

Quilt Assembly

1. Referring to *Quilt Top Assembly Diagram*, lay out blocks and setting triangles as shown.

2. Join into diagonal rows; join rows to complete quilt center.

3. Add red side borders to quilt. Add top and bottom borders.

4. Add black side borders to quilt. Add top and bottom borders.

Quilting and Finishing

1. Divide backing fabric into 3 (2½-yard) lengths. Join to make backing. Seams will run horizontally.

2. Layer backing, batting, and quilt top; baste. Quilt as desired. Quilt shown is quilted in-the-ditch around white pieces, with Cs filled with *Twist Quilting Pattern* below.

3. Join 2¼"-wide black print strips into 1 continuous piece for straight-grain French-fold binding. Add binding to quilt.

The numbers indicate block placement.

Quilt Top Assembly Diagram

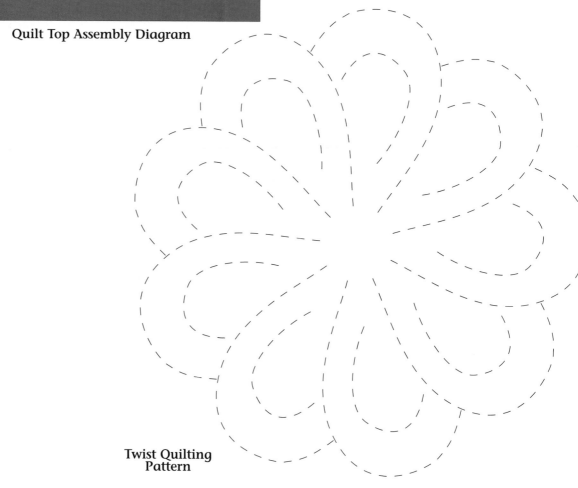

Twist Quilting Pattern

Crossed Canoes

A frequent sight on the American frontier, canoes were a
vital means of transportation for American Indians.
The constant presence of these wooden crafts was no doubt
an inspiration for an imaginative pioneer woman
who pieced her scraps into this design.

Quilt by Carolyn A. Tolliver

Finished Quilt Size
Lap size: 48" x 60"

Number of Blocks and Finished Size
12 (12") Crossed Canoe Blocks

Materials
2 yards navy print
¼ yard red print
2½ yards total light prints
2½ yards total dark prints
1 yard red stripe for bias binding
3 yards fabric for backing
Twin-size batting
Foundation material (paper, tear-away stabilizer, lightweight muslin)

Cutting
Measurements include ¼" seam allowances. Pattern is on page 175.

From navy print, cut:
• 4 (5½"-wide) lengthwise strips for outer border.

From red, cut:
• 5 (1½"-wide) strips. Piece to make 2 (1½" x 48½") inner side borders and 2 (1½" x 38½") inner top and bottom borders.

From light prints, cut:
• 24 (4" x 8") pieces for As.
• 24 sets of:
  • 2 (4½" x 7") pieces for Bs.
  • 1 (3½") square for Cs.

From dark prints, cut:
• 24 (4" x 8") pieces for As.
• 24 sets of:
  • 2 (4½" x 7") pieces for Bs.
  • 1 (3½") square for Cs.

From red stripe, cut:
• 1 (30") square for bias binding. Make 250" of 2¼"-wide bias strip. Fold and press to make bias binding.

Block Assembly
Set your machine to a short stitch length for greater ease in removing paper upon completion. Work with the paper pattern facing you. The fabric will be under the paper as you work.

1. Trace, scan, or photocopy 48 foundation patterns onto paper.

2. Choose 1 light A and 1 dark B/C set.

3. Place A fabric under paper with wrong sides facing *(Photo A).*

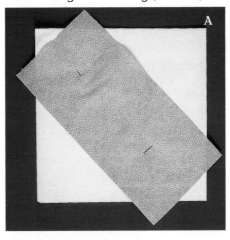

4. Pin in place (Photo B).

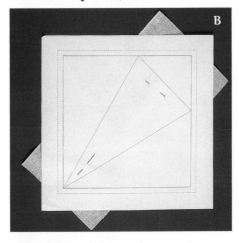

5. Pin B fabric in place so that it extends over A/B seam line. Stitch along line *(Photo C).*

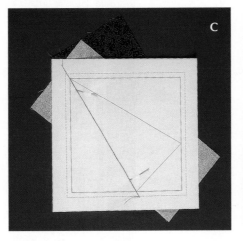

6. Trim excess fabric ¼" beyond seam line *(Photo D).* Press open.

7. Pin B fabric in place so that it extends over A/B seam line. Stitch along line *(Photo E).* Trim excess

fabric beyond stitching *(Photo F).* Press open.

8. Pin C fabric in place so that it extends over A/C line. Stitch along line *(Photo G)*. Trim excess fabric beyond stitching. Press open.

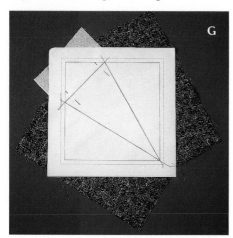

9. Trim excess fabric and paper from block, taking care to leave ¼" seam allowance on all sides *(Photo H)*.

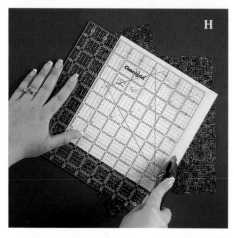

Each unit should measure 6½" *(Photo I)*.

10. Make 48 units.

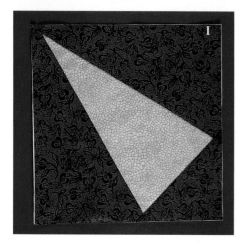

11. Lay out 4 units as shown in *Block Assembly Diagram*. Join to make 1 Crossed Canoe block *(Block Diagram)*. Carefully remove paper from back.

12. Make 12 Crossed Canoe blocks.

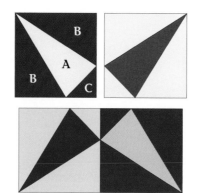

Block Assembly Diagram

Block Diagram

Quilt Assembly

1. Referring to *Quilt Top Assembly Diagram*, lay out blocks in 4 horizontal rows of 3 blocks each.

2. Join into rows; join rows to complete quilt center.

3. Add red inner side borders to quilt. Add top and bottom borders.

4. Center 1 navy outer border on each side of quilt top and add. Miter corners.

Quilting and Finishing

1. Divide backing fabric into 2 (1½-yard) lengths. Cut 1 piece in half lengthwise. Sew 1 narrow panel to each side of wide panel. Press seam allowances toward narrow panels. Seams will run horizontally.

2. Layer backing, batting, and quilt top; baste. Quilt as desired. Quilt shown is outline-quilted with diagonal fill.

3. Add bias binding to quilt.

Quilt Top Assembly Diagram

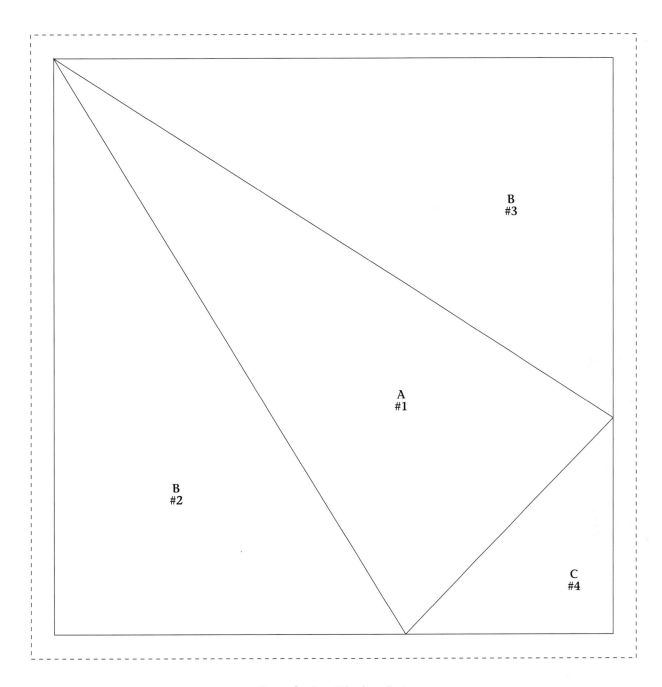

Foundation Piecing Pattern

If you prefer traditional piecing, trace the finished-size patterns and add ¼" seam allowance around each piece. Outer dashed line indicates seam allowance for foundation unit.

Snail's Trail

This seemingly complex design, also known as Virginia Reel and Indiana Puzzle, first appeared in the *Kansas City Star* in 1935. The easy-to-piece interlocking blocks give this quilt a dynamic spinning effect.

Finished Quilt Size
70" x 84"

Number of Blocks and Finished Size
49 (7") Snail's Trail Blocks

Materials
5 yards assorted dark prints
3 yards assorted light prints
¾ yard brown print for binding
5 yards fabric for backing
Twin-size batting

Cutting
Measurements include ¼" seam allowances.

From dark prints, cut:
- 116 (1¾") A squares.
- 58 (2⅝") squares. Cut squares in half diagonally to make 116 B triangles.
- 58 (3⅜") squares. Cut squares in half diagonally to make 116 C triangles.
- 58 (4⅜") squares. Cut squares in half diagonally to make 116 D triangles.
- 30 (7½") setting squares.
- 40 (4" x 7½") border strips.
- 4 (4") corner squares.

From light prints, cut:
- 80 (1¾") A squares.
- 40 (2⅝") squares. Cut squares in half diagonally to make 80 B triangles.
- 40 (3⅜") squares. Cut squares in half diagonally to make 80 C triangles.
- 40 (4⅜") squares. Cut squares in half diagonally to make 80 D triangles.
- 20 (7½") setting squares.

From brown print, cut:
- 9 (2¼"-wide) strips for binding.

Block Assembly
1. Referring to *Four-Patch Assembly Diagram*, join 2 light and 2 dark As to make 1 Four-Patch unit.

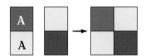

Four-Patch Assembly Diagram

2. Join 2 light B triangles to opposite sides of Four-patch, orienting as shown in *Center Block Assembly Diagram*. Join 2 dark Bs to complete center.

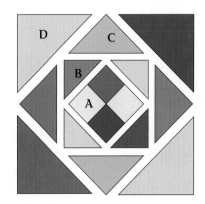

Center Block Assembly Diagram

3. In same manner, add 2 light and 2 dark Cs. Add 2 light and 2 dark Ds to complete 1 Snail's Trail center block (*Center Block Diagram*). Make 31 Snail's Trail center blocks.

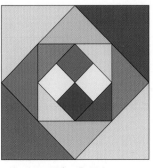

Center Block Diagram

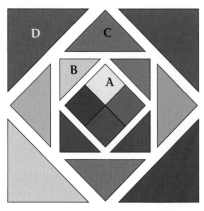

Side Block Assembly Diagram

4. Referring to *Side Block Assembly Diagram,* join 1 light and 3 dark As to make 1 four-patch. Join 1 light B and 1 dark B triangles to opposite sides of four-patch, orienting as shown. Join 2 dark Bs to complete center. In same manner, add 1 light and 3 dark Cs. Add 1 light and 3 dark Ds to complete 1 Snail's Trail side block *(Side Block Diagram).* Make 18 Snail's Trail side blocks.

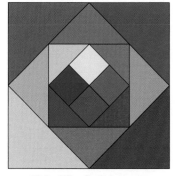

Side Block Diagram

Quilt Assembly

1. Referring to *Quilt Top Assembly Diagram,* lay out 2 corner squares and 9 border strips. Join to make top border row. Repeat to make bottom border row.

2. Lay out 2 border strips, 5 dark setting squares, and 4 side blocks as shown in *Quilt Top Assembly Diagram.* Join to make top block row. Repeat to make bottom block row.

3. Lay out 2 border strips, 2 side blocks, 3 center blocks, and 4 light setting squares as shown. Join to make Row 1. Make 5 of Row 1.

4. Lay out 2 border strips, 5 dark setting squares, and 4 center blocks as shown. Join to make Row 2. Make 4 of Row 2.

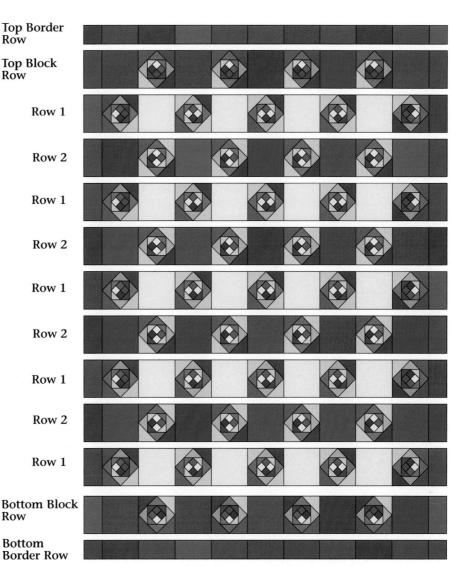

Top Border Row

Top Block Row

Row 1

Row 2

Row 1

Row 2

Row 1

Row 2

Row 1

Row 2

Row 1

Bottom Block Row

Bottom Border Row

Quilt Top Assembly Diagram

5. Referring to *Quilt Top Assembly Diagram,* lay out rows in order: top border, top block, alternate 5 Row 1s and 4 Row 2s, bottom block, and bottom border. Join rows to complete quilt.

Quilting and Finishing

1. Divide backing fabric into 2 (2½-yard) lengths. Cut 1 piece in half lengthwise. Sew 1 narrow panel to each side of wide panel. Press seam allowances toward narrow panels.

2. Layer backing, batting, and quilt top; baste. Quilt as desired. Quilt shown has no batting and is quilted in-the-ditch with a flannel backing.

3. Join 2¼"-wide brown print strips into 1 continuous piece for straight-grain French-fold binding. Add binding to quilt.

Pine Burr

The Chicago Tribune first published this pattern as
Pine Cones in 1936 as part of a quilting column
by Nancy Cabot. The pattern pre-dates this publication,
as this quilt was made prior to 1936.

Quilt by Adeline Webb Bowen; owned by Shirley T. Bowen

Finished Quilt Size
76" x 76"

Number of Blocks and Finished Size
16 (19") Pine Burr Blocks

Materials
16 (½-yard) pieces assorted light prints
16 (⅜-yard) pieces assorted dark prints
3½ yards pink stripe
1¼ yards brown print
¾ yard blue for binding
4½ yards fabric for backing
Full-size batting

Cutting
Measurements include ¼" seam allowances. Patterns are on page 182–183.

From light prints, cut:
- 16 sets of:
  - 1 (5½") square. Cut square in quarters diagonally to make 4 A triangles.
  - 1 (2½") C square.
  - 48 (2" x 3") pieces for Es.
  - 4 Fs.

From dark prints, cut:
- 16 sets of:
  - 4 Bs.
  - 4 Ds.
  - 40 (2" x 3") pieces for Es.

From pink stripe, cut:
- 48 Gs. Align long edge with stripe.

From brown print, cut:
- 16 Gs.

From blue, cut:
- 9 (2¼"-wide) strips for binding.

Block Assembly
1. Choose 1 set each light and dark pieces.

2. Trace, scan, or photocopy 128 paper piecing patterns from page 183. Place 1 light E on wrong side of pattern, with wrong sides facing. Align 1 dark E with seam line so that it will flip over and cover area #2 after stitching. With right sides together, stitch along line between #1 and #2. Trim seam allowance, if

needed, and flip #2 in place. Finger-press seam. Continue, alternating light and dark Es in numerical order. When paper pattern is complete, trim along seam allowance, remove paper, and press unit.

3. Make 8 E units.

4. Referring to *Block Assembly Diagram*, lay out 4 As, 4 Bs, and 1 C. Join to make center.

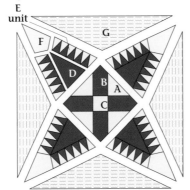

Block Assembly Diagram

5. Join 1 E unit to each long side of 1 D, dark side to inside. Set in 1 F to complete 1 burr unit. Make 4 burr units.

6. Join 1 burr unit to each side of center. Set in 1 G on each side to complete 1 Pine Burr block *(Block Diagram)*. Make 4 blocks for center.

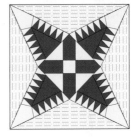

Block Diagram

7. Referring to *Side Block Diagram*, make 8 side blocks with 1 brown and 3 pink stripe Gs.

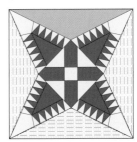

Side Block Diagram

8. Referring to *Corners Block Diagram,* make 4 corner blocks with 2 brown and 2 pink stripe Gs.

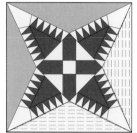

Corners Block Diagram

Quilt Assembly

1. Lay out blocks, orienting as shown in *Quilt Top Assembly Diagram.*

2. Join into rows; join rows to complete quilt.

Quilting and Finishing

1. Divide backing fabric into 2 (2¼-yard) lengths. Cut 1 piece in half lengthwise. Sew 1 narrow panel to each side of wide panel. Press seam allowances toward narrow panels.

2. Layer backing, batting, and quilt top; baste. Quilt as desired.

Quilt Top Assembly Diagram

Quilt shown is quilted in stripes in piecework and in diagonals in Gs.

3. Join 2¼"-wide blue strips into 1 continuous piece for straight-grain French-fold binding. Add binding to quilt.

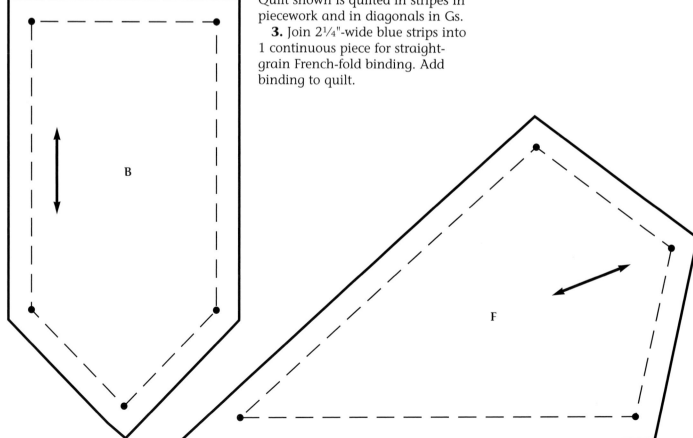

B

F

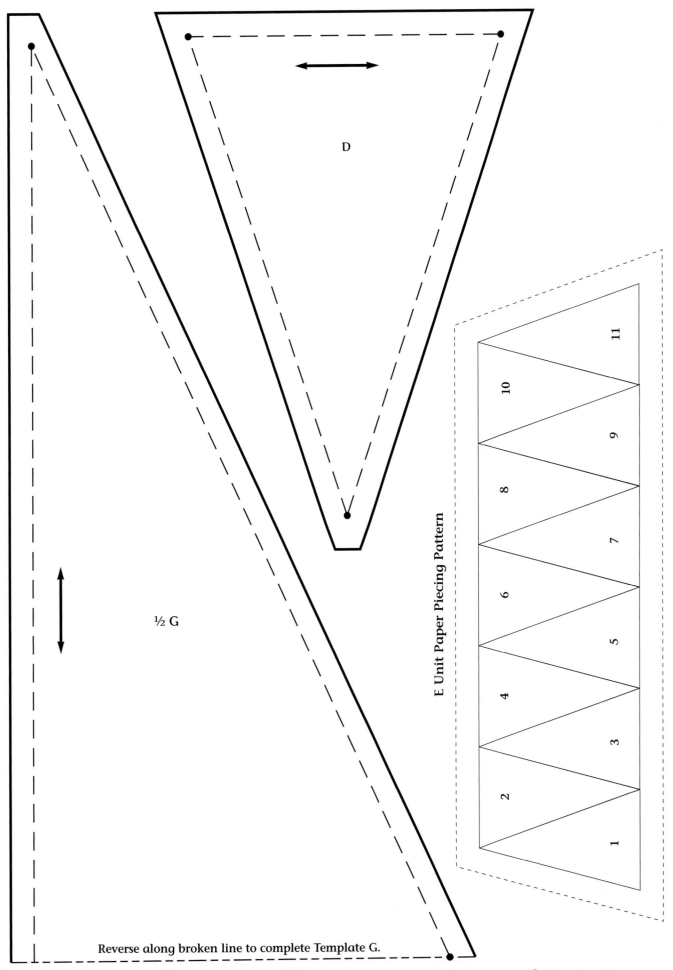

D

½ G

E Unit Paper Piecing Pattern

1 2 3 4 5 6 7 8 9 10 11

Reverse along broken line to complete Template G.

Ocean Waves

This quilt pattern is named for the numerous triangle pieces that recall the seemingly endless ocean waves that break along the shore. Because of this, many old examples are blue and white quilts. Modern quilters often nod to tradition by including at least a little bit of blue in their quilt.

Finished Quilt Size
68¼" x 82¼"

Number of Blocks and Finished Size
12 (14") Ocean Waves Blocks

Materials
1¾ yards assorted light prints
1¾ yards assorted dark prints
7 yards pink
1 yard blue tone-on-tone print
5 yards backing
Twin-size batting

Cutting
Measurements include ¼" seam allowances.

From light prints, cut:
• 48 (2⅝") squares. Cut squares in half diagonally to make 96 B triangles.
• 240 (2⅝") squares for quick pieced B units.

From dark prints, cut:
• 48 (2⅝") squares. Cut squares in half diagonally to make 96 B triangles.
• 240 (2⅝") squares for quick pieced B units.

From pink, cut:
• 2⅜ yards. Cut yardage into 4 (9¼"-wide) lengthwise strips for outer border.
• 6 (1⅞"-wide) strips. Piece to make 4 (1⅞" x 60") strips for inner border.
• 9 (2¼"-wide) strips for binding.
• 2 (5½"-wide) strips. Cut strips into 12 (5½") A squares.
• 24 (4⅜") squares. Cut squares in half diagonally to make 48 C triangles.

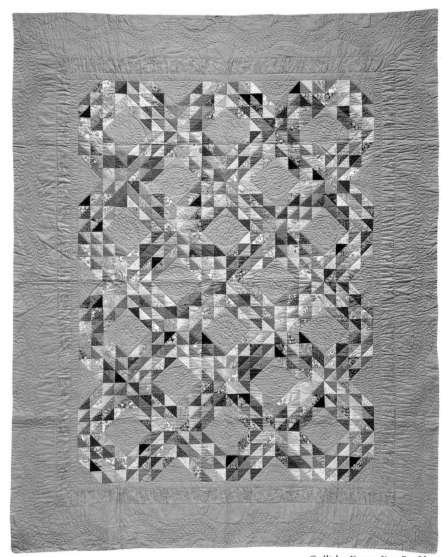

Quilt by Karen Kay Buckley

From blue tone-on-tone print, cut:
• 8 (3½"-wide) strips. Piece strips to make 4 (3½" x 70") middle border strips.

Block Assembly
1. Referring to *Triangle-Square Assembly Diagram,* draw a diagonal line from corner to corner on back of 1 light square. Place 1 light and 1 dark square together, right sides

facing. Stitch ¼" from line on both sides. Cut apart and press open to make 2 B units. Make 40 B units. (For traditional piecing, cut squares in half diagonally and sew together

Triangle-Square Assembly Diagram

...g edges to make triangle-
...)
...eferring to *Block Assembly*
...*am,* lay out 10 B units, 2 light
...angles and 2 dark triangles as
...nown. Join into sections; join sections. Add 1 C triangle to complete
1 unit. Make 4 triangle units,
noting direction of dark triangles
in each unit.

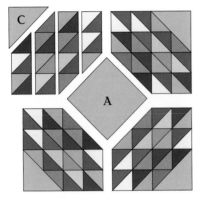

Block Assembly Diagram

3. Lay out 4 units and 1 A square
as shown in *Block Assembly Diagram.*
Join each unit to A, then set in
seams between triangle units to
complete 1 Ocean Waves block
(Block Diagram).
4. Make 12 Ocean Waves blocks.

Block Diagram

Quilt Assembly

1. Referring to *Quilt Top Assembly
Diagram,* lay out blocks in 4
horizontal rows of 3 blocks each.
Join into rows; join rows to
complete quilt center.
2. Fold each border strip in half
end to end; crease to find center
point. Join 1 each narrow pink,
blue, and wide pink strips, aligning
center creases, to make 1 border
strip. Make 4 border strips.
3. Center 1 border strip on each
side of quilt and join. Miter corners.

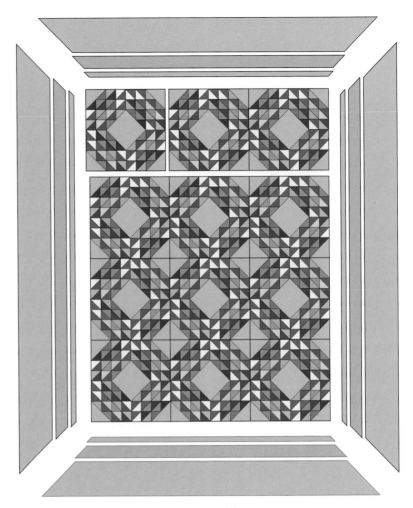

Quilt Top Assembly Diagram

Quilting and Finishing

1. Divide backing fabric into
2 (2½-yard) lengths. Cut 1 piece in
half lengthwise. Sew 1 narrow
panel to each side of wide panel.
Press seam allowances toward
narrow panels.
2. Layer backing, batting, and
quilt top; baste. Quilt as desired.
Quilt shown has a feather wreath
in As, with feathered plumes in
outer border.
3. Join pink strips into 1 continuous piece for straight-grain French-
fold binding. Add binding to quilt.

Friendship Album

To make this quilt, Mable Webb sent pieces of
muslin to celebrities for their signatures. She then
embroidered over the inked signatures to preserve them.
You may want to try this clever idea with your favorite
celebrities or with family and friends.
For ideas on getting started, see pages 352–353.

Quilt by Mable Azbill Webb

Finished Quilt Size
90" x 94"

Number of Blocks and Finished Size
25 (14") Friendship Album Blocks

Materials
25 fat eighths (9" x 22") assorted prints
25 (4½" x 17") strips assorted solids
4½ yards muslin
2 yards solid gold
7⅞ yards fabric for backing
Queen-size batting

Cutting
Measurements include ¼" seam allowances. Border strips are exact length needed. You may want to cut them longer to allow for piecing variations.

From each print, cut:
• 2 (7⅞") squares. Cut squares in half diagonally to make 4 A triangles.

From each solid, cut:
• 4 (4⅛") squares. Cut squares in half diagonally to make 8 B triangles.

From muslin, cut:
• 7 (5⅛"-wide) strips. Cut strips into 25 (5⅛" x 9¾") C rectangles.
• 3 (4⅛"-wide) strips. Cut strips into 25 (4⅛") squares. Cut squares in half diagonally to make 50 B triangles.
• 4 (14½"-wide) strips. Cut strips into 40 (3½" x 14½") sashing strips.
• 5 (2½"-wide) strips. Piece to make 2 (2½" x 82½") inner side borders.
• 5 (3½"-wide) strips. Piece to make 2 (3½" x 86½") inner top and bottom borders.

From solid gold, cut:
• 2 (3½"-wide) strips. Cut strips into 16 (3½") sashing squares.
• 5 (2½"-wide) strips. Piece strips to make 2 (2½" x 88½") outer side borders.
• 5 (3½"-wide) strips. Piece strips to make 2 (3½" x 90½") outer top and bottom borders.
• 10 (2¼"-wide) strips for binding.

Quilt Top Assembly Diagram

Block Assembly
1. Referring to *Block Assembly Diagram*, choose 1 print set and 1 solid set. Join 3 solid Bs and 1 muslin B to make 1 triangle unit. Make 2 triangle units.

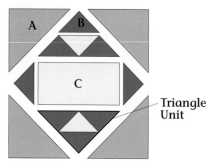

Block Assembly Diagram

2. Join 1 triangle unit to top of 1 C. Join remaining unit to bottom of C. Add 1 solid B triangle to each end to complete center.

3. Join 1 print A triangle to opposite sides of center. Repeat with remaining A triangles to complete 1 Friendship Album block (*Block Diagram*).

4. Make 25 Friendship Album blocks.

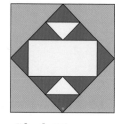

Block Diagram

Quilt Assembly
1. Referring to *Quilt Top Assembly Diagram*, alternate 5 blocks and 4 sashing strips. Join to make 1 block row. Make 5 block rows.

2. Alternate 5 sashing strips and 4 sashing squares. Join to make 1 sashing row. Make 4 sashing rows.

3. Alternate block rows and sashing rows. Join rows to complete quilt center.

4. Add muslin inner side borders to quilt. Add muslin top and bottom borders.

5. Add gold outer side borders to quilt. Add gold top and bottom borders.

Quilting and Finishing
1. Divide backing fabric into 3 (2⅝-yard) lengths. Join to make backing. Seams will run horizontally.

2. Layer backing, batting, and quilt top; baste. Quilt as desired. Quilt shown is outline-quilted in piecework, with diamond patterns in sashing and borders.

3. Join gold strips into 1 continuous piece for straight-grain French-fold binding. Add binding to quilt.

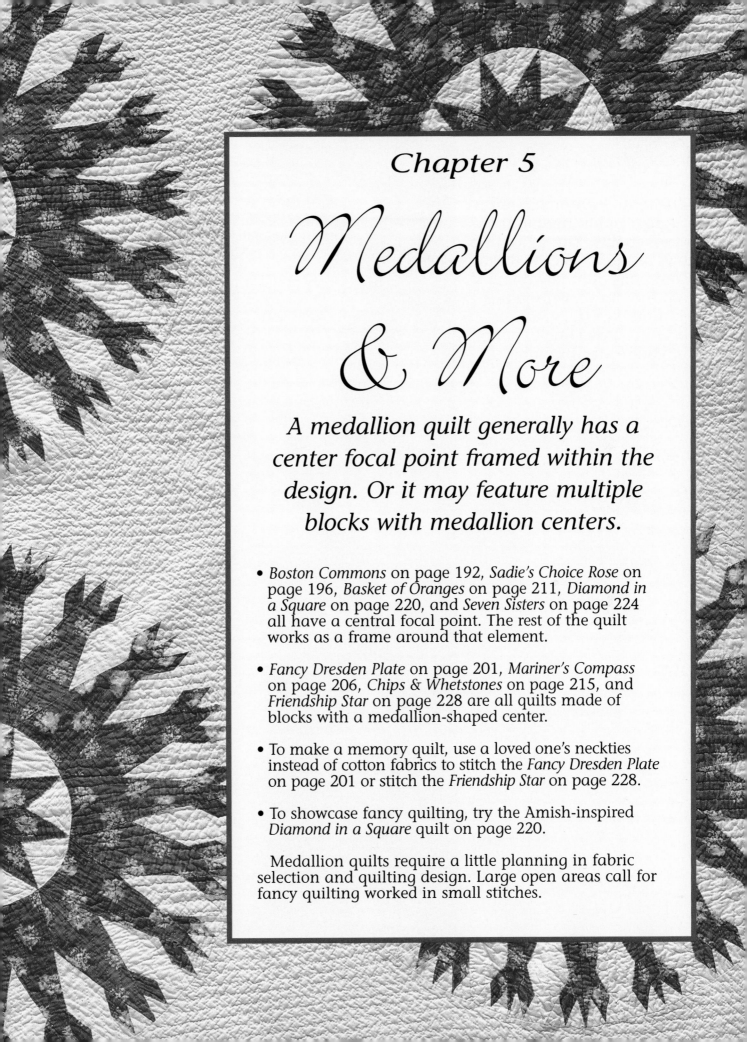

Chapter 5

Medallions & More

A medallion quilt generally has a center focal point framed within the design. Or it may feature multiple blocks with medallion centers.

- *Boston Commons* on page 192, *Sadie's Choice Rose* on page 196, *Basket of Oranges* on page 211, *Diamond in a Square* on page 220, and *Seven Sisters* on page 224 all have a central focal point. The rest of the quilt works as a frame around that element.

- *Fancy Dresden Plate* on page 201, *Mariner's Compass* on page 206, *Chips & Whetstones* on page 215, and *Friendship Star* on page 228 are all quilts made of blocks with a medallion-shaped center.

- To make a memory quilt, use a loved one's neckties instead of cotton fabrics to stitch the *Fancy Dresden Plate* on page 201 or stitch the *Friendship Star* on page 228.

- To showcase fancy quilting, try the Amish-inspired *Diamond in a Square* quilt on page 220.

Medallion quilts require a little planning in fabric selection and quilting design. Large open areas call for fancy quilting worked in small stitches.

Boston Commons

The term "commons" refers to a public area in a municipality. The concentric rows of squares in the Boston Commons quilt pay homage to the city's town squares and bustling areas of activity. Make one to honor your own community.

Quilt by Daisy V. Toland,
owned by Hazel O. Mannis

Finished Size

88" x 96"

Materials

5½" x 5½" scrap for Row 1
1 fat eighth (9" x 22") each for
  Rows 2–3
1 fat quarter (18" x 22") each for
  Rows 4–12
³⁄₈ yard each for Rows 13–19
½ yard each for Rows 20–27
⁵⁄₈ yard each for Rows 28–31
⁵⁄₈ yard pink for border (Bs and Cs)
¾ yard fabric for binding
7½ yards fabric for backing
Queen-size batting

Cutting

Measurements include ¼" seam
allowances. Refer to photo for color
selection.

From selected fabrics, cut 2½" squares as follows:

- Row 1—4 (2½") squares
- Row 2—10 (2½") squares
- Row 3—14 (2½") squares
- Row 4—18 (2½") squares
- Row 5—22 (2½") squares
- Row 6—26 (2½") squares
- Row 7—30 (2½") squares
- Row 8—34 (2½") squares
- Row 9—38 (2½") squares
- Row 10—42 (2½") squares
- Row 11—46 (2½") squares
- Row 12—50 (2½") squares
- Row 13—54 (2½") squares
- Row 14—58 (2½") squares
- Row 15—62 (2½") squares
- Row 16—66 (2½") squares
- Row 17—70 (2½") squares
- Row 18—74 (2½") squares
- Row 19—78 (2½") squares
- Row 20—82 (2½") squares
- Row 21—86 (2½") squares
- Row 22—90 (2½") squares
- Row 23—94 (2½") squares
- Row 24—98 (2½") squares
- Row 25—102 (2½") squares
- Row 26—106 (2½") squares
- Row 27—110 (2½") squares
- Row 28—114 (2½") squares
- Row 29—118 (2½") squares
- Row 30—122 (2½") squares
- Row 31—126 (2½") squares

From pink, cut:

- 4 (4⅛"-wide) strips. Cut strips into
  32 (4⅛") squares. Cut squares in
  quarters diagonally to make 126
  B triangles.
- 2 (2³⁄₈") squares. Cut in half diagonally to make 4 C triangles for
  corners.

From binding fabric, cut:

- 10 (2¼"-wide) strips for binding.

Quilt Assembly

1. *Piecing Diagram* shown is for ¼
of quilt top. Beginning with lower
left corner, lay out pieces in
diagonal rows as shown.

2. Join pieces into rows; join rows
to complete quilt top.

Quilting and Finishing

1. Divide backing fabric into
3 (2½-yard) lengths. Join to make
backing. Seams will run horizontally.

2. Layer backing, batting, and
quilt top; baste. Quilt as desired.
Quilt shown is outline-quilted.

3. Join 2¼"-wide binding strips
into 1 continuous piece for straight-
grain French-fold binding. Add
binding to quilt.

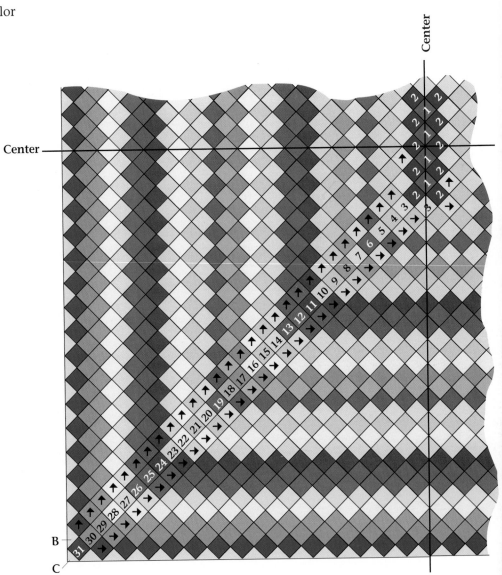

Piecing Diagram

Sadie's Choice Rose

The pattern for the center block in this quilt is a very old one known as Sadie's Choice Rose. The triangle design that surrounds the center block and forms the corners of the quilt are Broken Dishes units.

Finished Quilt Size
85½" x 85½"

Number of Blocks and Finished Size
1 (22") Sadie's Choice Block

Materials
5 yards cream
1 yard teal
1¼ yard navy
1 fat eighth (9" x 22") rose
1 yard light peach
1 yard dark peach
½ yard solid green
1½ yards green print
1 yard brown print
7½ yards fabric for backing
Queen-size batting

Cutting
Measurements include ¼" seam allowances. Patterns are on pages 199–200.

From cream, cut:
• 1 (22½") square for center.
• 17 (6"-wide) strips. Cut strips into 8 (6" x 11½") strips and 16 (6" x 17") strips. Piece as needed to make 2 (6" x 44½") strips and 2 (6" x 55½") strips for background.
• 3 (6⅜"-wide) strips. Cut strips into 12 (6⅜") squares. Cut squares in half diagonally to make 24 J triangles.
• 3 (6¾"-wide) strips. Cut strips into 15 (6¾") squares. Cut squares in quarters diagonally to make 60 L triangles.

From teal, cut:
• 4 Bs and 1 I for appliqué.
• 2 (6⅜"-wide) strips. Cut strips into 8 (6⅜") squares. Cut squares in half diagonally to make 16 J triangles.
• 2 (6¾"-wide) strips. Cut strips into 6 (6¾") squares. Cut squares in quarters diagonally to make 24 L triangles.

From navy, cut:
• 12 Fs for appliqué.
• 2 (6⅜"-wide) strips. Cut strips into 10 (6⅜") squares. Cut 6 squares in half diagonally to make 12 J triangles. Remaining 4 squares are for center block corners.

Quilt by Doris Amiss Rabey

• 2 (6¾"-wide) strips. Cut strips into 10 (6¾") squares. Cut squares in quarters diagonally to make 40 L triangles.
• 1 (8¾"-wide) strip. Cut strip into 2 (8¾") squares. Cut squares in half diagonally to make 4 K triangles.

From rose, cut:
• 4 As and 1 H for appliqué.

From light peach, cut:
• 12 Es for appliqué.
• 3 (6¾"-wide) strips. Cut strips into 14 (6¾") squares. Cut squares in quarters diagonally to make 56 L triangles.

From dark peach, cut:
• 4 (6¾"-wide) strips. Cut strips into 17 (6¾") squares. Cut squares in quarters diagonally to make 68 L triangles.

From solid green, cut:
• 1 G for appliqué.
• 1 (6⅜"-wide) strip. Cut strip into 4 (6⅜") squares. Cut squares in half diagonally to make 8 J triangles.
• 1 (6¾"-wide) strip. Cut strip into 4 (6¾") squares. Cut squares in quarters diagonally to make 16 L triangles.

From green print, cut:
• 4 Cs and 16 Ds for appliqué.
• 2 (6¾"-wide) strips. Cut strips into 10 (6¾") squares. Cut squares in quarters diagonally to make 40 L triangles.
• 10 (2¼" x 42") strips for binding.

From brown print, cut:
• 4 (6¾"-wide) strips. Cut strips into 16 (6¾") squares. Cut squares in quarters diagonally to make 64 L triangles.

Center Assembly

1. Referring to *Diagonal Seams Diagram*, place 1 navy (6³⁄₈") square atop 1 corner of appliqué block. Stitch diagonally from corner to corner. Trim excess fabric ¼" from stitching. Press open to reveal triangle. Repeat on all 4 corners.

Diagonal Seams Diagram

2. Referring to *Folding Diagram*, fold and press cream square horizontally, vertically, and diagonally to make guidelines for appliqué.

Folding Diagram

3. Appliqué shapes in alphabetical order, following *Block Diagram*.

Block Diagram

Triangle Section Assembly

1. Referring to *Side Section Assembly Diagram*, lay out 48 L triangles as shown (9 cream, 6 navy, 10 light peach, 6 dark peach, 3 teal, 4 green print, 2 solid green, and 8 brown print). Join triangles to make rows. Join rows to make 1 side section. Make 4 side sections. Lay in place on each side of center block.

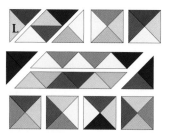

Side Section Assembly Diagram

2. Referring to *Inner Corner Assembly Diagram*, lay out 24 L triangles as shown (4 cream, 2 navy, 3 light peach, 6 dark peach, 4 green print, and 5 brown print). Join triangles into quarter-square triangle units. Lay out in position; add 3 (6" x 17") cream strips and 3 J triangles (1 each teal, navy, and solid green) as shown. Join into rows; join rows as shown to make corner unit. Make 4 corner units, matched to position.

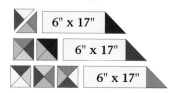

Inner Corner Assembly Diagram

3. Refer to *Outer Corner Assembly Diagrams*. For top left and lower right corners *(Diagram 1)*, lay out 20 L (2 cream, 2 navy, 1 light peach, 5 dark peach, 3 teal, 2 green print, 2 solid green, and 3 brown print), 8 J (6 cream and 2 navy), and 1 navy K triangles as shown with 2 (6" x 11½") and 2 (6" x 17") cream strips. Join into sections; join sections to complete corner unit, setting in seams as needed. Repeat.

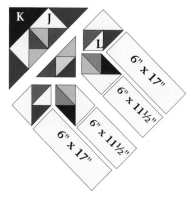

Outer Corner Assembly Diagram 1
Top Left and Lower Right
Corner Assembly

Repeat for top right and lower left corners *(Diagram 2)*, using 2 (6" x 11½") cream strips and 2 edge J triangles.

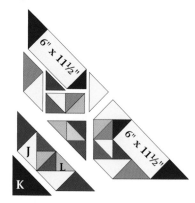

Outer Corner Assembly Diagram 2
Top Right and Lower Left
Corner Assembly

Quilt Assembly

1. Lay all sections as shown in *Quilt Top Assembly Diagram*.

2. Join into diagonal strips; join strips to complete quilt top.

Quilting and Finishing

1. Divide backing fabric into 3 (2½-yard) lengths. Cut 1 piece in half lengthwise. Sew 1 narrow panel between wide panels. Press seam allowances toward narrow panel. Seams will run horizontally.

2. Layer backing, batting, and quilt top; baste. Quilt as desired. Quilt shown has feathered motifs in corners, with diagonal grid fill in cream areas.

3. Join 2¼"-wide green print strips into 1 continuous piece for straight-grain French-fold binding. Add binding to quilt.

Quilt Top Assembly Diagram

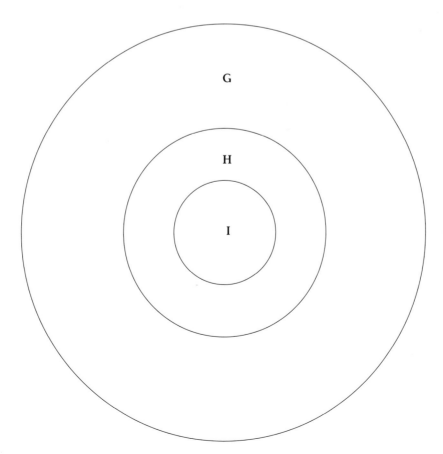

E

B A

F

D

C

Fancy Dresden Plate

This pattern is named for the dainty ornate porcelain that originated in Dresden, Germany. In this example, Georgean Kruger made a memory quilt in honor of her father by using his silk neckties for the fan blades.

Quilt by Georgean Kruger

A quilt's top border receives much wear from being pulled, and prairie points can tickle your chin. In this example, the quiltmaker used what is called a "chin tuck," by placing a dark border at the top, which is more durable and will help conceal soil from skin oils or makeup.

Finished Quilt Size

77⅝" x 96⅜"

Number of Blocks and Finished Size

12 (15") Fancy Dresden Plate Blocks

Materials

7 yards muslin
2½ yards navy
60–90 neckties or 3½ yards assorted prints
5¾ yards backing
Queen size batting

Cutting

Measurements include ¼" seam allowances. Patterns are on page 204–205.

From muslin, cut:
- 2 yards. Cut yardage into 1 (22½"-wide) lengthwise strip. Cut strip into 3 (22½") squares. Cut squares in quarters diagonally to make 12 side setting triangles. You will have 2 extra.
- From remainder, cut 1 (15½"-wide) lengthwise strip. Cut strip into 4 (15½") squares for appliqué background.
- 7 (15½"-wide) strips. Cut strips into 8 (15½") squares for appliqué background (total of 12) and 6 (15½") setting squares.
- 1 (11½"-wide) strip. Cut strip into 2 (11½") squares. Cut squares in half diagonally to make 4 corner setting triangles.
- 7 (4¾"-wide) strips. Piece to make 1 (4¾" x 80") bottom border and 2 (4¾" x 100") side borders.

From navy, cut:
- 7 (3¼"-wide) strips. Piece to make 1 (3¼" x 80") bottom border and 2 (3¼" x 100") side borders.
- 2 (5"-wide) strips. Join to make 1 (5" x 80") top border.
- 10 (4½"-wide) strips. Cut strips into 87 (4½") squares for prairie points.

From neckties or prints, cut:
- 12 sets of 4 As and 4 Bs (Set 1).
- 48 sets of 4 As (Set 2).

Quilt Top Assembly Diagram

Block Assembly

1. Choose 1 of Set 1 and 4 of Set 2. Join 1 A from each set to make 1 quadrant. Make 4 matching quadrants. Join quadrants to make plate *(Block Assembly Diagram)*.

and basting inside edges of As in place. Appliqué Bs in center to complete 1 Fancy Dresden Plate block *(Block Diagram)*. Make 12 Fancy Dresden Plate blocks.

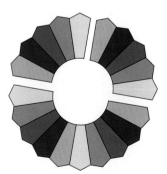

Block Assembly Diagram

2. Appliqué plate to 1 background square, aligning as shown

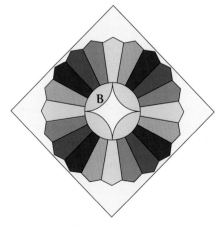

Block Diagram

Quilt Assembly

1. Referring to *Quilt Top Assembly Diagram*, lay out blocks, setting squares, and setting triangles as shown. Join into diagonal rows; join rows to complete center.

2. Join 1 navy and 1 muslin strip to make 1 border strip. Make 3 border strips.

3. Center navy border strip on top edge of quilt and join. Center navy and muslin border strips on remaining quilt sides and join. Miter corners at 45º. Top corners will not match evenly.

Quilting and Finishing

1. Divide backing fabric into 2 (2⅞-yard) lengths. Cut 1 piece in half lengthwise. Sew 1 narrow panel to each side of wide panel. Press seam allowances toward narrow panels.

2. Layer backing, batting, and quilt top; baste. Quilt as desired. Quilt shown is outline-quilted in blocks, with a Fancy Dresden Plate pattern in setting pieces. (Pattern is on page 205.) Background is filled with diagonal grid.

3. Refer to instructions on page 365 to fold prairie points and baste in place to quilt top. There are 25 across bottom edge and 31 on each side. For top edge, turn to inside and slipstitch closed.

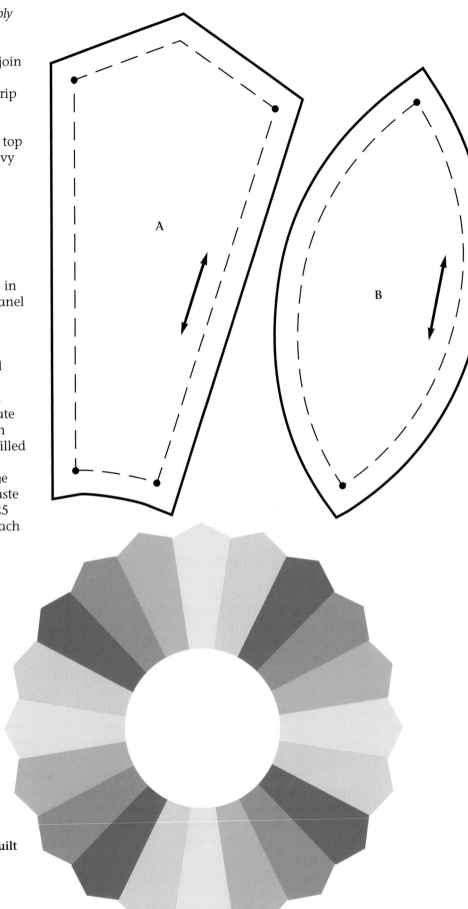

Quilt Label
Trace, scan, or photocopy this quilt label to finish your quilt.

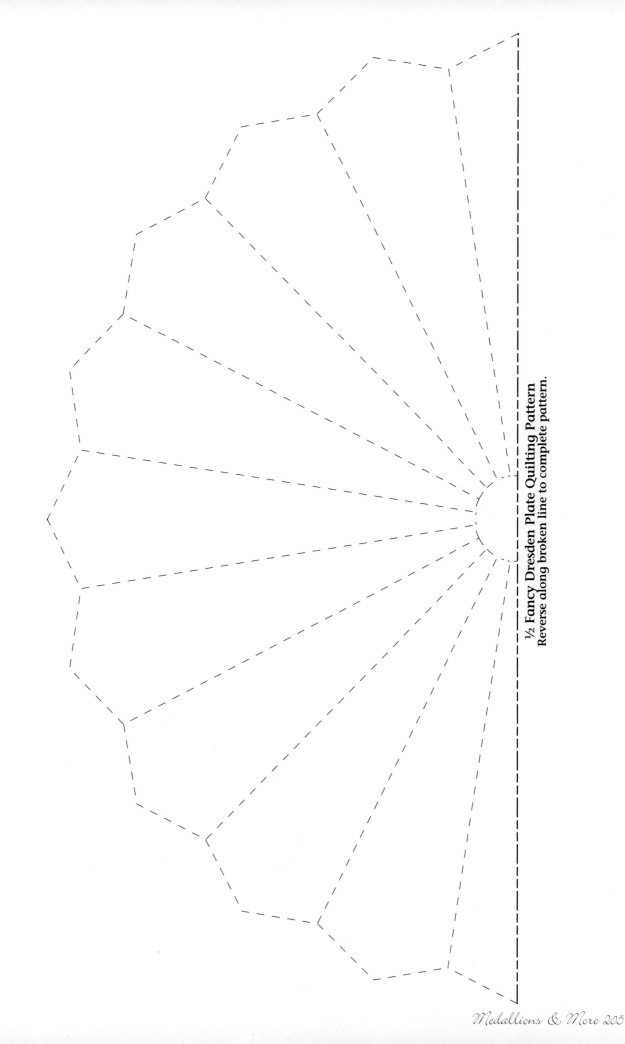

½ Fancy Dresden Plate Quilting Pattern
Reverse along broken line to complete pattern.

Mariner's Compass

Mariner's Compass is considered among the most challenging pieced blocks because of its many sharp points and tiny pieces. However, paper piecing can make assembling those bits much easier. This late 1800s example with 24 points is sometimes called Sunburst.

Finished Quilt Size
70" x 70"

Number of Blocks and Finished Size
16 (14") Mariner's Compass Blocks

Materials
3 yards total assorted prints
1 fat quarter (18" x 22") red
3½ yards muslin
3 yards floral print
2 yards plaid for border
¾ yard check for binding
4½ yards fabric for backing
Twin-size batting

Cutting
Measurements include ¼" seam allowances. Border strips are exact length needed. You may want to cut them longer to allow for piecing variations. Patterns are on pages 209–210.

From prints, cut:
• 192 (2½" x 5") pieces for Cs.
• 192 (2" x 3½") pieces for Es.

From red, cut:
• 16 As.

From muslin, cut:
• 384 (2" x 2") squares for Bs and Ds.
• 384 (2½" x 3") pieces for Fs.

From floral print, cut:
• 64 Gs.

From plaid, cut:
• 4 (7½"-wide) lengthwise strips. Trim strips to make 2 (7½" x 56½") top and bottom borders and 2 (7½" x 70½") side borders.

From check, cut:
• 8 (2¼"-wide) strips for binding.

Block Assembly
1. Trace, scan, or photocopy 192 each of Paper Piecing Patterns B/C and D/E/F on page 209.

2. Beginning with 1 B/C unit, place 1 print C on wrong side of pattern, with wrong sides facing. Align 1 muslin B with seam line so that it will flip over and cover area #2 after stitching. With right sides together, stitch along line between #1 and #2. Trim seam allowance, if needed, and flip #2 in place. Finger-press seam. When paper pattern is complete, trim along seam allowance, remove paper, and press unit.

3. Paper piece 1 muslin B and print C unit. Repeat to make 12 B/C units.

4. Paper piece 1 D/E/F unit with 1 print E, 1 muslin D, and 2 muslin Fs. Repeat to make 12 D/E/F units.

5. Referring to *Assembly Diagram 1,* join 1 B/C unit and 1 D/E/F unit to make 1 section. Make 12 sections.

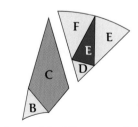

Assembly Diagram 1

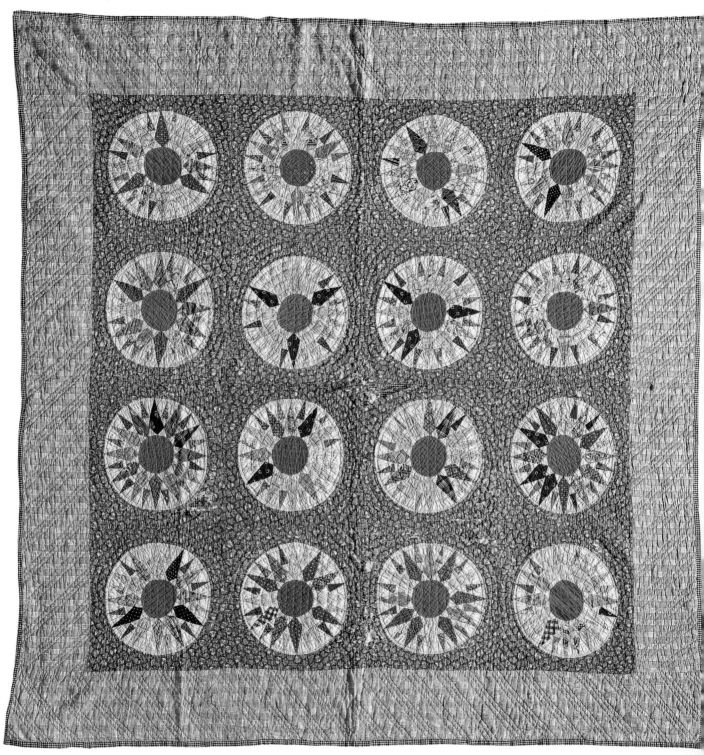

Quilt owned by Rebecca B. Mondorf

6. Referring to *Assembly Diagram 2,* join 3 sections. Add 1 G to make 1 quadrant. Make 4 quadrants.

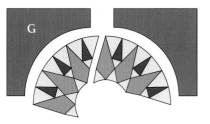

Assembly Diagram 2

7. Join 4 quadrants to make compass circle. Appliqué 1 A in center to complete 1 Mariner's Compass block *(Block Diagram).*

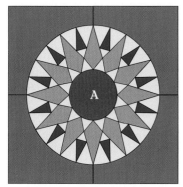

Block Diagram

8. Make 16 Mariner's Compass blocks.

Quilt Assembly

1. Referring to *Quilt Top Assembly Diagram,* lay out blocks in 4 horizontal rows of 4 blocks each.
2. Join into rows; join rows to complete quilt center.
3. Add top and bottom borders to quilt. Add side borders.

Quilting and Finishing

1. Divide backing fabric into 2 (2¼-yard) lengths. Cut 1 piece in half lengthwise. Sew 1 narrow panel to each side of wide panel. Press seam allowances toward narrow panels
2. Layer backing, batting, and quilt top; baste. Quilt as desired. Quilt shown is quilted in concentric circles with diagonal fill in borders.
3. Join 2¼"-wide check strips into 1 continuous piece for straight-grain French-fold binding. Add binding to quilt.

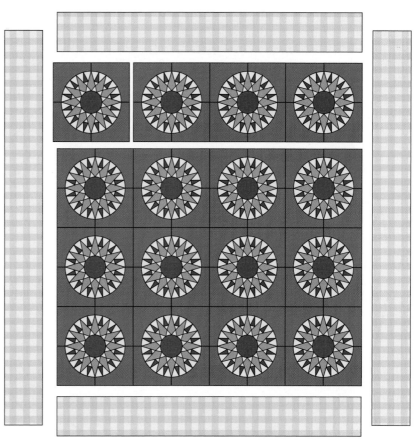

Quilt Top Assembly Diagram

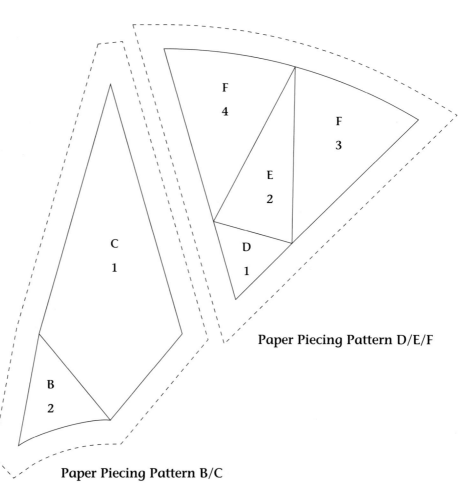

Paper Piecing Pattern D/E/F

Paper Piecing Pattern B/C

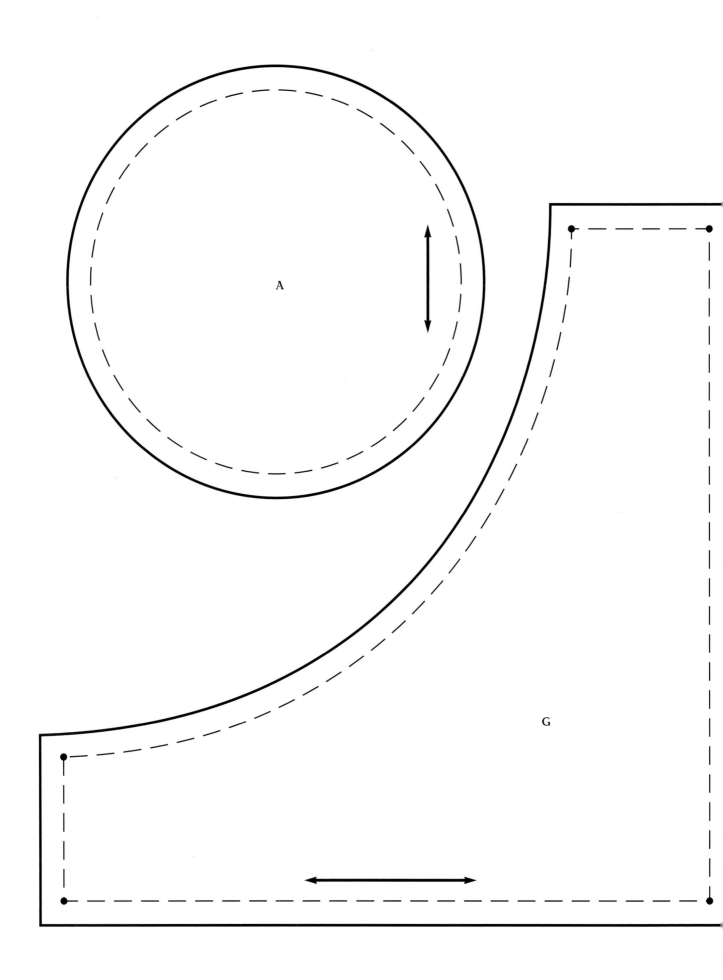

A

G

2. Join 1 light
orange and 1 green
print C to make 1 C
unit *(C Unit
Diagram).* Make 5 C
units.

**C Unit
Diagram**

3. Referring to *Block Assembly
Diagram,* lay out C units with 6
green print Cs, 1 A, 1 A reversed,
1 D and 1 B. Join into sections;
join sections to make basket
unit.

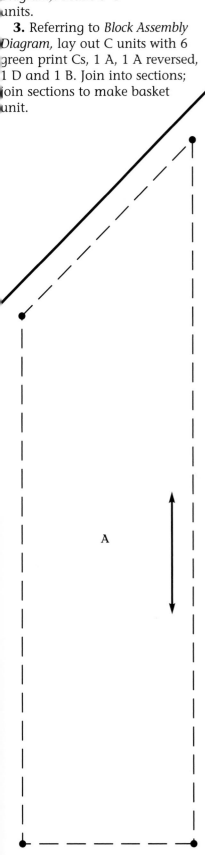

A

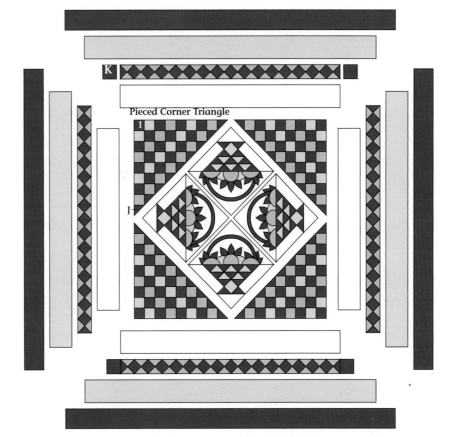

Pieced Corner Triangle

Quilt Top Assembly Diagram

4. Join 1 handle unit and 1
basket unit to make 1 Basket of
Oranges block. Make 4 blocks.

5. To make pieced corner triangles,
lay out 16 green print, 8 light
orange, and 12 solid orange Is with
9 green print J triangles. Join into
rows; join rows to complete 1 pieced
corner triangle. Make 4 pieced
corner triangles.

Quilt Assembly

1. Lay out 4 basket blocks as
shown in *Quilt Top Assembly Diagram*
and join. Center 1 pieced corner triangle on each side and add to basket
center. Triangles will overlap on sides.

2. Add white inner side borders to
quilt. Add top and bottom borders.

3. Join 1 orange triangle to each
side of 1 green print square to make
1 border unit *(Border Unit Diagram).*
Make 60 border units.

Border Unit Diagram

4. Join 15 border units. Add 1
orange and 1 green print triangle to

each end to complete 1 border strip.
Make 4 border strips.

5. Add 1 pieced border strip to
sides of quilt. Add 1 green print K to
each end of remaining strips and
add to top and bottom.

6. Add light orange middle side
borders to quilt. Add top and
bottom borders.

7. Add green print outer side
borders to quilt. Add top and
bottom borders.

Quilting and Finishing

1. Divide backing fabric into
2 (1⅞-yard) lengths. Cut 1 piece in
half lengthwise. Sew 1 narrow panel
to each side of wide panel. Press
seam allowances toward narrow
panels.

2. Layer backing, batting, and
quilt top; baste. Quilt as desired.
Quilt shown is outline-quilted in
appliqué and piecing, with orange
peels in inner border. Outer borders
have diagonal fill.

3. Join 2¼"-wide green print
strips into 1 continuous piece for
straight-grain French-fold binding.
Add binding to quilt.

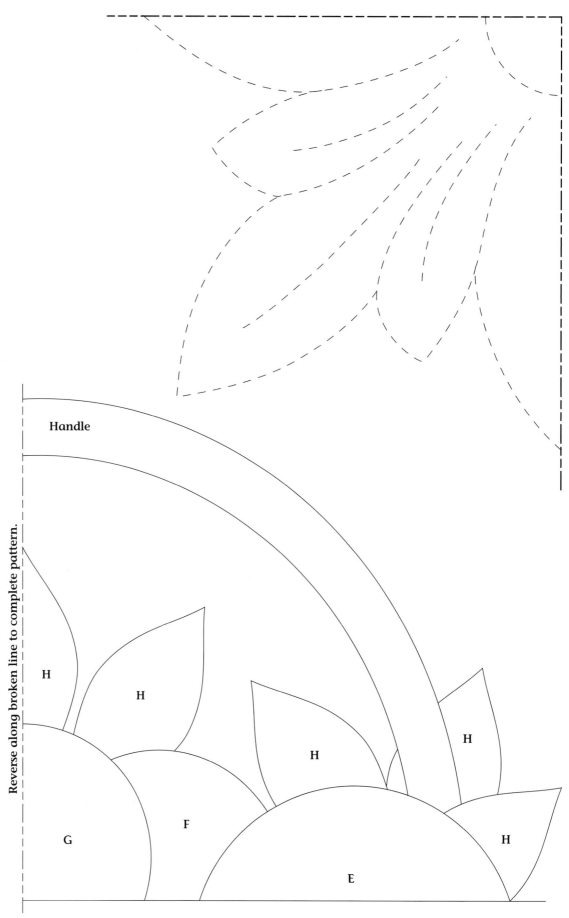

Quilting Pattern
Reverse along broken line to complete pattern.

Handle

Reverse along broken line to complete pattern.

H

H

H

H

H

G

F

E

Chips & Whetstones

Perhaps the wife of a carpenter long ago made a pattern similar to this one, where the center wheel represents the whetstone, used for sharpening tools, and the small points represent the chips that flake away.

Quilt owned by Edith T. Springer

Finished Quilt Size
76" x 76"

Number of Blocks and Finished Size
9 (22") Chips & Whetstones Blocks

Materials
6½ yards red
11½ yards muslin
4½ yards fabric for backing
Full-size batting

Cutting
Note: Measurements include ¼" seam allowances. Patterns are on pages 218–219.

From red, cut:
- 90 As.
- 90 Cs.
- 90 Ds.
- 14 (3½"-wide) strips. Cut strips into 360 (1½" x 3½") pieces for Fs.
- 216 Is.
- 4 Ks.

From muslin, cut:
- 8 (3"-wide) strips. Piece to make 4 (3" x 80") border strips.
- 9 (2¼"-wide) strips for binding.
- 90 Bs.
- 180 Es.
- 36 (1¾"-wide) strips. Cut strips into 720 (1¾" x 2") pieces for Gs.
- 36 Hs.
- 424 Js.
- 4 Ls and 4 Ls reversed.

Block Assembly
1. Join 2 red As and 2 muslin Bs to make 1 A/B unit *(A/B Unit Diagram)*. Make 5 A/B units. Join A units to make center star.

A/B Unit Diagram

2. Trace, scan, or photocopy 180 F/G and 180 F/G Reversed Paper Piecing Patterns from page 219. Paper piece 1 red F and 2 muslin Gs

to make 1 F/G unit. Make 20 F units and 20 reversed F units.

3. Join 1 F/G unit to left side and 1 reversed F/G unit to right side of 1 muslin E to make 1 E/F/G unit *(E/F/G Unit Diagram)*. Make 20 E units.

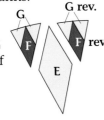

E/F/G Unit Diagram

4. Join 1 E/F unit to each side of 1 red D to make 1 D/E/F unit *(D/E/F Unit Diagram)*. Make 10 D/E/F units.

D/E/F Unit Diagram

5. Referring to *Block Assembly Diagram,* join D units with red Cs to make circle. Appliqué center star, positioning as shown.

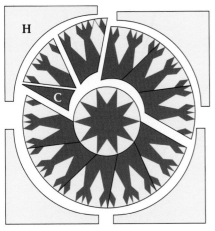

Block Assembly Diagram

Block Diagram

Quilt Top Assembly Diagram

6. Add muslin Hs as shown to complete 1 Chips & Whetstones block *(Block Diagram)*. Make 9 blocks.

Quilt Assembly

1. Referring to *Quilt Top Assembly Diagram,* lay out blocks in 3 horizontal rows of 3 blocks each. Join into rows; join rows to complete quilt center.

2. Referring to *Border Assembly Diagram,* join 2 muslin Js to opposite sides of 1 I diamond to make 1 border unit. Join 52 border units, 2 Is, and 2 Js (total of 106 muslin Js and 54 red Is) as shown in *Quilt Top Assembly Diagram* to make 1 border strip. Make 4 border strips.

3. Check fit of border strips; adjust if needed. Add 1 border strip to each side of quilt, matching end I points to block corners.

4. Set in 1 K on each corner. Add 1 L and 1 L reversed to each corner.

5. Center 1 border strip on each side of quilt and join. Miter corners.

Quilting and Finishing

1. Divide backing fabric into 2 (2¼-yard) lengths. Cut 1 piece in half lengthwise. Sew 1 narrow panel to each side of wide panel. Press seam allowances toward narrow panels.

2. Layer backing, batting, and quilt top; baste. Quilt as desired. Quilt shown is quilted in an all-over crosshatch pattern.

3. Join 2¼"-wide muslin strips into 1 continuous piece for straight-grain French-fold binding. Add binding to quilt.

Border Assembly Diagram

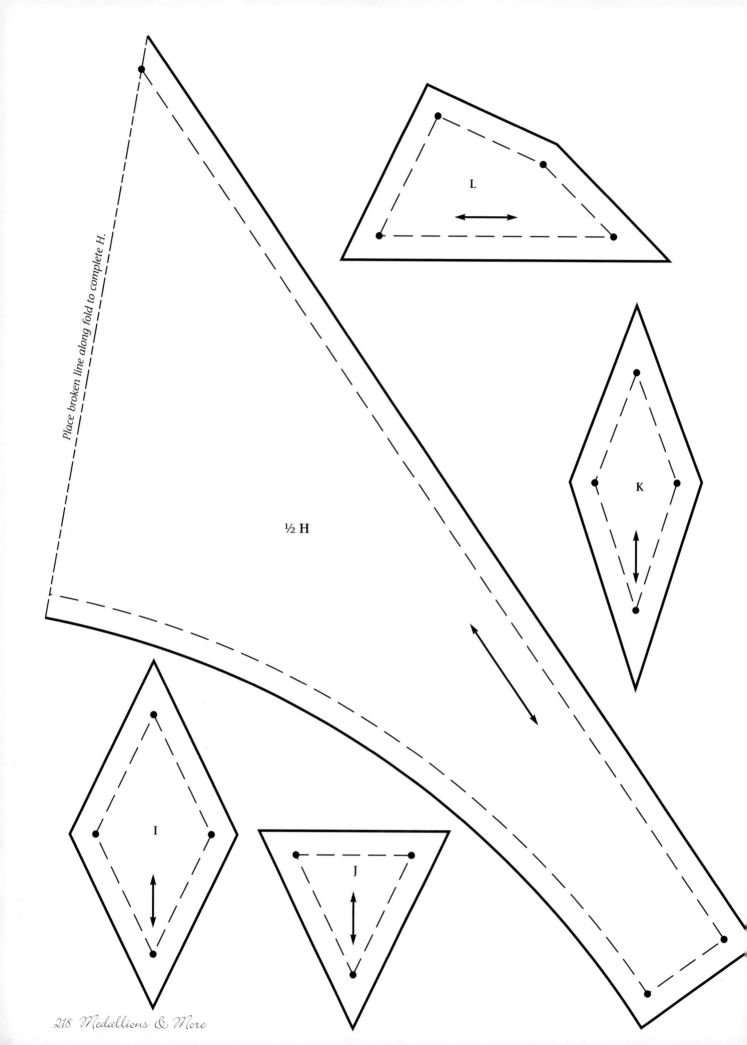

Place broken line along fold to complete H.

½ **H**

L

K

I

J

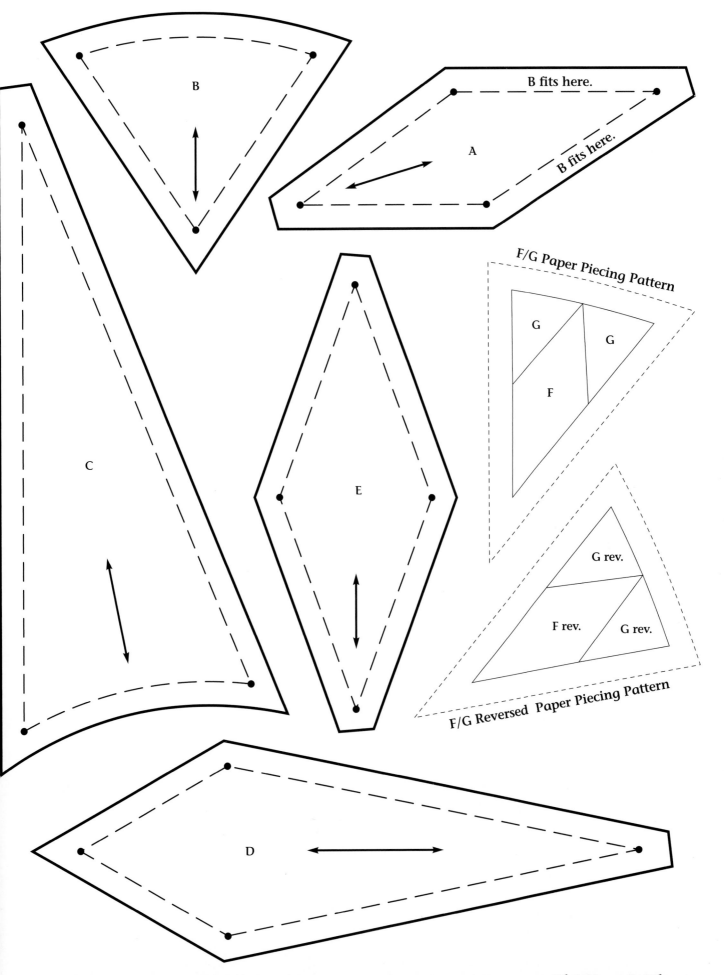

B

B fits here.

B fits here.

A

F/G Paper Piecing Pattern

G

G

F

C

E

G rev.

F rev.

G rev.

F/G Reversed Paper Piecing Pattern

D

Diamond in a Square

The Amish are known for their extensively quilted, brightly colored quilts. Because the religious doctrine of the Amish prohibits the use of printed fabrics or the making of representational forms, the quilts are showcases for elaborate quilting. Although this quilt's maker is not Amish, the quilt contains all of the elements that make Amish quilts so spectacular.

Quilt by Meg Irizarry

Finished Quilt Size

58" x 68"

Materials

2¾ yards black
2 yards blue
1 yard red
1 yard gold
4 yards fabric for backing
Twin-size batting

Cutting

Measurements include ¼" seam allowances. Border strips are exact length needed. You may want to cut them longer to allow for piecing variations.

From black, cut:

- 2 yards. Cut yardage into 8 (2"-wide) lengthwise strips. Trim strips to make 2 (2" x 44½") G strips, 2 (2" x 47½") H strips, 2 (2" x 65½") L strips, and 2 (2" x 68½") M strips.
- From remainder, cut 1 (21¼") A square.
- From remainder, cut 2 (2"-wide) lengthwise strips. Cut strips into 8 (2" x 9½") J strips.
- From remainder, cut 1 (2¾"-wide) lengthwise strip. Cut strip into 16 (2¾") K squares.
- 8 (2¼"-wide) strips for binding.

From blue, cut:

- 1¼ yards. Cut yardage into 4 (9½" x 44½") lengthwise I strips.
- 4 (3½"-wide) strips. Cut strips into 4 (3½" x 21¼") B strips and 4 (3½") F squares.
- 2 (2¾"-wide) strips. Cut strips into 16 K squares.

From red, cut:

- 1 (3½"-wide) strip. Cut strip into 4 (3½") C squares.
- 4 (3½"-wide) strips. Cut strips into 4 (3½" x 38½") E strips.
- 2 (2¾"-wide) strips. Cut strips into 16 K squares.

From gold, cut:

- 1 (20"-wide) strip. Cut strip into 2 (20") squares. Cut squares in half diagonally to make 4 D triangles.
- 2 (2¾"-wide) strips. Cut strips into 16 (2¾") K squares.

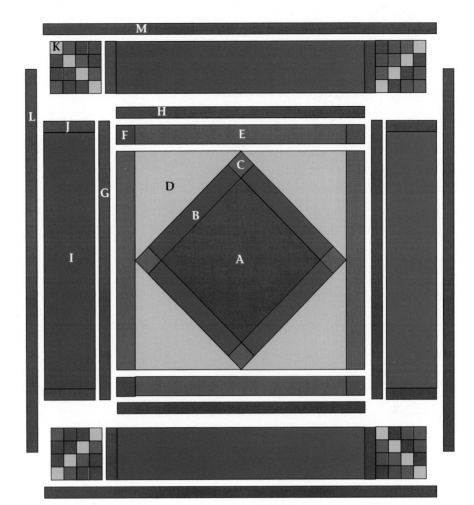

Quilt Top Assembly Diagram

Quilt Assembly

1. Referring to *Quilt Top Assembly Diagram,* join 2 B strips to opposite sides of 1 A square. Join 1 red C square to each end of remaining B strips. Add to A square.

2. Add 1 gold D triangle to each side of center, working in opposite pairs.

3. Add 2 E strips to opposite sides of center. Join 1 blue F square to each end of remaining E strips and add to center.

4. Add 2 G strips to sides. Add 2 H strips to top and bottom.

5. Join 2 Js and 1 I to make side border. Repeat. Add to sides of center.

6. Lay out 4 each black, gold, red, and blue K squares as shown in *Corner Block Assembly Diagram* for

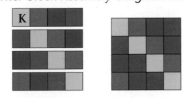

Corner Block Assembly Diagram

corner block. Join into rows; join rows to make 1 corner block. Make 4 matching corner blocks.

7. Lay out 2 corner blocks, 2 Js, and 1 I as shown, rotating corners. Join to make top border and add. Repeat for bottom border.

8. Add L strips to sides. Add M strips to top and bottom.

Quilting and Finishing

1. Divide backing fabric into 2 (2-yard) lengths. Cut 1 piece in half lengthwise. Sew 1 narrow panel to each side of wide panel. Press seam allowances toward narrow panels.

2. Layer backing, batting, and quilt top; baste. Quilt as desired. Quilt shown has extensive quilting, including stars, feather wreaths, cabling, feathered swags, and cross-hatching. Patterns are on pages 222-223.

3. Join black strips into 1 continuous piece for straight-grain French-fold binding. Add binding to quilt.

Reverse along broken line for complete quilting pattern.

Quilting Patterns

Diagram at right shows placement of quilting patterns as used in the original quilt.

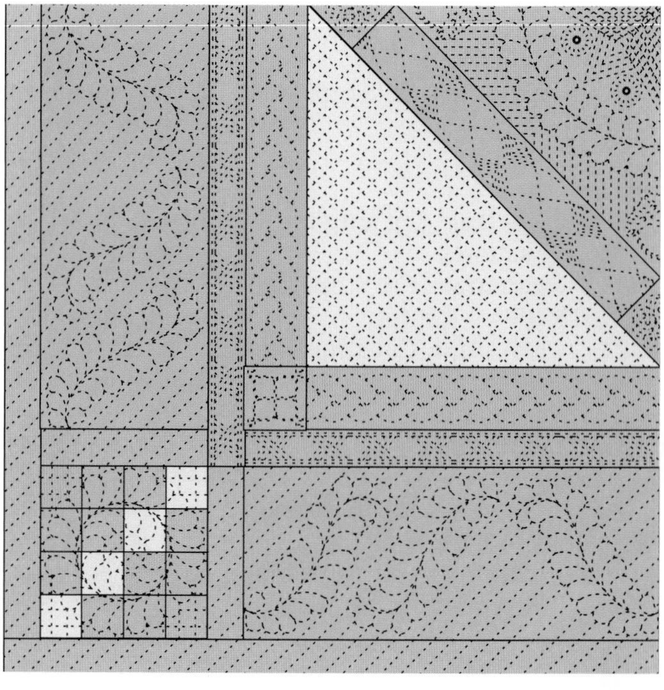

Quilting Patterns

Seven Sisters

In Greek mythology, the seven daughters of Atlas are represented in the constellation Pleiades. The name of this quilt pattern, a favorite among many quilters, came from this astrological configuration.

Finished Quilt Size
78½" x 87½"

Number of Blocks and Finished Size
7 (19½" x 22½") Seven Sisters Blocks

Materials
2½ yards peach
5 yards off-white
⅝ yard each of 7 different prints
5 yards fabric for backing
Full-size batting

Cutting
Measurements include ¼" seam allowances. Border strips are exact length needed. You may want to cut them longer to allow for piecing variations. Patterns are on page 227.

From peach, cut:
- 7 (4½"-wide) strips. Piece to make 2 (4½" x 59") top and bottom borders and 2 (4½" x 75½") side borders.
- 9 (2¼"-wide) strips for binding.
- 1 (24½"-wide) strip. Cut strip into 2 (10½" x 24½") strips. Referring to *Setting Triangle Cutting Diagram* and using 60° markings on ruler, cut 6 equilateral setting triangles.

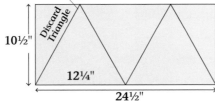

Setting Triangle Cutting Diagram

From off-white, cut:
- 8 (6½"-wide) strips. Piece to make 2 (6½" x 67") top and bottom borders and 2 (6½" x 88") side borders.

- 1 (24½"-wide) strip. Cut strip into 2 (10½" x 24½") strips. Referring to *Setting Triangle Cutting Diagram* and using 60° markings on ruler, cut 6 equilateral setting triangles.
- 1 (30½"-wide) strip. Cut strip into 2 (17⅝" x 30½") rectangles. Referring to *Corner Triangle Cutting Diagram*, cut each rectangle diagonally corner to corner as shown to make 4 corner triangles.

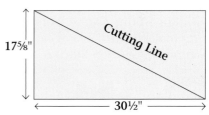

Corner Triangle Cutting Diagram

- 14 (2½"-wide) strips. Referring to *Diamond Cutting Diagram* and using 60° markings on ruler, cut strips in 2½"-wide increments to make 126 As. Check cut pieces against template on page 227, or use template to cut diamonds.
- 42 Bs.

From each of 7 different prints, cut:
- 5 (2½"-wide) strips. Referring to *Diamond Cutting Diagram* and using 60° markings on ruler, cut strips 2½"-wide increments to make 42 As. Check cut pieces against template on page 227, or use template to cut diamonds.

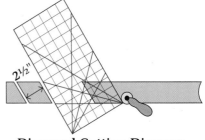

Diamond Cutting Diagram

Block Assembly

1. Choose 1 print set, 18 off-white As, and 6 Bs. Join 6 print As as shown in *Star Assembly Diagram* to make center star.

Star Assembly Diagram

2. Join 6 print As and 4 off-white As to make 1 Star #1 *(Star #1 Diagram)*. Make 3 of Star #1.

Star #1 Diagram

3. Join 6 print As and 2 off-white As to make 1 Star #2 *(Star #2 Diagram)*. Make 3 of Star #2.

Star #2 Diagram

Quilt by Mable Azbill Webb

4. Referring to *Block Assembly Diagram*, alternate Stars #1 and #2 around center star. Join to center, setting in seams. Add Bs to complete 1 Seven Sisters block *(Block Diagram)*. Make 7 Seven Sisters blocks.

Quilt Assembly

1. Lay out blocks and setting triangles as shown in *Quilt Top Assembly Diagram.* Join into diagonal rows; join rows. Add corner triangles to complete center.

2. Add top and bottom peach borders. Add side borders.

3. Add top and bottom off-white borders. Add side borders.

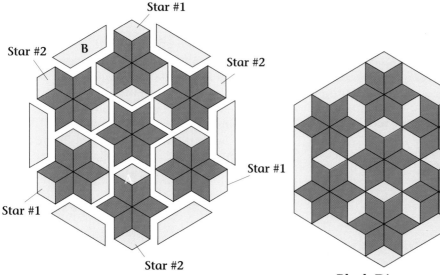

Block Assembly Diagram

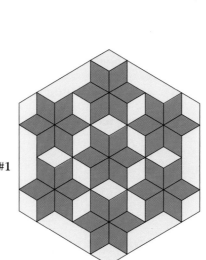

Block Diagram

Quilting and Finishing

1. Divide backing fabric into 2 (2½-yard) lengths. Cut 1 piece in half lengthwise. Sew 1 narrow panel to each side of wide panel. Press seam allowances toward narrow panels.

2. Layer backing, batting, and quilt top; baste. Quilt as desired. Quilt shown is outline-quilted in piecing, with diamond fill in background. Peach border has a chain pattern, and off-white border features a feather-wrapped ribbon pattern.

3. Join 2¼"-wide peach strips into 1 continuous piece for straight-grain French-fold binding. Add binding to quilt.

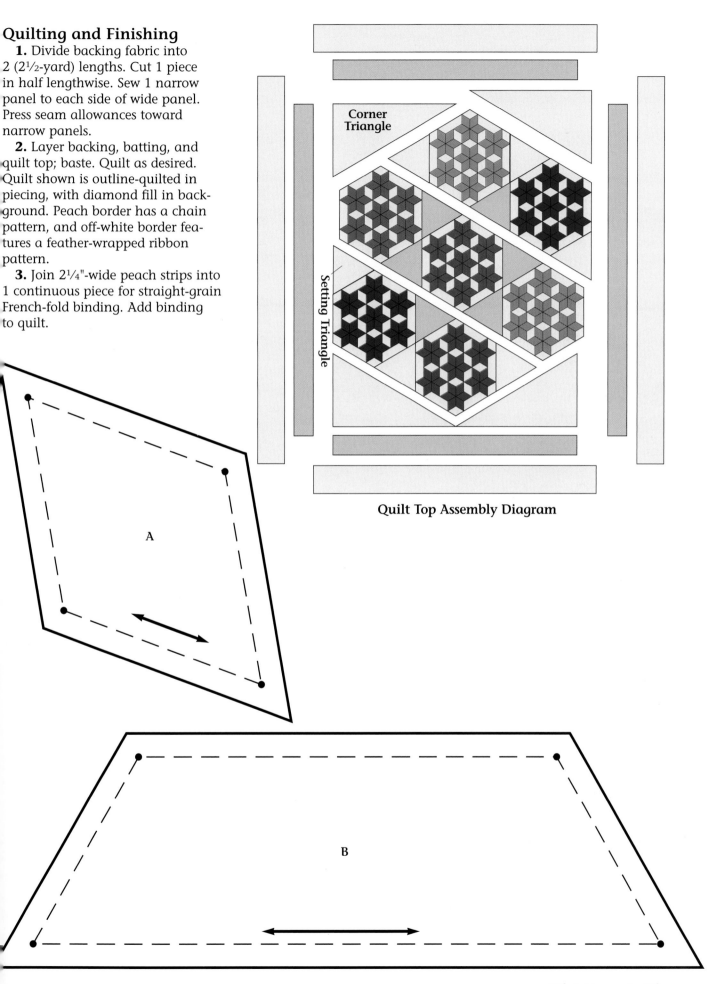

Quilt Top Assembly Diagram

A

B

Friendship Star

Mona Richards found this antique quilt in
a small shop in Harrison, Arkansas,
while she was traveling in the Ozarks.
Research indicated that the quilt was first published
in the 1930s under the name Friendship Star.

Finished Quilt Size

66" x 77"

Number of Blocks and Finished Size

42 (11") Friendship Star Blocks

Materials

4 yards total assorted 1930s prints
for blocks (or 24 [18" x 22"] fat
quarters)
5 yards solid yellow for blocks and
binding
4 yards fabric for backing
Twin-size batting

Cutting

Measurements include ¼" seam
allowances. Patterns are on pages
230–231.

From assorted 1930s prints, cut:
• 42 sets of 8 Bs.

From solid yellow, cut:
• 42 As.
• 7 (5⅞"-wide) strips. Cut strips into
42 (5⅞") squares. Cut squares in
quarters diagonally to make 168
C quarter-square triangles.
• 17 (3¾"-wide) strips. Cut strips
into 168 (3¾") D squares.
• 8 (2¼"-wide) strips for binding.

Block Assembly

1. Join 8 Bs into a circle as shown
in *Block Assembly Diagram*. Add 1 A
to center.

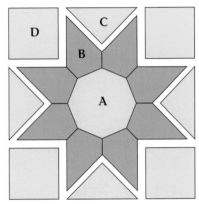

Block Assembly Diagram

2. Set in C triangles on opposite
sides of block. Set in D squares in
each corner of block (*Block Assembly
Diagram*).

3. Make 42 Friendship Star blocks
(*Block Diagram*).

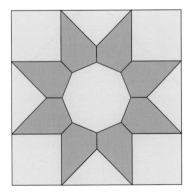

Block Diagram

Quilt Assembly

1. Referring to *Quilt Top Assembly
Diagram*, arrange blocks in 7
horizontal rows of 6 blocks each.

2. Join blocks into rows.

3. Join rows to complete quilt top.

Quilting and Finishing

1. Divide backing fabric into
2 (2-yard) lengths. Cut 1 piece
in half lengthwise. Sew 1 narrow
panel to each side of wide panel.
Press seam allowances toward
narrow panels. Seams will run
horizontally.

2. Layer backing, batting, and
quilt top; baste. Quilt as desired.
Quilt shown is outline-quilted in
centers, petals, and triangles. The
yellow squares formed by 4 blocks
coming together feature a star burst
pattern.

3. Join 2¼"-wide yellow strips
into 1 continuous piece for straight-
grain French-Fold binding. Add
binding to quilt.

Perhaps only the quiltmaker
knew the name of the person who
made this special block.

Quiltmaker unknown; owned by Mona M. Richard.

Although we don't know the full names of the
people who made these blocks, we do know that they took
a lot of pride in their work. In addition to embroidering their names,
notice how some added small flowers
in the center of the blocks.

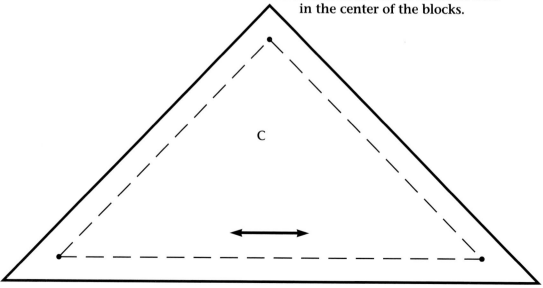

C

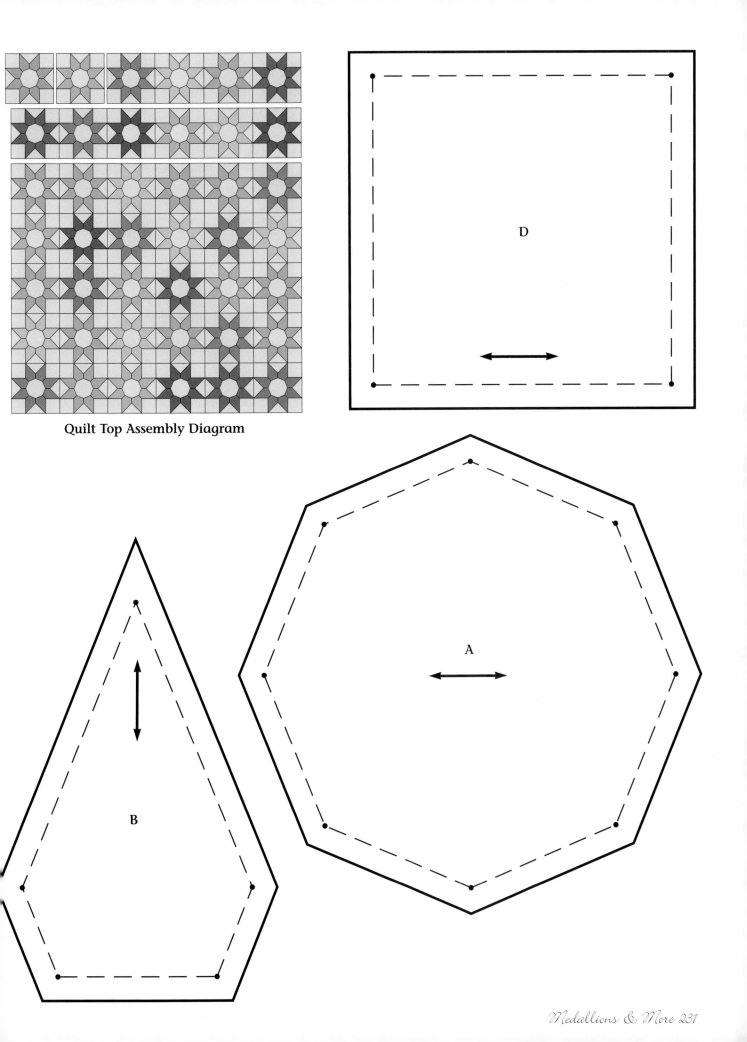

Quilt Top Assembly Diagram

D

A

B

Chapter 6

Picture Blocks

Picture block quilts form an easily-recognizable design by piecing fabric shapes together, rather than by using appliqué.

- Because of their clear graphic impact, picture block quilts are easily identified and well-loved. The *Schoolhouse* quilt on page 234 is an example of an ever-popular picture block quilt. Consider making one for a teacher, a student, or a new home owner.

- *Lucky Lindy* on page 259 is perfect for a pilot, a history buff, or someone who has recently overcome a fear of flying.

- By changing the color scheme, you can turn the *Pine Tree* quilt on page 270 into a Christmas heirloom.

- Gardening enthusiasts and nature lovers will appreciate the *Butterfly Quilt* on page 246.

We naturally associate certain people with hobbies or objects that they enjoy. Therefore, picture block quilts are natural choices for gift-giving. Each one is sure to remind you of someone you know who needs a quilt.

Schoolhouse

This pattern originated in the United States in the mid-1800s. The design and its variations include House, Schoolhouse, Little Red Schoolhouse, House on the Hill, Old Kentucky Home, The Old Homestead, and Jack's House.

Finished Quilt Size
64" x 94"

Number of Blocks and Finished Size
8 (12") Schoolhouse Blocks

Materials
4½ yards muslin
1¼ yards blue
2½ yards brown
5½ yards backing fabric
Full-size batting

Cutting
Measurements include ¼" seam allowances. You may want to cut borders longer to allow for piecing variations. Patterns are on pages 236–237.

From muslin, cut:
- 2¼ yards. Cut yardage into 4 (8½"-wide) lengthwise strips. Cut strips into 2 (8½" x 48½") top and bottom borders and 2 (8½" x 78½") side borders.
- From remainder, cut 24 (3½") sashing squares.
- 3 (12½"-wide) strips. Cut strips into 7 (12½") squares for alternate blocks.
- 4 (2½"-wide) strips. Cut strips into 16 (2½" x 3") As, 8 (2½" x 5½") Cs, and 8 (2½" x 5") Ks.
- 8 Ds and 8 Ds reversed.
- 8 Fs.
- 3 (1½"-wide) strips. Cut strips into 8 (1½" x 7") Hs and 8 (1½" x 6½") Is.
- 2 (1¾"-wide) strips. Cut strips into 16 (1¾" x 4") Ls.

From blue, cut:
- 5 (1½"-wide) strips. Cut strips into 16 (1½" x 2½") Bs, 16 (1½" x 6½") Is, and 8 (1½" x 4") Ms.

- 2 (2½"-wide) strips. Cut strips into 8 (2½" x 5½") Cs.
- 8 Es.
- 8 Gs.
- 2 (2"-wide) strips. Cut strips into 16 (2" x 5") Js.
- 2 (1¾"-wide) strips. Cut strips into 16 (1¾" x 4") Ls.

From brown, cut:
- 13 (3½"-wide) strips. Cut strips into 38 (3½" x 12½") sashing strips.
- 1 (8½"-wide) strip. Cut strip into 4 (8½") border corner squares.
- 9 (2¼"-wide) strips for binding.

Block Assembly
1. Referring to *Block Assembly Diagram,* join 2 As, 2 Bs, and 1 C to make chimney row.

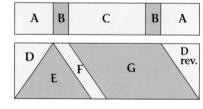

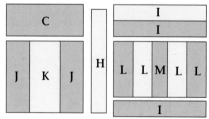

Block Assembly Diagram

2. Join 1 each D, E, F, G, and D reversed to make roof row. Join to chimney row to make block top half.

3. Join 2 Js and 1 K. Add 1 C to top. Add 1 H to right side to make door section.

4. Join 2 blue Ls, 2 muslin Ls, and 1 M. Add 1 blue I to top and bottom of strip. Add 1 muslin I to top to

make window section. Join to door section to make bottom half of block.

5. Join top and bottom halves to complete 1 Schoolhouse block *(Block Diagram).*

6. Make 8 Schoolhouse blocks.

Block Diagram

Quilt Assembly
1. Referring to *Quilt Top Assembly Diagram,* lay out Schoolhouse blocks, alternate blocks, sashing strips, and sashing squares. Join into rows; join rows to complete quilt center.

2. Add side borders to quilt. Join 1 brown square to each end of remaining borders. Add top and bottom borders to quilt.

Quilting and Finishing
1. Divide backing fabric into 2 (2¾-yard) lengths. Cut 1 piece in half lengthwise. Sew 1 narrow panel to each side of wide panel. Press seam allowances toward narrow panels.

2. Layer backing, batting, and quilt top; baste. Quilt as desired. Quilt shown is outline-quilted in blocks and sashing, with a hearts and diamond pattern in alternate blocks *(Quilting Diagram).* Border is filled with crosshatching.

3. Join brown strips into 1 continuous piece for straight-grain French-fold binding. Add binding to quilt.

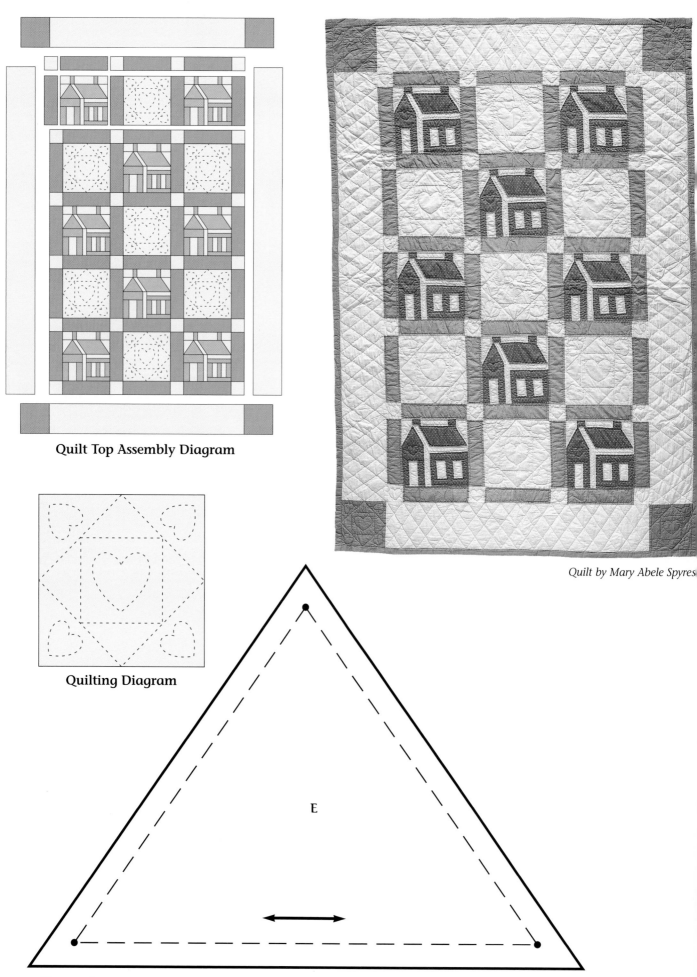

Quilt Top Assembly Diagram

Quilting Diagram

Quilt by Mary Abele Spyres

E

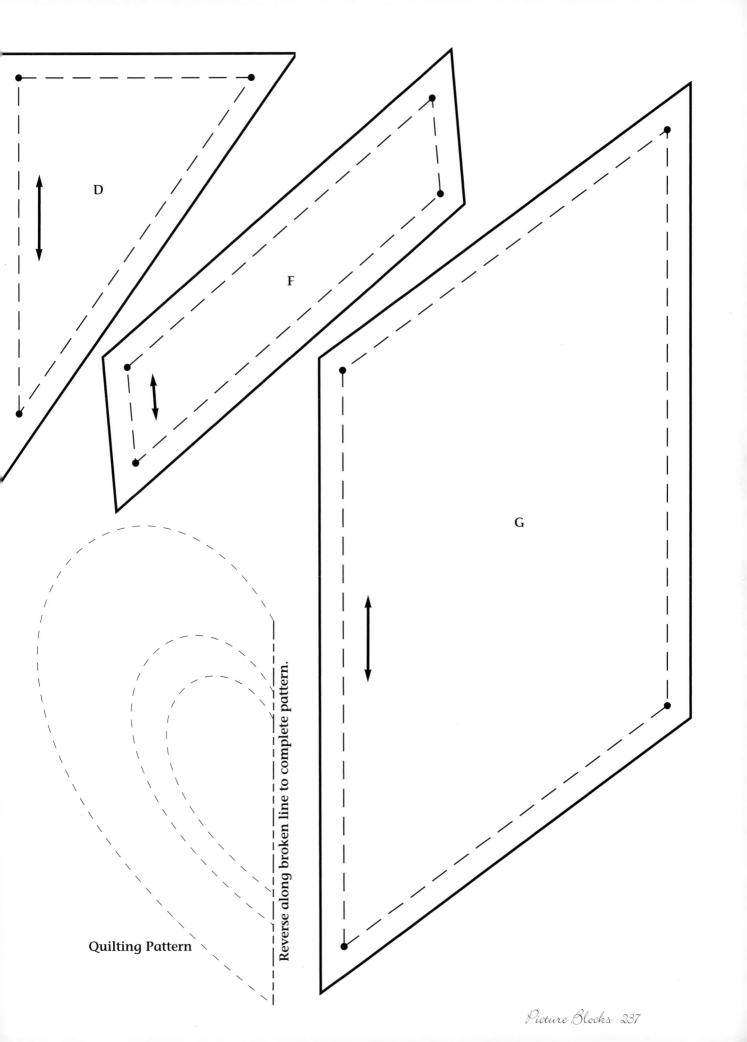

D

F

G

Quilting Pattern

Reverse along broken line to complete pattern.

Cherry Basket

Baskets abound in traditional American patchwork designs, and most of them are of New England origin. The design pictured below, Cherry Basket, is one of the most popular.

Finished Quilt Size
77" x 94"

Number of Blocks and Finished Size
12 (12") Cherry Basket Blocks

Materials
4 yards blue
6½ yards white
5½ yards backing fabric
Full-size batting

Cutting
Measurements include ¼" seam allowances. Patterns are on page 241.

From blue, cut:
- 2¾ yards. Cut yardage into 4 (3"-wide) lengthwise strips for inner borders and 4 (5"-wide) lengthwise strips for outer borders.
- 5 (2⅞"-wide) strips. Cut strips into 66 (2⅞") squares. Cut squares in half diagonally to make 132 A triangles.
- 12 (1¼" x 17") bias strips. Press raw edges under ¼" to make basket handles.

From white, cut:
- 2¾ yards. Cut yardage into 4 (6½"-wide) lengthwise strips for borders.
- From remainder, cut 6 (12½") setting squares.
- 10 (2¼"-wide) strips for binding.
- 2 (18¼"-wide) strips. Cut strips into 3 (18¼") squares. Cut squares in quarters diagonally to make 12 side setting triangles. You will have 2 extra.
- 1 (9⅜"-wide) strip. Cut strip into 2 (9⅜") squares. Cut squares in half diagonally to make 4 corner setting triangles.
- 3 (2⅞"-wide) strips. Cut strips into 30 (2⅞") squares. Cut squares in half diagonally to make 60 A triangles.
- 1 (2½"-wide) strip. Cut strip into 12 (2½") B squares.
- 1 (4⅞"-wide) strip. Cut strip into 6 (4⅞") squares. Cut squares in half diagonally to make 12 C triangles.
- 12 Ds and 12 Ds reversed.
- 2 (12⅞"-wide) strips. Cut strips into 6 (12⅞") squares. Cut squares in half diagonally to make 12 E triangles.

Block Assembly
1. Join 1 blue and 1 white A triangles to make 1 A unit (*A Unit Diagram*). Make 5 A units.

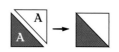

A Unit Diagram

2. Referring to *Block Assembly Diagram,* lay out A units with 6 blue A triangles and 1 each B, C, D, and D reversed. Join into sections as shown. Join sections to complete basket portion of block.

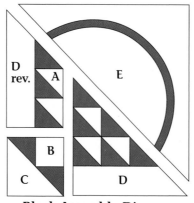

Block Assembly Diagram

3. Appliqué 1 handle to 1 E triangle as shown. Add E triangle to basket portion to complete 1 Cherry Basket block (*Block Diagram*).

4. Make 12 Cherry Basket blocks.

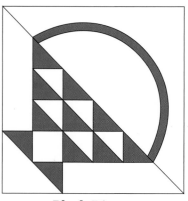

Block Diagram

Quilt Assembly
1. Lay out blocks and setting pieces as shown in *Quilt Top Assembly Diagram.* Join into diagonal rows; join rows to complete quilt center.

2. Join 1 (3"-wide) blue border, 1 white border, and 1 (5"-wide) blue border to make 1 border strip. Make 4 border strips.

3. Center 1 border strip on each side of quilt, narrow blue border to inside. Join to quilt; miter corners.

Quilting and Finishing
1. Divide backing fabric into 2 (2¾-yard) lengths. Cut 1 piece in half lengthwise. Sew 1 narrow panel to each side of wide panel. Press seam allowances toward narrow panels.

2. Layer backing, batting, and quilt top; baste. Quilt as desired. Quilt shown is quilted in-the-ditch in piecing, with leaf patterns around handles. Setting blocks have a basket and leaf pattern. Borders feature a hearts and flowers pattern.

3. Join 2¼"-wide white strips into 1 continuous piece for straight-grain French-fold binding. Add binding to quilt.

Quilt Top Assembly Diagram

Quilt Label
Trace, scan, or photocopy this quilt label to finish your quilt

Quilt by Mable Azbill Webb

Quilting Pattern
Reverse along broken line to complete pattern.

D

Amish Lily

This design is known by many regional names.
In the Midsouth it's the Mountain Lily. In the Midwest
it's Prairie Lily, Fire Lily, or Noon Day Lily.
In New England it's Wood Lily or Meadow Lily.
In California it's Mariposa Lily.

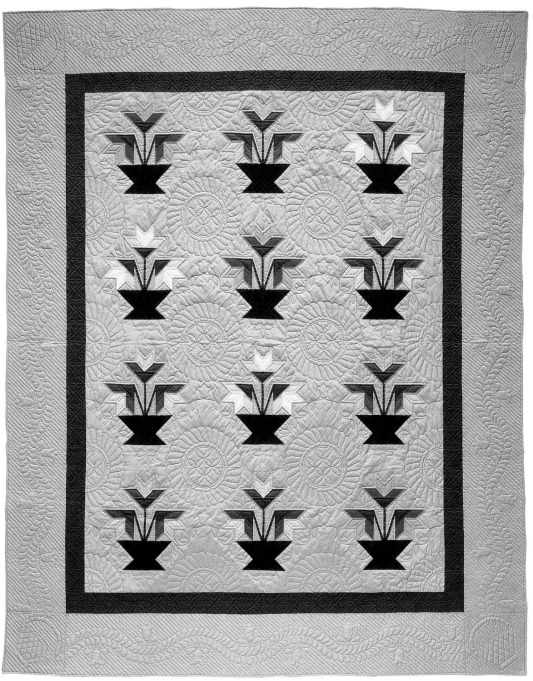

Quilt by Doris Angell Dunlap; owned by Ellen Angell Dunlap

Finished Quilt Size
86½" x 106¼"

Number of Blocks and Finished Size
12 (14") Amish Lily Blocks

Materials
9 yards gray
2¼ yards green
¾ yard black
1 fat eighth (9" x 22") each of solid
   light and dark red, blue, yellow,
   and purple (8 fabrics)
7½ yards backing fabric
Queen-size batting

Cutting
Measurements include ¼" seam
allowances. Patterns are on pages
244–245.

From gray, cut:
- 2½ yards. Cut yardage into
  4 (10½"-wide) lengthwise strips
  for outer borders.
- 11 (2¼"-wide) strips for binding.
- 3 (14½"-wide) strips. Cut strips
  into 6 (14½") setting squares.
- 2 yards. Cut yardage into
  1 (21⅛"-wide) lengthwise strip.
  Cut strip into 3 (21⅛") squares.
  Cut squares in quarters diagonally
  to make 12 side setting triangles.
  You will have 2 extra.
- From remainder, cut 2 (11")
  squares. Cut squares in half
  diagonally to make 4 corner
  setting triangles.
- 3 (2½"-wide) strips. Cut strips into
  36 (2½") A squares.
- 2 (4⅛"-wide) strips. Cut strips into
  18 (4⅛") squares. Cut squares in
  quarters diagonally to make 72 B
  triangles.
- 2 (5⅝"-wide) strips. Cut strips into
  12 (5⅝") squares. Cut squares in
  half diagonally to make 24 E
  triangles.
- 2 (4½"-wide) strips. Cut strips into
  12 (4½" x 5¼") F rectangles.
- 1 (5⅞"-wide) strip. Cut strip into
  6 (5⅞") squares. Cut squares in
  half diagonally to make 12 I
  triangles.
- 6 (3"-wide) strips. Cut strips into
  24 (3" x 9½") J rectangles.

From green, cut:
- 4 (4"-wide) lengthwise strips for
  inner borders.
- 1 (3⅝"-wide) lengthwise strip. Cut
  strip into 18 (3⅝") squares. Cut
  squares in half diagonally to
  make 36 D triangles.
- 36 (¾" x 5½") bias strips. Press
  under ¼" on long sides to make
  stems.

From black, cut:
- 2 (7⅝"-wide) strips. Cut strips into
  6 (7⅝") squares. Cut squares in
  half diagonally to make 12 G
  triangles.
- 1 (3⅜"-wide) strip. Cut strip into
  12 (3⅜") squares. Cut squares in
  half diagonally to make 24 H
  triangles.

*From each light or dark solid color,
cut:*
- 18 Cs. Divide by color into 24 sets
  of 6 Cs each.

Block Assembly
1. Choose 1 light red and 1 dark
red C set. Join 1 light and 1 dark C

as shown in *Block Assembly Diagram*.
Repeat. Join Cs to make flower. Set in
2 B triangles. Set in 1 A square. Add
1 D triangle to base. Add 2 E triangles
to make 1 center flower unit.

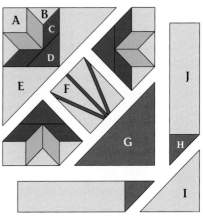

Block Assembly Diagram

2. To make side flower units, join
1 light and 1 dark C as shown in
Block Assembly Diagram. Repeat. Join
Cs to make flower. Set in 2 B
triangles. Set in 1 A square. Add
1 D triangle to base. Repeat to
make 2 side flower units, noting
position of A square.

3. Appliqué 3 stems to 1 F rectangle, placing as shown. Join side flower units to F. Add center flower unit. Join 1 G triangle to bottom.

4. Join 1 H triangle to 1 J. Add to side of block. Repeat for adjacent side. Add 1 I triangle to complete 1 Amish Lily block *(Block Diagram)*.

5. Make 12 Amish Lily blocks, 3 in each colorway.

Block Diagram

Quilt Assembly

1. Lay out blocks and setting pieces as shown in *Quilt Top Assembly Diagram*. Join into diagonal rows; join rows to complete quilt center.

2. Measure length of quilt and trim 2 green borders to that length (approximately 79¾"). Add green side borders to quilt. Measure width of quilt (approximately 67") and trim green borders to this measurement. Add green top and bottom borders to quilt.

3. Measure and add gray side borders to quilt (approximately 86¾"). Measure and add top and bottom borders (approximately 87").

Quilting and Finishing

1. Divide backing fabric into 3 (2½-yard) lengths. Join to make backing. Seams will run horizontally.

2. Layer backing, batting, and quilt top; baste. Quilt as desired. Quilt shown is outline-quilted in blocks, with feather wreaths in setting pieces. Inner border has a cable pattern, and outer border has a feathered vine with diagonal fill.

3. Join 2¼"-wide gray strips into 1 continuous piece for straight-grain French-fold binding. Add binding to quilt.

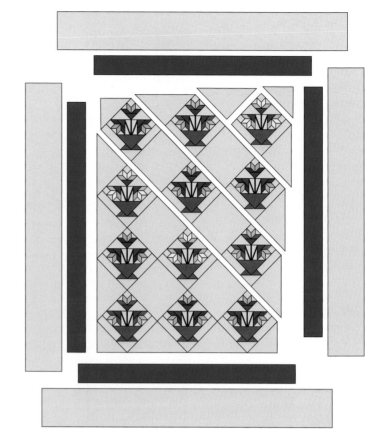

Quilt Top Assembly Diagram

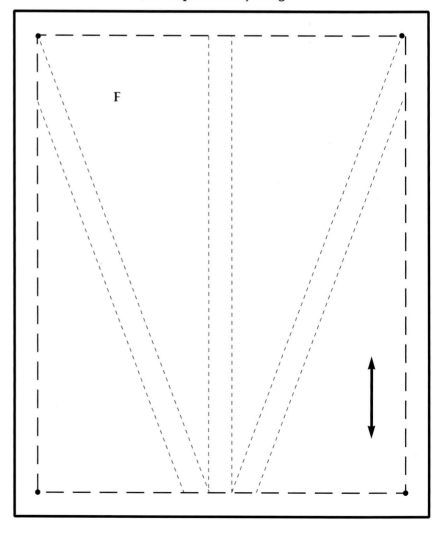

F

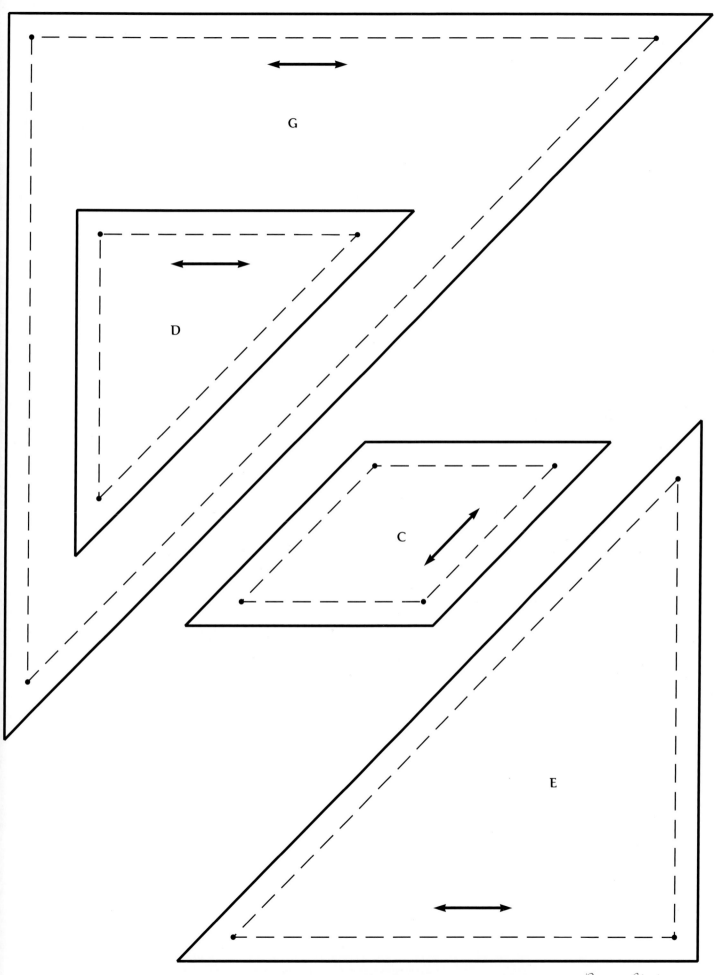

Butterfly Quilt

In the 1920s and 1930s, Ruby Short McKim published a syndicated newspaper column of quilt patterns. Her company, McKim Studios, also published quilting pamphlets. It was in one of these pamphlets that June Wolpert discovered this pattern.

Finished Quilt Size

64" x 84"

Number of Blocks and Finished Size

18 (10") Butterfly Blocks

Materials

2 yards tan
⅝ yard white
18 fat eighths (9" x 22") assorted medium prints
18 fat eighths (9" x 22") assorted dark prints
1 fat eighth (9" x 22") black
2⅜ yard each inner, middle, and outer border fabric
5 yards backing fabric
Twin-size batting
Black embroidery floss

Cutting

Measurements include ¼" seam allowances. Patterns are on pages 248–249.

From tan, cut:
• 6 (10½"-wide) strips. Cut strips into 17 (10½") setting squares.

From white, cut:
• 1 (5¼"-wide). Cut strip into 5 (5¼") squares. Cut squares in quarters diagonally to make 20 Is. You will need 18 Is; 2 are extra.
• 18 As.
• 36 Ds.

From medium prints, cut:
• 18 sets of:
  • 1 B and 1 B reversed.
  • 2 Cs.

From dark prints, cut:
• 18 sets of:
  • 2 Es.

• 1 F and 1 F reversed.
• 1 H and 1 H reversed.

From black, cut:
• 18 (1" x 4¾") G rectangles.

From inner border fabric, cut:
• 4 (2½"-wide) lengthwise strips for inner border.

From middle border fabric, cut:
• 4 (1½"-wide) lengthwise strips for middle border.
• 4 (2¼"-wide) lengthwise strips for binding.

From outer border fabric, cut:
• 4 (4½"-wide) lengthwise strips for outer border.

Block Assembly

Refer to *Block Assembly Diagram* throughout.

1. To make top row, join 1 B, 1 A, and 1 B reversed. Embroider antennae in black with stem stitch (*Stem Stitch Diagram*).

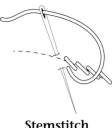

Stemstitch Diagram

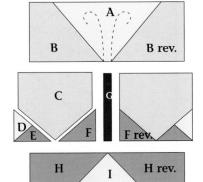

Block Assembly Diagram

2. To make middle row, join 1 D and 1 E as shown. Add to 1 C. Add 1 F to remaining angle of C to complete 1 section. Repeat to make second section, noting placement. Join sections to 1 G to complete middle row.

3. To make bottom row, join 1 H, 1 I, and 1 H reversed.

4. Join rows to complete 1 Butterfly block (*Block Diagram*). Make 18 Butterfly blocks.

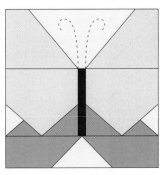

Block Diagram

Quilt Assembly

1. Lay out blocks and tan setting squares as shown in *Quilt Top Assembly Diagram*. Join into rows; join rows to complete center.

2. Join 1 inner, 1 middle, and 1 outer border strips to make 1 pieced border strip. Make 4 pieced border strips.

3. Center 1 pieced border strip on each side of quilt and join. Miter corners.

Quilting and Finishing

1. Divide backing fabric into 2 (2½-yard) lengths. Cut 1 piece in half lengthwise. Sew 1 narrow panel to each side of wide panel. Press seam allowances toward narrow panels.

Quilt Top Assembly Diagram

2. Layer backing, batting, and quilt top; baste. Quilt as desired. Quilt shown is echo-quilted in wings, with outline-quilting in remaining piecework. Alternate blocks have a rose pattern. Borders feature cable patterns.

3. Join 2¼"-wide binding strips into 1 continuous piece for straight-grain French-fold binding. Add binding to quilt.

Quilt by June Wolpert

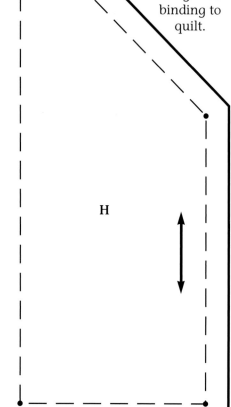

H

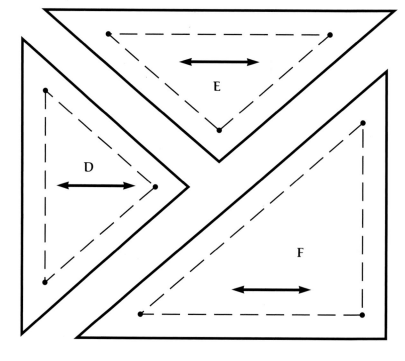

E

D

F

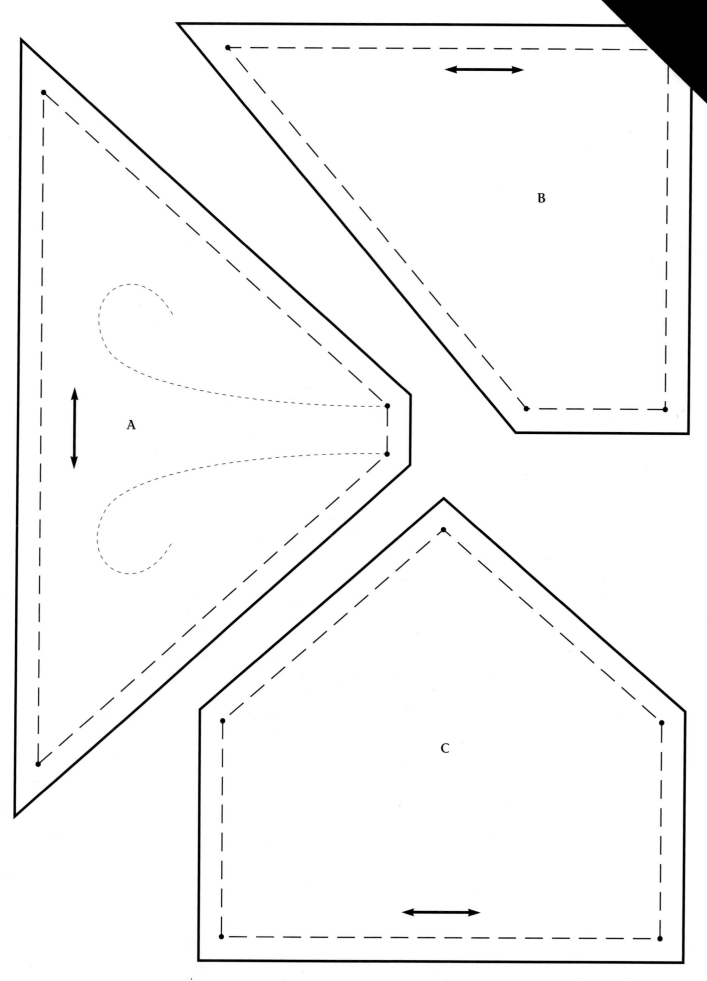

dmother's Fan

In Victorian times, ladies pieced this pattern with lavish silks, satins, and velvets, and embellished it with embroidery, lace, ribbons, and beading. During the lean Depression years, quilters dug into their scrap bags to make this favorite design.

Finished Quilt Size
82" x 100"

Number of Blocks and Finished Size
40 (9") Grandmother's Fan Blocks

Materials
3½ yards assorted floral prints
6½ yards unbleached muslin
2 yards solid rose
7½ yards fabric for backing
Queen-size batting

Cutting
Measurements include ¼" seam allowances. Patterns are on pages 252–253.

From assorted floral prints, cut:
• 360 Bs.

From unbleached muslin, cut:
• 40 Cs.
• 10 (9½"-wide) strips. Cut strips into 40 (9½") setting squares.
• 10 (2¼"-wide) strips for binding.

From solid rose, cut:
• 10 (5½"-wide) strips. Piece strips to make 2 (5½" x 84") and 2 (5½" x 104") border strips.
• 40 As.

Block Assembly
1. Referring to *Block Assembly Diagram*, join 9 Bs to make fan. Appliqué or piece in 1 A for handle.

2. Appliqué or piece in fan to 1 C to complete 1 Grandmother's Fan block. (For more on piecing curves, see page 356.)

3. Make 40 Grandmother's Fan blocks.

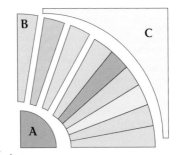

Block Assembly Diagram

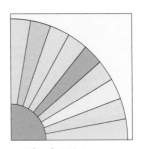

Block Diagram

Quilt Assembly
1. Referring to *Quilt Top Assembly Diagram*, lay out blocks and setting squares. Join into rows; join rows to complete quilt center.

2. Center 1 border strip on each side of quilt and join, mitering corners.

Quilting and Finishing
1. Divide backing fabric into 3 (2½-yard) lengths. Join to make backing. Seams will run horizontally.

2. Layer backing, batting, and quilt top; baste. Quilt as desired. Quilt shown is outline-quilted in piecework. Setting squares have fan pattern, and border has a cable pattern.

3. Join 2¼"-wide muslin strips into 1 continuous piece for straight-grain French-fold binding. Add binding to quilt.

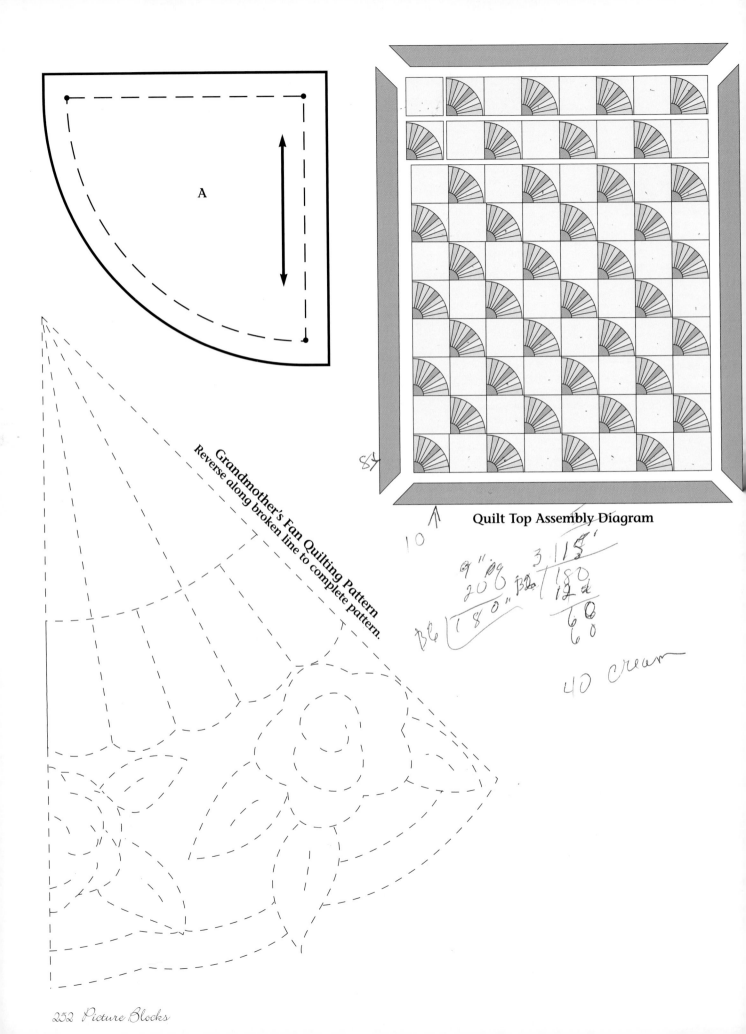

A

Grandmother's Fan Quilting Pattern
Reverse along broken line to complete pattern.

Quilt Top Assembly Diagram

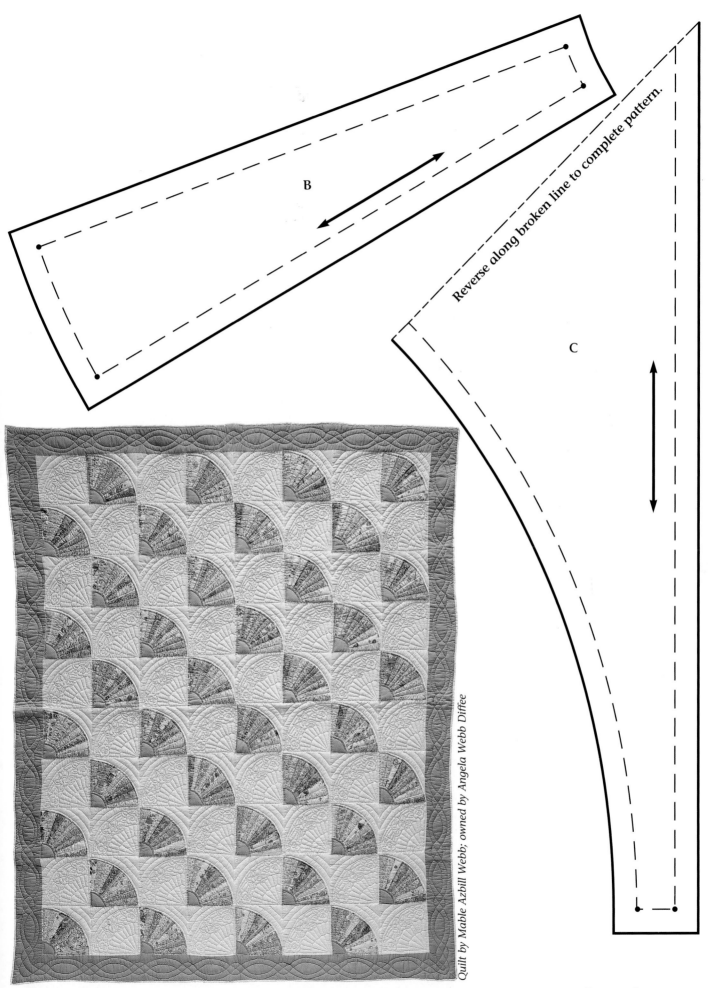

B

Reverse along broken line to complete pattern.

C

Quilt by Mable Azbill Webb; owned by Angela Webb Diffee

Fruit Basket

Basket patterns evoke memories of beautiful gardens past and hopes of bountiful harvests to come. This lovely Fruit Basket, pieced in rich autumn colors, probably dates from the 1930s and may have represented the quilter's longing for more prosperous times.

Finished Quilt Size
66½" x 89"

Number of Blocks and Finished Size
35 (8") Fruit Basket Blocks

Materials
3½ yards red print
3 yards white print
2½ yards brown print
6 yards fabric for backing
Twin-size batting

Cutting
Measurements include ¼" seam allowances. Because E is 1⁹⁄₁₆" finished and D is 4¹¹⁄₁₆" finished, we recommend using the templates on pages 256–258 to make this quilt. Rotary-cutting instructions are also given below.

From red print, cut:
- 8 (2⁷⁄₁₆"-wide) strips. Cut strips into 123 (2⁷⁄₁₆") squares for E units.
- 3 (5⁹⁄₁₆"-wide) strips. Cut strips into 18 (5⁹⁄₁₆") squares. Cut squares in half diagonally to make 36 D triangles. You will have 1 extra.
- 3 (2⁵⁄₈"-wide) strips. Cut strips into 35 (2⁵⁄₈") squares. Cut squares in half diagonally to make 70 C triangles.
- 10 (4"-wide) strips. Piece to make 4 (4" x 90") outer border strips.
- 9 (2¼"-wide) strips for binding.

From white print, cut:
- 8 (2⁷⁄₁₆"-wide) strips. Cut strips into 123 (2⁷⁄₁₆") squares for E units.
- 9 (2¼"-wide) strips. Cut strips into 70 (2¼" x 5") A rectangles.
- 2 (4³⁄₈"-wide) strips. Cut strips into 18 (4³⁄₈") squares. Cut squares in half diagonally to make 36 B triangles. You will have 1 extra.
- 3 (5⁹⁄₁₆"-wide) strips. Cut strips into 18 (5⁹⁄₁₆") squares. Cut squares in half diagonally to make 36 D triangles. You will have 1 extra.
- 10 (2"-wide) strips. Piece to make 4 (2" x 90") inner border strips.

Quilt from Hanna Antiques, Birmingham, Alabama

From brown print, cut:
- 6 (8½"-wide) strips. Cut strips into 24 (8½") setting squares.
- 2 (12⅝"-wide) strips. Cut strips into 5 (12⅝") squares. Cut squares in quarters diagonally to make 20 side setting triangles.
- From remainder, cut 2 (6⅝") squares. Cut squares in half diagonally to make 4 corner setting triangles.

Block Assembly

1. Referring to *E Unit Diagram,* draw a diagonal line from corner to corner on back of white print 2⁷⁄₁₆" squares. Place 1 white and 1 red print square together, right sides facing. Stitch ¼" from line on both sides. Cut apart and press open to make 2 E units. Make 245 E units (7 per block). You will have 1 extra.

E Unit Diagram

2. Referring to *Block Assembly Diagram,* join 1 white and 1 red D to make 1 D unit. Join 3 E units into a strip. Join E strip to left side of D unit. Join 4 E units into a strip. Add to top of D unit.

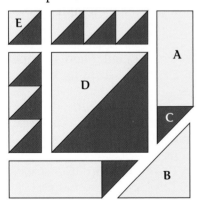

Block Assembly Diagram

3. Join 1 red C triangle to 1 A. Add to right side of D unit. Repeat for bottom of D unit. Add 1 B triangle to complete 1 Fruit Basket block *(Block Diagram).*

4. Make 35 Fruit Basket blocks.

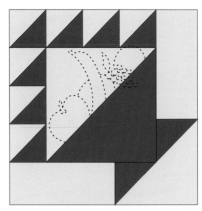

Block Diagram

Quilt Assembly

1. Lay out blocks and setting pieces as shown in *Quilt Top Assembly Diagram* on page 257. Join into diagonal rows; join rows to complete center.

2. Join 1 white and 1 red border strip to make 1 border strip. Make 4 border strips.

3. Center 1 border strip on each side of quilt and join, mitering corners.

Quilting and Finishing

1. Divide backing fabric into 3 (2-yard) lengths. Cut 1 piece in half lengthwise. Sew 1 narrow panel between wide panels. Press seam allowances toward narrow panel. Remaining panel is extra and may be used to make a hanging sleeve. Seams will run horizontally.

2. Layer backing, batting, and quilt top; baste. Quilt as desired. Quilt shown is outline-quilted in blocks, with fruit pattern quilted into basket. Setting squares have a pineapple pattern. Patterns are on pages 256–258.

3. Join 2¼"-wide red print strips into 1 continuous piece for straight-grain French-fold binding. Add binding to quilt.

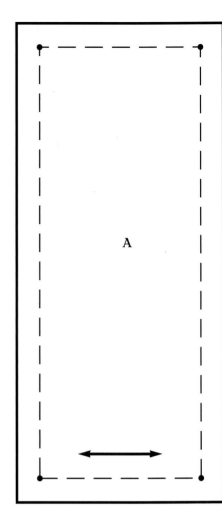

A

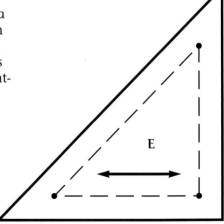

E

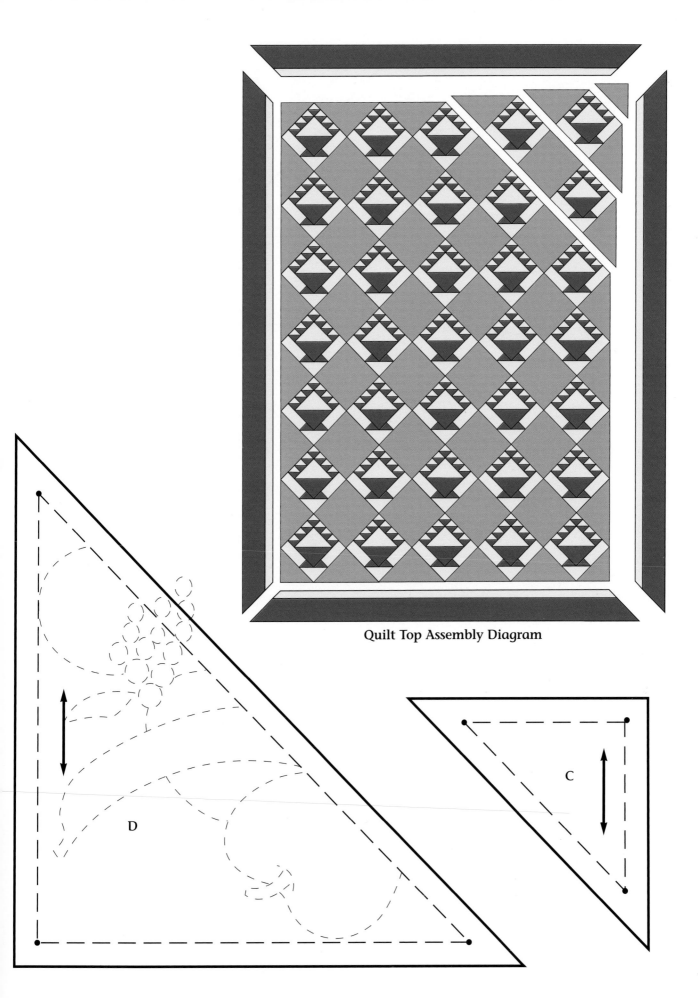

Quilt Top Assembly Diagram

C

D

B

Pineapple Quilting Pattern for Setting Squares

Lucky Lindy

With Charles Lindbergh's nonstop solo flight
from New York to Paris in 1927, the imagination of
quilters took wing. Several pieced airplane patterns date
from this time. The publication of Lindbergh's book,
The Spirit of St. Louis, in 1953 inspired new ones.

Quilt by Shirley E. Pepi; owned by Neil Pepi

Finished Quilt Size
78" x 100½"

Number of Blocks and Finished Size
54 (8") Lucky Lindy Blocks

Materials
6 yards muslin
54 (5" x 20") strips assorted prints
1 yard brown print
1¼ yards navy print
¾ yard red for binding
6¾ yards fabric for backing
Queen-size batting

Cutting
Measurements include ¼" seam allowances. Patterns are on pages 261–262.

From muslin, cut:
• 7 (8½"-wide) strips. Cut strips into 28 (8½") setting squares.
• 3 (12⅝"-wide) strips. Cut strips into 7 (12⅝") squares. Cut squares into quarters diagonally to make 28 setting triangles.
• 54 Ds and 54 Ds reversed.
• 54 Es and 54 Es reversed.
• 54 Fs and 54 Fs reversed.
• 54 Hs.

From each strip assorted prints, cut:
• 1 A.
• 1 B.
• 1 C.
• 1 G.

From brown print, cut:
• 10 (2½"-wide) strips. Piece to make 2 (2½" x 82") and 2 (2½" x 102") inner border strips.

From navy print, cut:
• 10 (3½"-wide) strips. Piece to make 2 (3½" x 82") and 2 (3½" x 102") outer border strips.

From red, cut:
• 10 (2¼"-wide) strips for binding.

Block Assembly
1. Choose 1 print set. Referring to *Block Assembly Diagram,* join D, C and D reversed to make top row. Add B strip.
2. Join E, A and E reversed to make 1 strip. Add to B strip.

3. Join H to G. Join F and F reversed to each side of G/H unit to make bottom row. Add to bottom of unit to complete 1 Lucky Lindy block *(Block Diagram).*
4. Make 54 Lucky Lindy blocks.

Quilt Assembly
1. Lay out blocks and setting pieces as shown in *Quilt Top Assembly Diagram.* Join into diagonal rows; join rows to complete quilt center.
2. Join 1 brown and 1 navy strips, matching lengths, to make 1 border strip. Make 4 border strips.
3. Center 1 border strip on each side of quilt and join, mitering corners.

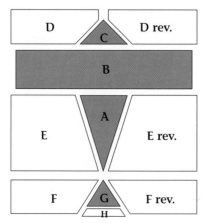

Block Assembly Diagram

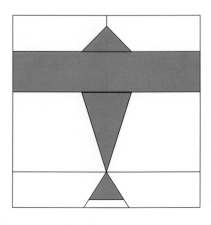

Block Diagram

Quilting and Finishing

1. Divide backing fabric into 3 (2¼-yard) lengths. Join to make backing. Seams will run horizontally.

2. Layer backing, batting, and quilt top; baste. Quilt as desired. Quilt shown is outline-quilted in blocks, with crosshatch fill.

3. Join 2¼"-wide red strips into 1 continuous piece for straight-grain French-fold binding. Add binding to quilt.

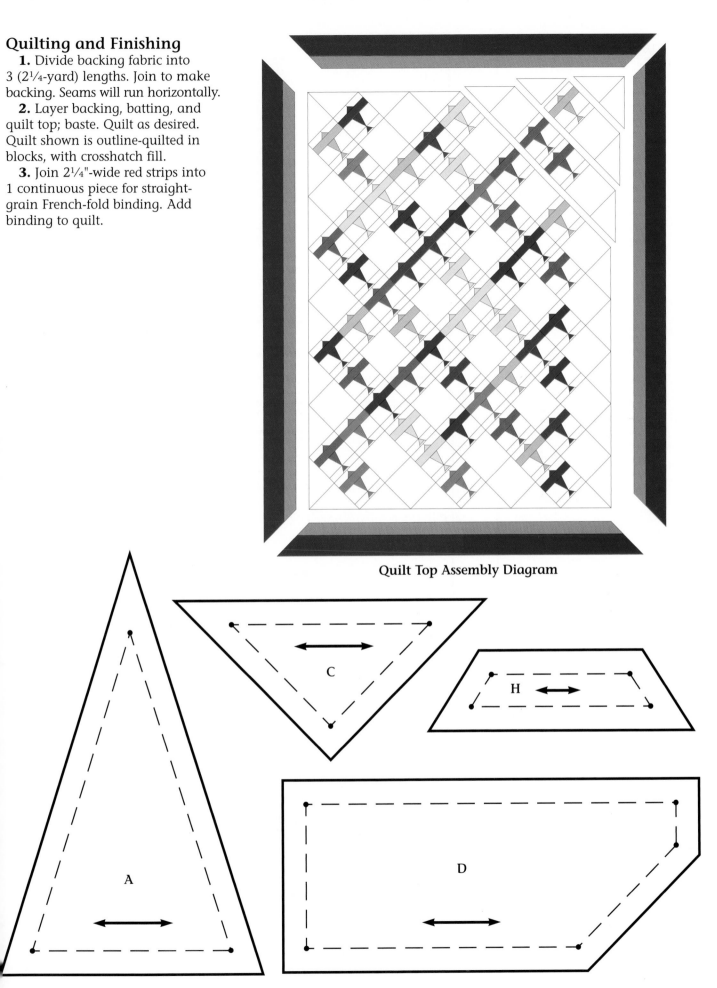

Quilt Top Assembly Diagram

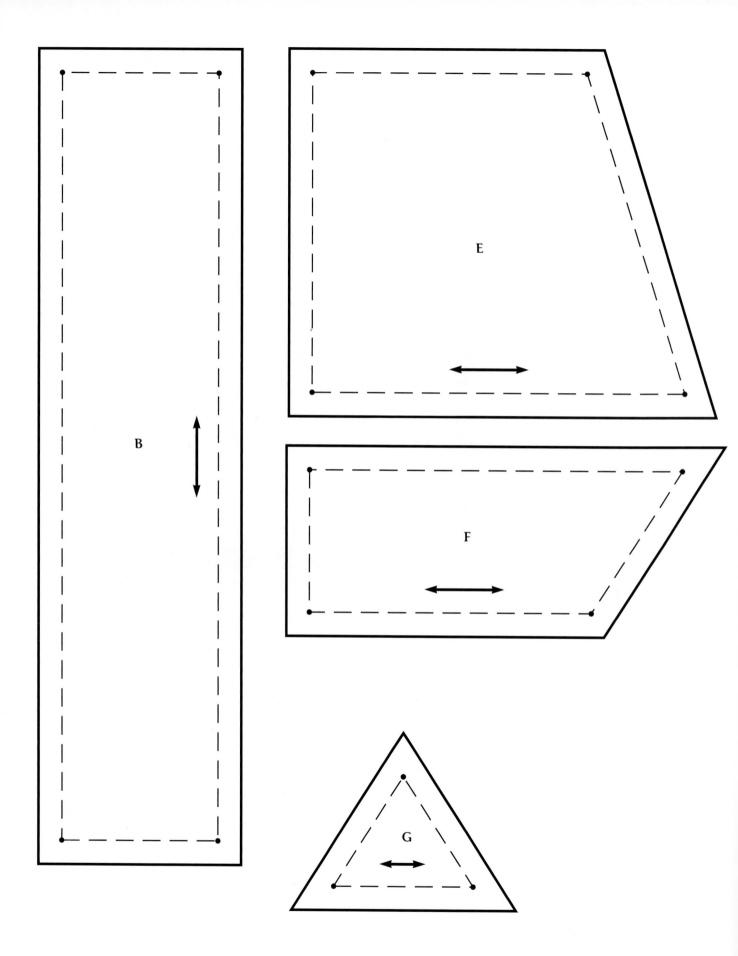

B

E

F

G

Fanny's Fan

The blocks in this beautiful fan quilt were made in
the 1930s, when Judia Chapman Mitchel pieced together
fabric scraps and muslin feedsacks. Judia's daughter,
Bertha Mitchel Sikes, and granddaughter,
Karen Sikes Collins, assembled the top after Judia's death.

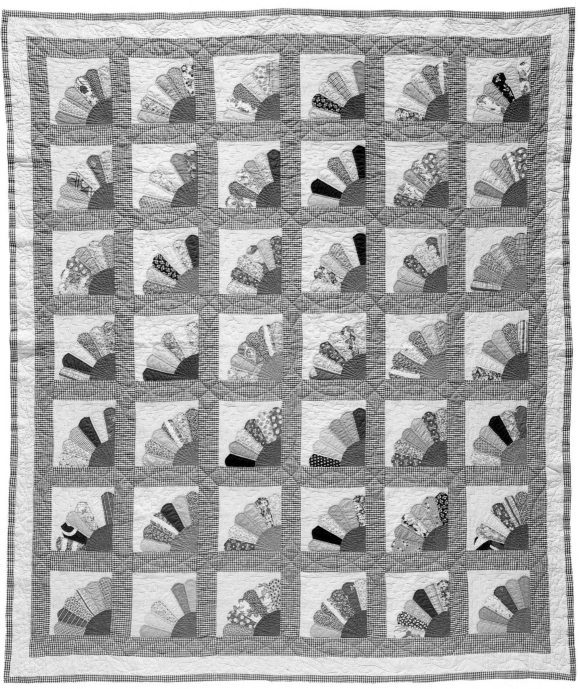

Quilt owned by Bertha Mitchel Sikes

Finished Quilt Size

71½" x 82"

Number of Blocks and Finished Size

42 (8") Fan Blocks

Materials

¾ yard solid blue
2 yards total assorted prints and
   solids
3¾ yards muslin
3½ yards blue gingham
5 yards fabric for backing
Twin-size batting

Cutting

Measurements include ¼" seam allowances. Border strips are exact length needed. You may want to cut them longer to allow for piecing variations. Patterns are on page 266.

From solid blue, cut:
• 42 As.

From assorted prints and solids, cut:
• 252 Bs.

From muslin, cut:
• 11 (8½"-wide) strips. Cut strips into 42 (8½") blocks.
• 8 (3½"-wide) strips. Piece to make 2 (3½" x 76½") side borders and 2 (3½" x 72") top and bottom borders.

From blue gingham, cut:
• 16 (3"-wide) strips. Piece to make 8 (3" x 66") horizontal sashing strips.
• 12 (3"-wide) strips. Cut strips into 49 (3" x 8½") vertical sashing strips.
• 9 (2¼"-wide) strips for binding.

Block Assembly

1. Referring to *Block Assembly Diagram*, join 6 assorted Bs to make fan. Appliqué 1 A to fan for handle.
2. Appliqué fan to 1 block square to make 1 Fan block (*Block Diagram*).
3. Make 42 Fan blocks.

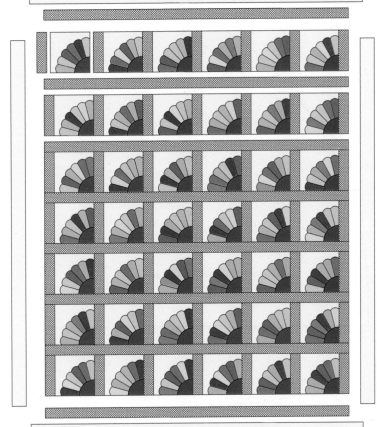

Quilt Top Assembly Diagram

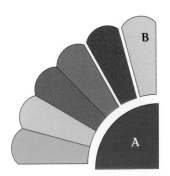

Block Assembly Diagram

Block Diagram

Quilt Assembly

1. Referring to *Quilt Top Assembly Diagram*, alternate 7 sashing strips and 6 blocks. Join to make 1 block row. Make 7 block rows.
2. Alternate horizontal sashing with block rows and join to complete center.
3. Add muslin side borders to quilt. Add top and bottom borders.

Quilting and Finishing

1. Divide backing fabric into 2 (2½-yard) lengths. Cut 1 piece in half lengthwise. Sew 1 narrow panel to each side of wide panel. Press seam allowances toward narrow panels.
2. Layer backing, batting, and quilt top; baste. Quilt as desired. Quilt shown is outline-quilted in piecework, with outlines extending through A pieces. Block corners and borders have a flower pattern.
3. Join 2¼"-wide blue gingham strips into 1 continuous piece for straight-grain French-fold binding. Add binding to quilt.

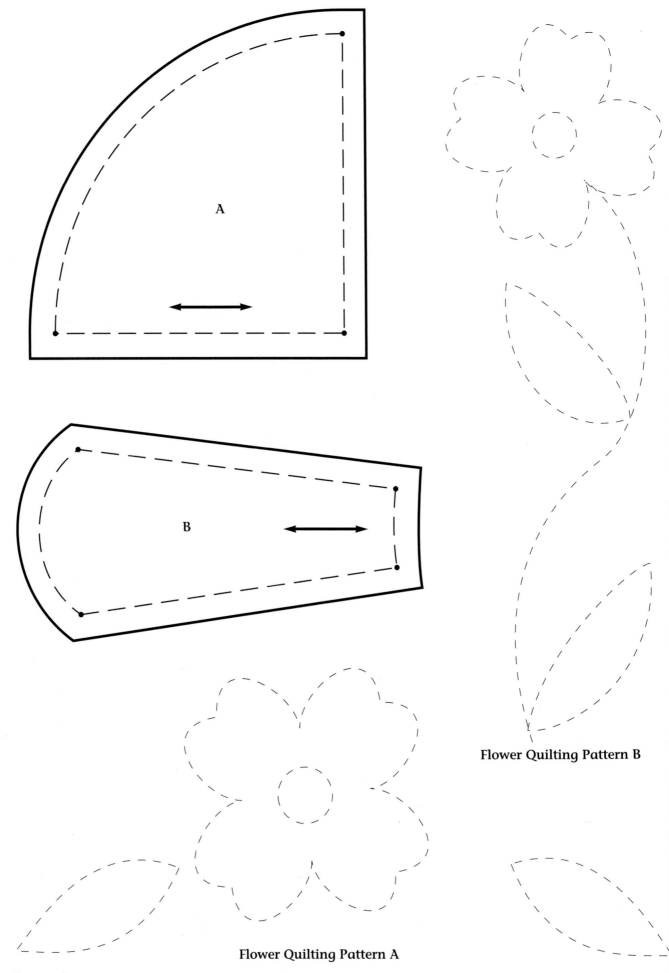

A

B

Flower Quilting Pattern B

Flower Quilting Pattern A

Bow Tie

The Bow Tie block was first published in the 1930s as an Aunt Martha pattern. It was included among booklets, kits, and patterns that were advertised in a syndicated column under various names including Aunt Ellen, Aunt Matilda, and Betsy Ross.

Quilt by CeCe Lewis

Finished Quilt Size
76" x 92"

Number of Blocks and Finished Size
309 (4") Bow Tie Blocks

Materials
4 yards assorted prints
5 yards white
¾ yard dark fabric for binding
5½ yards fabric for backing
Full-size batting

Cutting
Measurements include ¼" seam allowances. Border strips are exact length needed. You may want to cut them longer to allow for piecing variations. Patterns are on page 269.

From assorted prints, cut:
• 309 sets of:
  • 2 As.
  • 1 B.

From white, cut:
• 618 As.
• 14 (4½"-wide) strips. Piece strips to make 2 (4½" x 60½") inner side borders, 2 (4½" x 52½") inner top and bottom borders, 2 (4½" x 76½") outer side borders, and 2 (4½" x 68½") outer top and bottom borders.

From dark fabric, cut:
• 9 (2¼"-wide) strips for binding.

Block Assembly
1. Choose 1 print set. Join 2 white As to 1 print B as shown in *Block Assembly Diagram*. Set in 2 print As to complete 1 Bow Tie block *(Block Diagram)*.
2. Make 309 Bow Tie blocks.

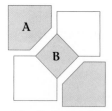

Block Assembly Diagram

Block Diagram

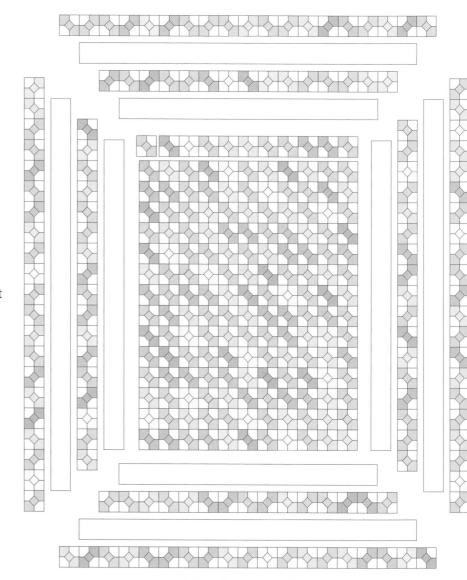

Quilt Top Assembly Diagram

Quilt Assembly
1. Referring to *Quilt Top Assembly Diagram*, lay out 165 blocks in 15 rows of 11 blocks each for center section. Join into rows; join rows to complete center.
2. Add inner side borders to quilt. Add inner top and bottom borders.
3. Join 17 blocks to make inner side pieced border. Repeat. Add to quilt.
4. Join 15 blocks to make inner top pieced border. Repeat for bottom border. Add to quilt.
5. Add outer side borders to quilt. Add top and bottom borders.
6. Join 21 blocks to make outer side pieced border. Repeat. Add to quilt.

7. Join 19 blocks to make outer top pieced border. Repeat for bottom border. Add to quilt.

Quilting and Finishing
1. Divide backing fabric into 2 (2¾-yard) lengths. Cut 1 piece in half lengthwise. Sew 1 narrow panel to each side of wide panel. Press seam allowances toward narrow panels.
2. Layer backing, batting, and quilt top; baste. Quilt as desired. Quilt shown is outline-quilted in blocks with half-circles in borders.
3. Join dark strips into 1 continuous piece for straight-grain French-fold binding. Add binding to quilt.

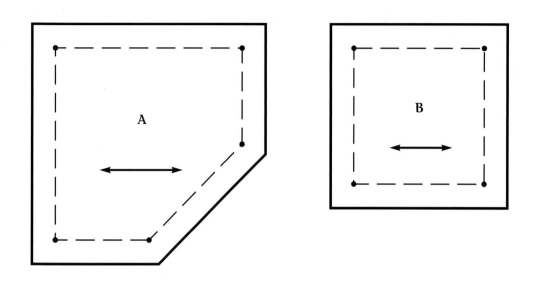

A

B

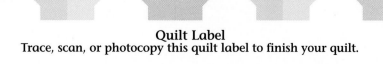

Quilt Label
Trace, scan, or photocopy this quilt label to finish your quilt.

Pine Tree

A stately image of the American frontier, the pine tree was the inspiration for this pattern—one of the oldest representational quilt designs. Other variations and names for the pattern include Temperance Tree, Christmas Tree (when stitched in red and green), Tree of Paradise, Tree of Life, and Proud Pine.

Finished Quilt Size
68" x 68"

Number of Blocks and Finished Size
16 (12") Pine Tree Blocks

Materials
3 yards pink print
2½ yards muslin
1 yard solid brown
½ yard total assorted red prints
¾ yard total assorted brown prints
4 yards backing fabric
Twin-size batting

Cutting
Note: Measurements include ¼" seam allowances. Patterns are on page 272–273.

From pink print, cut:
- 3 (12½"-wide) strips. Cut strips into 9 (12½" x 12½") setting squares.
- 2 (18¼"-wide) strips. Cut strips into 3 (18¼") squares. Cut squares in quarters diagonally to make 12 side setting triangles.
- From remainder, cut 2 (9⅜") squares. Cut squares in half diagonally to make 4 corner setting triangles.
- 8 (2¼"-wide) strips for binding.

From muslin, cut:
- 12 (2⅜"-wide) strips. Cut strips into 192 (2⅜") squares for A units.
- 2 (2"-wide) strips. Cut strips into 32 (2") B squares.
- 3 (5⅜"-wide) strips. Cut strips into 16 (5⅜") squares. Cut squares in half diagonally to make 32 C triangles.
- 16 Es and 16 Es reversed.
- 1 (4⅝"-wide) strip. Cut strip into 8 (4⅝") squares. Cut squares in

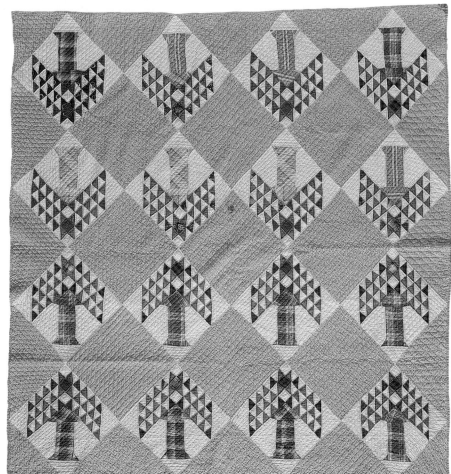

Quilt owned by Laura Earnest Leatherwood

half diagonally to make 16 G triangles.

From solid brown, cut:
- 10 (2⅜"-wide) strips. Cut strips into 160 (2⅜") squares for A units.
- 1 (2⅜"-wide) strip. Cut strip into 16 (2⅜") squares. Cut squares in half diagonally to make 32 A triangles for side units.

From assorted red prints, cut:
- 32 (2⅜") squares for A units.

- 32 (2⅜") squares. Cut squares in half diagonally to make 64 A triangles for side units.
- 16 (2") B squares.

From assorted brown prints, cut:
- 8 (3⅝") squares. Cut squares in half diagonally to make 16 D triangles.
- 16 (1⅞") squares. Cut squares in half diagonally to make 32 F triangles.
- 16 (3¼" x 6½") H rectangles.

Block Assembly

1. Referring to *A Unit Diagram*, draw a diagonal line from corner to corner on back of 192 (2⅜") muslin squares. Place 1 muslin and 1 solid brown squares together, right sides facing. Stitch ¼" from line on both sides. Cut apart and press open to make 2 A units. Make 320 A units with solid brown and 64 A units with red.

A Unit Diagram

2. To make top left corner, lay out 4 brown and 2 red A units as shown in *Block Assembly Diagram.* Add 2 muslin and 1 red B squares. Join pieces to make top corner.

3. To make sides, lay out 8 brown and 1 red A units as shown in *Block Assembly Diagram.* Add 2 red A triangles, 1 brown A triangle, and 1 muslin C triangle as shown. Join pieces to make 1 side unit. Repeat for second side unit.

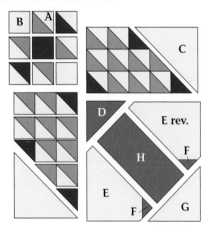

Block Assembly Diagram

4. Join 1 F to bottom of 1 E. Repeat with E reversed. Join E units to each side of 1 H rectangle. Add 1

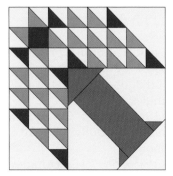

Block Diagram

Quilt Top Assembly Diagram

D triangle to top. Add 1 G triangle to bottom to complete trunk section.

5. Add 1 side unit to trunk unit. Join top and remaining side units; add to top to complete 1 Pine Tree block *(Block Diagram).*

6. Make 16 Pine Tree blocks.

Quilt Assembly

1. Lay out blocks and setting pieces as shown in *Quilt Top Assembly Diagram.*

2. Join into diagonal rows; join rows to complete quilt.

Quilting and Finishing

1. Divide backing fabric into 2 (2-yard) lengths. Cut 1 piece in half lengthwise. Sew 1 narrow panel to each side of wide panel. Press seam allowances toward narrow panels.

2. Layer backing, batting, and

quilt top; baste. Quilt as desired. Quilt shown is outline-quilted in patchwork with diagonal fill in blocks. Setting pieces have hanging diamond gridwork.

3. Join 2¼"-wide pink strips into 1 continuous piece for straight-grain French-fold binding. Add binding to quilt.

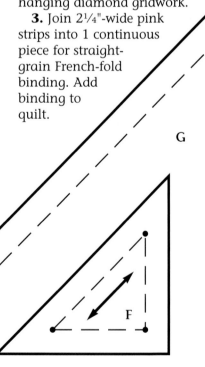

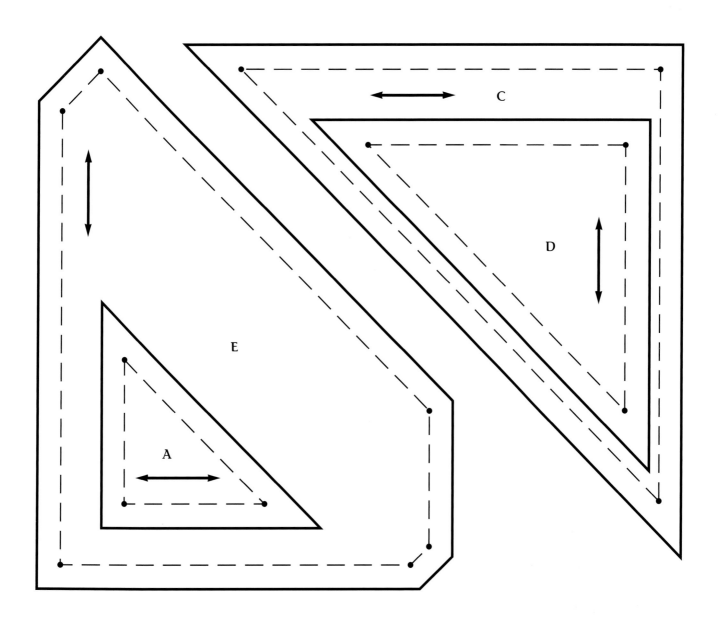

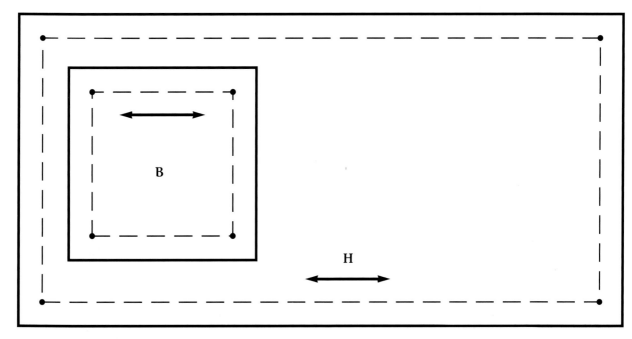

Chapter 7

Appliqué

Like their picture block counterparts, appliqué quilts form shapes of objects we are quick to recognize.

• While traditionally stitched by hand, there are many appliqué techniques, including those that can be done by machine. See pages 350–351 to choose the technique that will work best for you.

• Some of the quilts in this chapter are very old, such as the *Whig Rose* on page 300 and *Currants & Coxcombs* on page 317. Because appliquéd bed quilts were saved for special occasions or for company, they survived the ages better than their well-used pieced cousins that served as everyday quilts.

• If you choose to stitch them by hand, appliqué blocks make wonderful take-along projects for travel or for everyday errands that require waiting.

• When purchasing thread for an appliqué quilt, remember to match the thread to the appliqué fabrics rather than to the background material.

Appliqué quilts are often considered masterpiece quilts, especially if they are completely done by hand. The soothing activity of handwork can even reduce your stress level.

Tulip Garden

This pattern is one of several variations on the tulip appliqué theme. Others include Spring Tulip, Egyptian Tulip, Rare Old Tulip, Colonial Tulip, Conventional Tulip, Tennessee Tulip, and Cottage Tulips.

Finished Quilt Size
86" x 105"

Number of Blocks and Finished Size
12 (16") Tulip Blocks

Materials
8 yards muslin
2½ yards dark green
1 yard dark peach
4½ yards light peach
8¼ yards fabric for backing
Queen-size batting

Cutting
Measurements include ¼" seam allowances. Patterns are on page 279.

From muslin, cut:
- 11 (13½"-wide) strips. Piece strips to make 2 (13½" x 89") top and bottom borders and 2 (13½" x 108") side borders.
- 6 (16½"-wide) strips. Cut strips into 12 (16½") appliqué background squares.
- 1 (16½"-wide) strip. Cut strip and above remainder into 31 (1½" x 16½") strips for sashing.
- 4 (1½"-wide) strips for Nine-Patch sashing squares.

From dark green, cut:
- 12 Cs and 12 Cs reversed.
- 30 Ds and 30 Ds reversed.
- 30 (1¼" x 16") bias strips and 12 (1" x 7") bias strips for appliqué. Fold under ¼" on long edges and press.

From dark peach, cut:
- 1 (1½"-wide) strip for Nine-Patch sashing squares.
- 72 As.

Quilt by Gladys E. Love

From light peach, cut:
- 4 (1½"-wide) strips for Nine-Patch sashing squares.
- 72 Bs and 72 Bs reversed.
- 3 (16½"-wide) strips. Cut strips into 62 (1½" x 16½") strips for sashing.
- 1 (35") square for bias binding.

Block Assembly
1. Fold 1 (16½") square in quarters in both directions as shown in *Folding Diagram.* Press to make guidelines for appliqué.

2. Referring to *Appliqué Placement Diagram,* position and appliqué 1 each: 1 D, 1 D reversed, 1 C, 1 C reversed. Appliqué 1 (7"-long) bias strip for straight stem. Place 1 (16"-long) bias strip over pressing guide and

Folding Diagram

Appliqué Placement Diagram

press. Appliqué in place as shown.

3. For each tulip, appliqué 1 B, 1 B reversed, and 1 A as shown to complete 1 Tulip Garden block.

4. Make 12 Tulip Garden blocks.

Quilt Assembly

1. Referring to *Sashing Diagram,* join 1 muslin and 2 light peach (1½" x 16½") strips as shown to make 1 sashing strip. Make 31 sashing strips.

Sashing Diagram

2. Referring to *Strip Set A Diagram,* join 1 muslin and 2 light peach 1½"-wide strips to make 1 Strip Set A. Make 2 strip sets. Cut strip sets into 40 (1½"-wide) segments for Nine-Patch sashing squares.

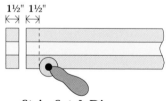

Strip Set A Diagram

3. Referring to *Strip Set B Diagram,* join 1 dark peach and 2 muslin 1½"-wide strips to make 1 Strip Set B. Cut strip sets into 20 (1½"-wide) segments for Nine-Patch sashing squares.

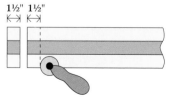

Strip Set B Diagram

Quilt Top Assembly Diagram

4. Referring to *Nine-Patch Sashing Square Assembly Diagram,* lay out 2 A and 1 B segments. Join to make 1 Nine-Patch sashing square. Make 20 Nine-Patch sashing squares.

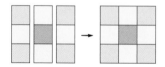

Nine-Patch Sashing Square Assembly Diagram

5. Referring to *Quilt Top Assembly Diagram,* lay out blocks, sashing squares, and sashing strips. Join into rows; join rows to complete quilt center.

6. Center 1 border strip on each side of quilt and join, mitering corners.

7. For each set of border tulips, appliqué in order 1 D, 1 D reversed, 1 (16"-long) bias strip, 2 Bs, 2 Bs reversed, and 2 As as shown in *Border Tulips Diagram.* Appliqué 18 sets of border tulips, positioned as shown in quilt photo.

8. Mark corners for rounding with

Border Tulips Diagram

a large dinner plate. Do not trim corners yet.

Quilting and Finishing

1. Divide backing fabric into 3 (2¾-yard) lengths. Join to make backing. Seams will run horizontally.

2. Layer backing, batting, and quilt top; baste. Quilt as desired. Quilt shown is outline-quilted in appliqué, with crosshatch fill. Sashing is quilted in-the-ditch.

3. Make 11¼ yards of 2¼"-wide bias strip from light peach square. Fold and press to make bias-grain French-fold binding. Add binding to quilt. Trim corners after applying binding to front.

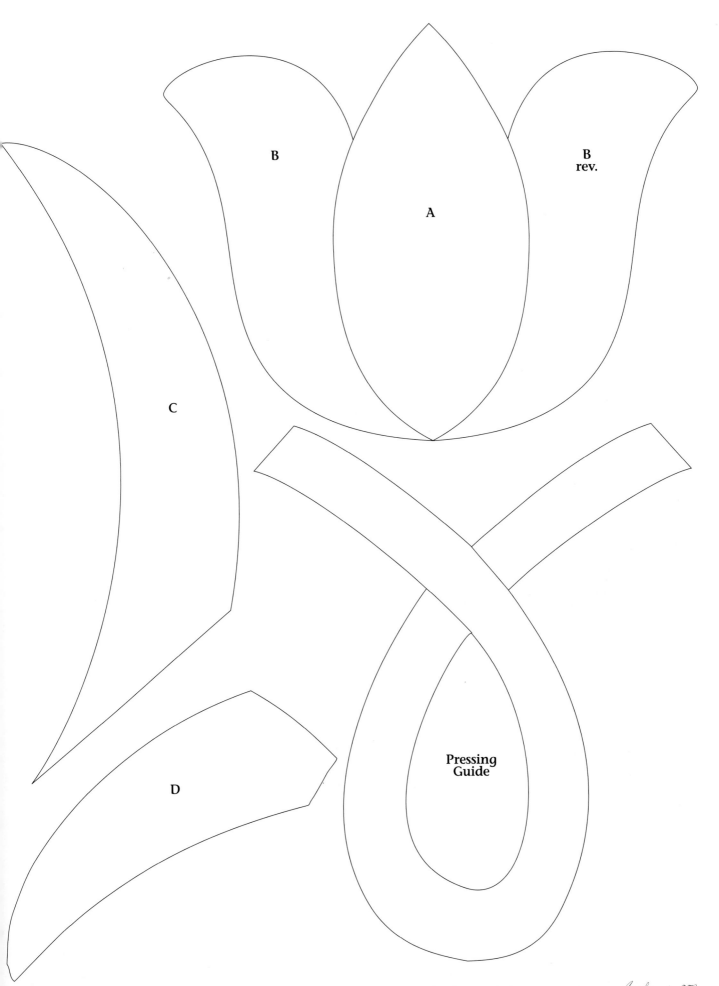

B

B
rev.

A

C

D

Pressing
Guide

Country Hearts

The heart, a longstanding symbol of love,
is a popular motif in casual country decor.
Maker Jackie Underwood stitched her blocks
while waiting on her children
at piano and karate lessons.

Finished Quilt Size
60" x 72"

Number of Blocks and Finished Size
84 (6") Heart Blocks

Materials
3 yards muslin
30 (6") squares assorted prints
2 yards rust print
4 yards fabric for backing
Twin-size batting

Cutting
Measurements include ¼" seam allowances. Border strips are exact length needed. You may want to make them longer to allow for piecing variations. Pattern is on page 282.

From muslin, cut:
• 14 (6½"-wide) strips. Cut strips into 84 (6½") squares.

From each square of assorted prints, cut:
• 1 heart.

From rust print, cut:
• 6 (6½"-wide) strips. Piece to make 2 (6½" x 48½") top and bottom borders and 2 (6½" x 60½") side borders.
• 8 (2¼"-wide) strips for binding.
• 4 hearts.

Quilt by Jackie S. Underwood

Block Assembly
1. Appliqué 1 heart to each muslin square *(Block Diagram).*
2. Set aside rust hearts for border corners.

Block Diagram

Quilt Assembly

1. Referring to *Quilt Top Assembly Diagram*, lay out blocks in 10 horizontal rows of 8 blocks each. Join into rows; join rows to complete quilt center.

2. Add side borders to quilt. Add rust heart blocks to ends of remaining borders. Add top and bottom borders to quilt.

Quilting and Finishing

1. Divide backing fabric into 2 (2-yard) lengths. Cut 1 piece in half lengthwise. Sew 1 narrow panel to each side of wide panel. Press seam allowances toward narrow panels. Seams will run horizontally.

2. Layer backing, batting, and quilt top; baste. Quilt as desired. Quilt shown is quilted around appliqué, and in-the-ditch between blocks. Borders have diagonal fill.

3. Join 2¼"-wide rust strips into 1 continuous piece for straight-grain French-fold binding. Add binding to quilt.

Quilt Top Assembly Diagram

Heart Template

Sunbonnet Sue

Sunbonnet Sue first appeared in Bertha Corbett's *The Sunbonnet Babies Primer* in 1900. Much of Sue's enduring charm results from the bright scraps from which her dresses are always made—often bits of fabric left over from dresses the quiltmaker stitched for a daughter.

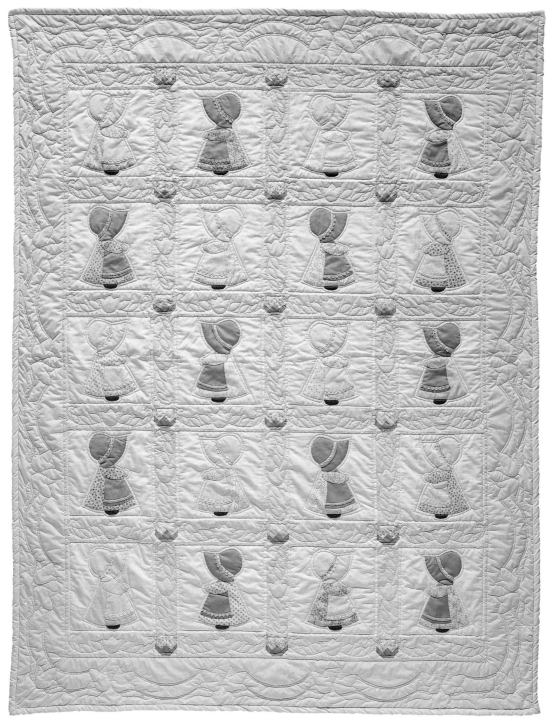

Quilt by Arlet Collie; owned by Jeannette Sisson

Finished Quilt Size
70" x 90"

Number of Blocks and Finished Size
20 (12") Sunbonnet Sue Blocks

Materials
3 yards white
4 yards yellow
1 yard green
2 yards total assorted yellow prints
3" x 22" strip black
3" x 15" strip pink
5½ yards fabric for backing
Twin-size batting
6 yards of ¼"-wide Cluny lace edging

Cutting
Measurements include ¼" seam allowances. Border strips are exact length needed. You may want to make them longer to allow for piecing variations. Patterns are on pages 285–287.

From white, cut:
- 7 (12½"-wide) strips. Cut strips into 20 (12½") squares for appliqué blocks.
- 1 (2¾"-wide) strip. Cut strip into 9 (2¾") squares. Cut squares in quarters diagonally to make 36 H triangles for sashing squares.
- 1 (1⅝"-wide) strip. Cut strip into 18 (1⅝") squares. Cut squares in half diagonally to make 36 J triangles for sashing squares.

From yellow, cut:
- 4 (6½"-wide) strips. Piece to make 2 (6½" x 70½") top and bottom borders.
- 4 (7"-wide) strips. Piece to make 2 (7" x 78½") side borders.
- 13 (3½"-wide) strips. Cut strips into 39 (3½" x 12½") sashing strips.
- 9 (2¼"-wide) strips for binding.

From green, cut:
- 4 Ds and 6 Ds reversed for aprons.
- 4 Fs and 6 Fs reversed for bonnets.
- 18 G squares.
- 36 Is.

From assorted yellow prints, cut:
- 10 Cs and 10 Cs reversed for dresses.

- 20 (½" x 5") bias strips for hatbands to match dresses.
- 6 Ds and 4 Ds reversed for aprons.
- 10 Es and 10 Es reversed for sleeves.
- 6 Fs and 4 Fs reversed for bonnets.
- 18 (1⁹⁄₁₆") G squares.
- 9 (2¾") squares. Cut squares in quarters diagonally to make 36 H triangles. Divide into 18 matching sets of 1 G and 2 Hs.
- 18 sets of 2 (1⁹⁄₁₆") G squares.

From black, cut:
- 10 As and 10 As reversed for shoes.

From pink, cut:
- 10 Bs and 10 Bs reversed for hands.

From Cluny lace edging, cut:
- 40 (5"-long) pieces.

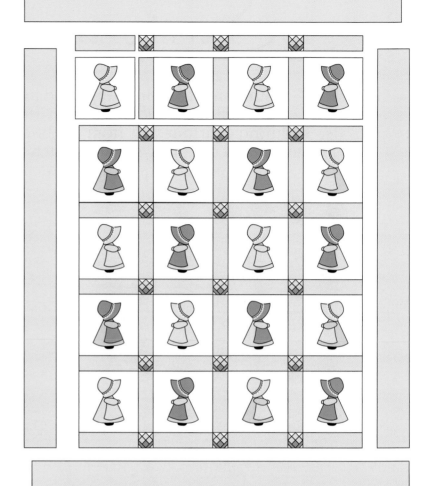

Quilt Top Assembly Diagram

Block Assembly
1. Center appliqué on 1 block. Referring to *Appliqué Placement Diagram*, appliqué in order: shoe (A), hand (B), dress (C), apron (D), sleeve (E), bonnet (F). Appliqué bias hatband strip to bonnet. Add lace to bonnet and apron to complete 1 Sunbonnet Sue block.

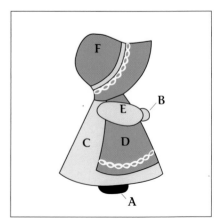

Appliqué Placement Diagram

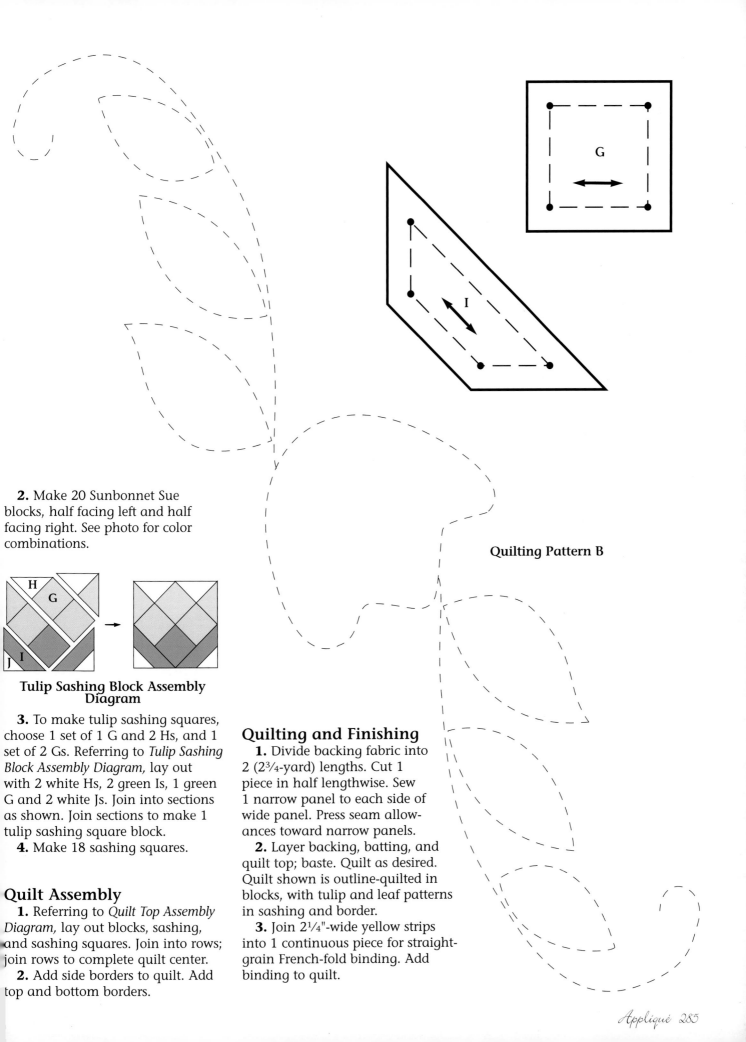

G

I

Quilting Pattern B

2. Make 20 Sunbonnet Sue blocks, half facing left and half facing right. See photo for color combinations.

H
G
J I

Tulip Sashing Block Assembly Diagram

3. To make tulip sashing squares, choose 1 set of 1 G and 2 Hs, and 1 set of 2 Gs. Referring to *Tulip Sashing Block Assembly Diagram,* lay out with 2 white Hs, 2 green Is, 1 green G and 2 white Js. Join into sections as shown. Join sections to make 1 tulip sashing square block.

4. Make 18 sashing squares.

Quilt Assembly

1. Referring to *Quilt Top Assembly Diagram,* lay out blocks, sashing, and sashing squares. Join into rows; join rows to complete quilt center.

2. Add side borders to quilt. Add top and bottom borders.

Quilting and Finishing

1. Divide backing fabric into 2 (2¾-yard) lengths. Cut 1 piece in half lengthwise. Sew 1 narrow panel to each side of wide panel. Press seam allowances toward narrow panels.

2. Layer backing, batting, and quilt top; baste. Quilt as desired. Quilt shown is outline-quilted in blocks, with tulip and leaf patterns in sashing and border.

3. Join 2¼"-wide yellow strips into 1 continuous piece for straight-grain French-fold binding. Add binding to quilt.

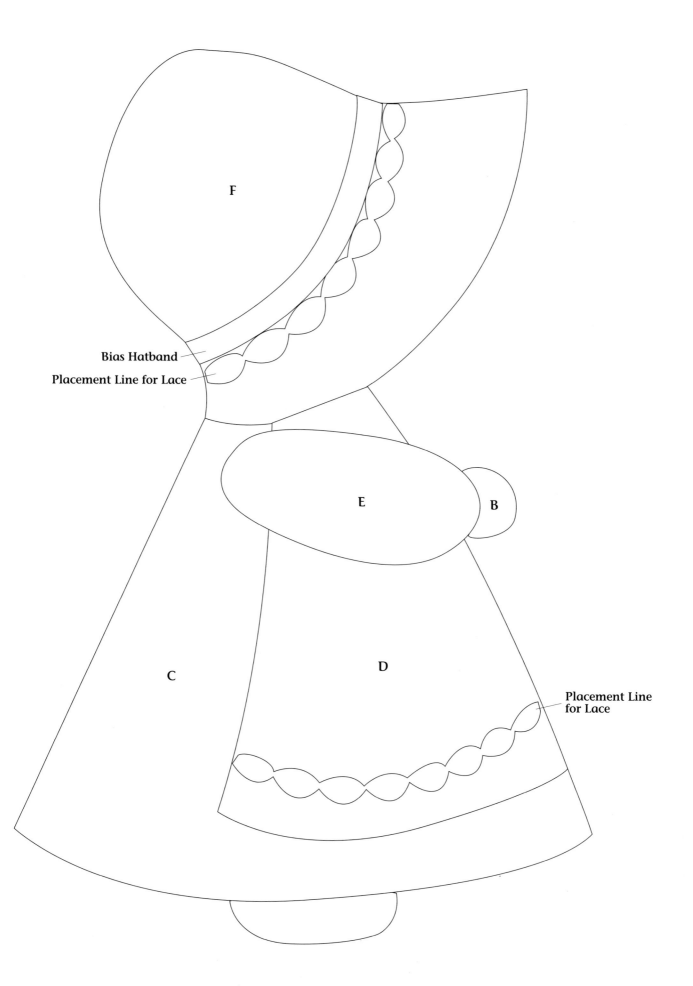

Bias Hatband

Placement Line for Lace

F

E

B

C

D

Placement Line
for Lace

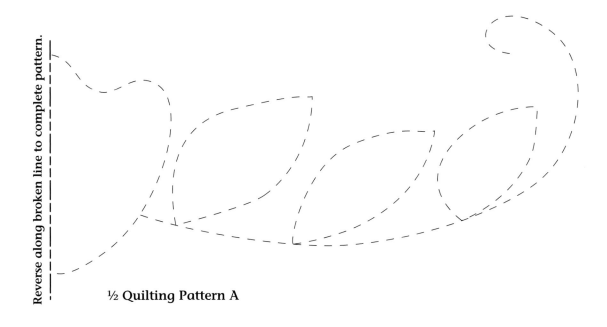

Reverse along broken line to complete pattern.

½ **Quilting Pattern A**

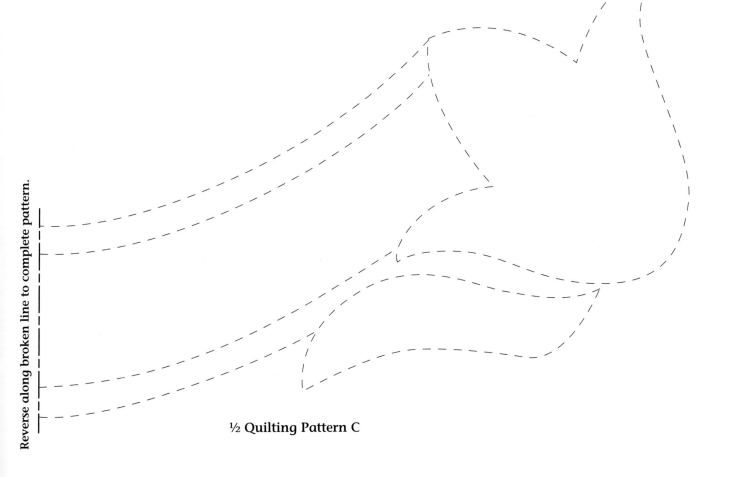

Reverse along broken line to complete pattern.

½ **Quilting Pattern C**

Fisherman Fred

This cheerful friend of Sunbonnet Sue made his debut in the 1930s on his way to the river with an empty fishing line. By the mid-1950s, he was headed home, having acquired both a name and a fish on his line.

Finished Quilt Size
73" x 94"

Number of Blocks and Finished Size
20 (12") Fisherman Fred Blocks

Materials
3½ yards plaid print
2¾ yards white
1¾ yards blue
¾ yard yellow print
20 (4" x 8") pieces assorted plaids
¾ yard navy
1 fat eighth (9" x 22") gray
1 fat eighth (9" x 22") pink
1 fat quarter (18" x 22") brown print
1 fat eighth (9" x 22") light brown print
5½ yards backing fabric
Full-size batting
Embroidery floss in brown and gray

Cutting
Measurements include ¼" seam allowances. Patterns are on pages 290–291.

From plaid print, cut:
• 2¾ yards. Cut yardage into 4 (8½"-wide) lengthwise strips for borders. Adjust cuts for matching borders.
• 9 (2¼"-wide) strips for binding.

From white, cut:
• 7 (12½"-wide) strips. Cut strips into 20 (12½") squares for appliqué blocks.

From blue, cut:
• 13 (3½"-wide) strips. Cut strips into 39 (3½" x 12½") sashing strips.

From yellow print, cut:
• 2 (3½"-wide) strips. Cut strips into 18 (3½") sashing squares.
• 20 hats G.

From plaids, cut:
• 1 shirt D and 1 sleeve E from each plaid.

From navy, cut:
• 20 pants F.

From gray, cut:
• 20 buckets H.

From pink, cut:
• 20 hands B.
• 20 hands C.

From brown print, cut:
• 40 shoes A.

From light brown print, cut:
• 21 fish I.

Block Assembly
1. Fold blocks into quarters and press to make guidelines.

2. Referring to *Appliqué Placement Diagram* on page 290, appliqué in order onto 1 block: 2 shoes (A), 1 hand (B), 1 hand (C), 1 shirt (D), 1 sleeve (E), 1 pants (F), 1 hat (G), 1 bucket (H) and 1 fish (I).

3. Using 3 strands of brown floss, embroider fishing pole using satin stitch (*Satin Stitch Diagram*). Embroider fishing line and pants using outline stitch (*Outline Stitch Diagram*).

Satin Stitch Diagram

Quilt by Cynthia Moody Wheeler

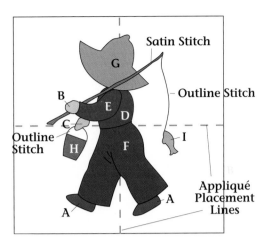

Appliqué Placement Diagram

Outline Stitch Diagram

4. Using 3 strands of gray floss, outline stitch bucket handle to complete 1 Fisherman Fred block.

5. Make 20 Fisherman Fred blocks, giving 1 fisherman 2 fish.

Quilt Assembly

1. Lay out blocks, sashing strips, and sashing squares as shown in *Quilt Top Assembly Diagram.* Join into rows; join rows to complete quilt center.

2. Center 1 border strip on each side of quilt, matching pattern at corners. Add to quilt, mitering corners.

Quilting and Finishing

1. Divide backing fabric into 2 (2¾-yard) lengths. Cut 1 piece in half lengthwise. Sew 1 narrow panel to each side of wide panel. Press seam allowances toward narrow panels.

2. Layer backing, batting, and quilt top; baste. Quilt as desired. Quilt shown is outline-quilted in blocks, with fish patterns in sashing. Borders have straight line quilting.

3. Join plaid strips into 1 continuous piece for straight-grain French-fold binding. Add binding to quilt.

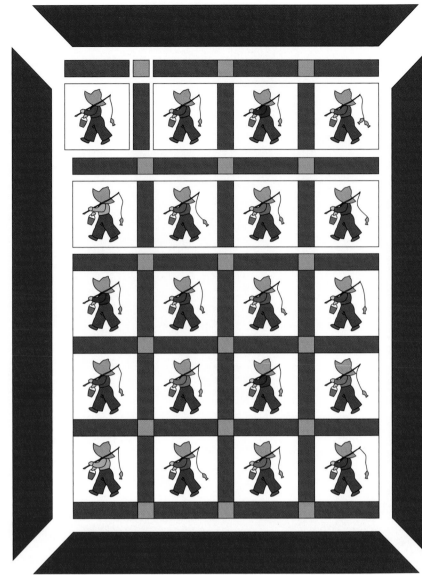

Quilt Top Assembly Diagram

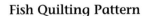

Fish Quilting Pattern

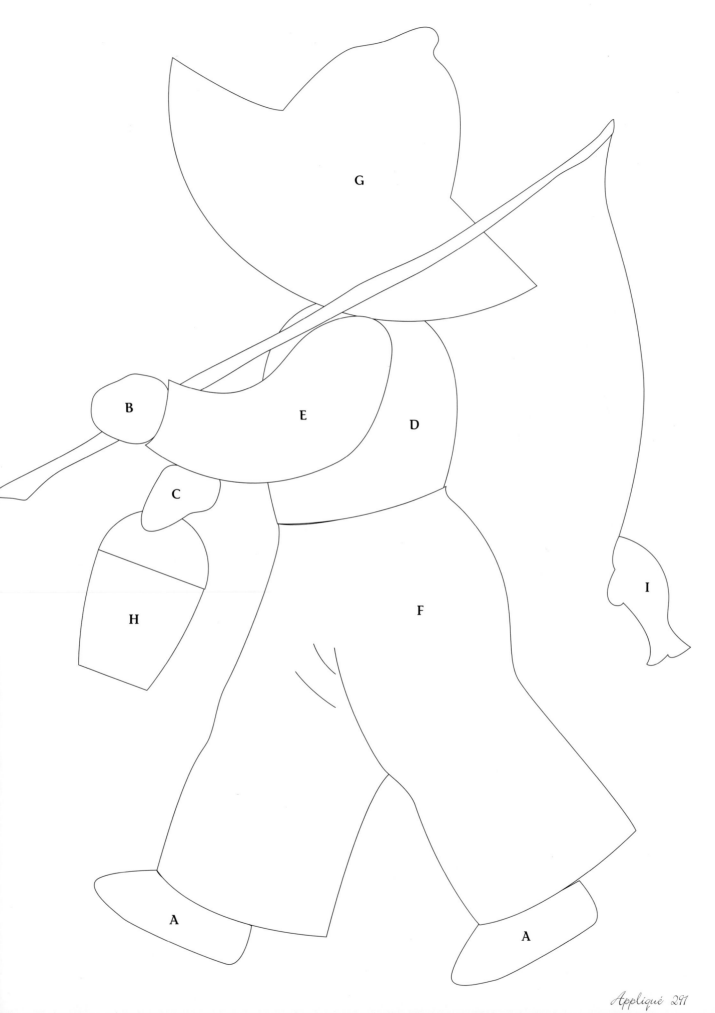

Appliqué 291

Nancy's Tulips

This elegant appliqué quilt was likely the quiltmaker's
prized piece and would have just been brought
out when company came to visit.

Quit made by Anna Margaret Hopper Brandon
owned by Robert and Joyce Stark

Finished Quilt Size
74" x 74"

Number of Blocks and Finished Size
9 (12½") Nancy's Tulips Blocks

Materials
5½ yards white
2 yards red
1¼ yards green
4½ yards fabric for backing
Full-size batting

Cutting
Measurements include ¼" seam allowances. Border strips are exact length needed. You may want to cut them longer to allow for piecing variations. Patterns are on page 295.

From white, cut:
• 7 (8"-wide) strips. Piece to make 2 (8" x 59½") top and bottom borders and 2 (8" x 74½") side borders.
• 5 (13"-wide) strips. Cut strips into 13 (13") blocks and setting squares.
• From remainder, cut 2 (9¾") squares. Cut squares in half diagonally to make 4 corner setting triangles.
• 2 (19"-wide) strips. Cut strips into 4 (19") squares. Cut squares in quarters diagonally to make 8 side setting triangles.
• 140 G pieced border diamonds.
• Optional: 176 M triangles, 16 (1¼") L squares, 4 I circles, and 4 (2¼") squares. Cut 2¼" squares in quarters diagonally to make 16 K triangles for corner blocks.

From red, cut:
• 8 (2¼"-wide) strips for binding.
• 36 As.
• 9 Es.
• 272 H triangles for pieced border triangles.
• 8 Fs and 8 Fs reversed for pieced border ends.
• Optional: 176 M triangles and 32 Js for corner block pieces.
• If not piecing corner blocks, cut 4 (3½") squares for pieced border corners.

One block is a bright yellow-green. Although at one time all of the leaves were the same color green, the quilter used a different fabric for that block. In that cloth, the fabric was dyed yellow first and then blue to achieve green. The fading has left the block with a yellow cast.

From green, cut:
• 36 Bs.
• 36 Cs.
• 36 Ds and 36 Ds reversed.

Block Assembly
1. Fold background square in quarters and diagonally. Press blocks to make appliqué guidelines *(Folding Diagram)*.

2. Referring to *Appliqué Placement Diagram*, appliqué in order : 4 As, 4 Ds, 4 Ds reversed, 4 Cs, 4 Bs, 1 E.
3. Make 9 Nancy's Tulips blocks.

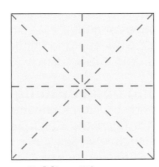

Folding Diagram

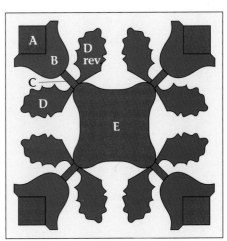

Appliqué Placement Diagram

Quilt Assembly

1. Referring to *Quilt Top Assembly Diagram,* lay out blocks and setting pieces. Join into diagonal rows; join rows to complete quilt center.

2. Referring to *Pieced Border Assembly Diagram,* join 2 Fs, 2 Fs reversed, 35 Gs, and 68 Hs to make 1 pieced border strip. Make 4 pieced border strips. Adjust seams to fit sides of quilt.

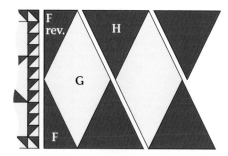

Pieced Border Assembly Diagram

3. Because of the curves and tiny triangles in the Pieced Border Corner Blocks, these 3" blocks are not recommended for beginners. Feel free to substitute solid red 3½" squares for your own borders. To piece the border corner blocks, refer to the *Pieced Border Corner Block Assembly Diagram* to join 1 red and 1 white M triangles to make 1 M unit. Make 44 M units. Join 2 Js and 1 K as shown. Make 4 J/K units. Join J/K units with L squares. Appliqué I in center. Join 10 M units and join to 1 side. Repeat. Join 12 M units and join to top. Repeat. Make 4 pieced border corner blocks.

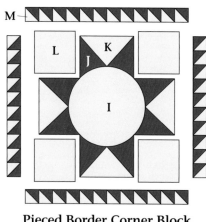

Pieced Border Corner Block Assembly Diagram

4. Join 1 pieced border strip to opposite sides of quilt. Join 1 pieced block or red square to ends of

Quilt Top Assembly Diagram

Pieced Border Corner Block

remaining strips and join to top and bottom of quilt.

5. Add white top and bottom borders. Add side borders.

Quilting and Finishing

1. Divide backing fabric into 2 (2¼-yard) lengths. Cut 1 piece in half lengthwise. Sew 1 narrow panel to each side of wide panel. Press seam allowances toward narrow panels.

2. Layer backing, batting, and quilt top; baste. Quilt as desired. Quilt shown is outline-quilted in appliqué blocks. Setting squares have a feathered wreath design. Background is filled with a cross-hatch pattern.

3. Join 2¼"-wide red strips into 1 continuous piece for straight-grain French-fold binding. Add binding to quilt.

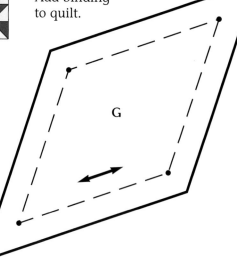

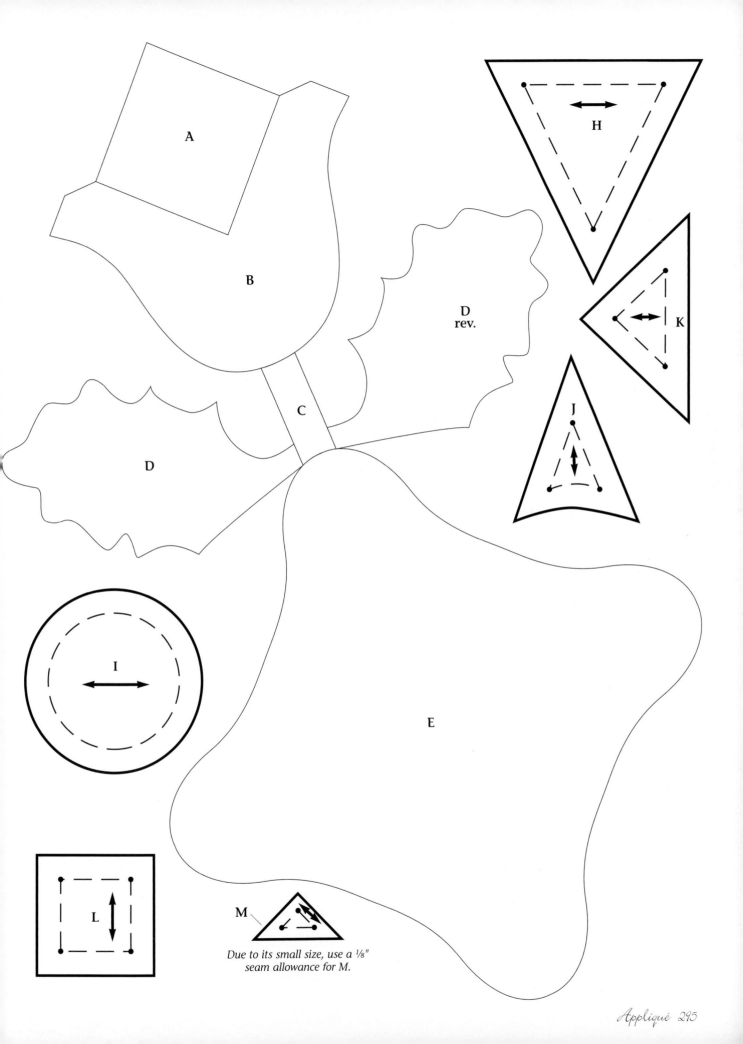

A

B

C

D

D rev.

E

H

K

J

I

L

M

Due to its small size, use a ⅛"
seam allowance for M.

Lancaster Rose

The name of this quilt pattern commemorates the 15th-century British War of the Roses. In this conflict, the Lancasters were symbolized by a red rose, and their enemies, the Yorks, by a white rose. Perhaps it is because the Lancasters won that there is no York Rose quilt pattern.

Finished Quilt Size

74½" x 106½"

Number of Blocks and Finished Size

15 (13½") Lancaster Rose Blocks

Materials

7 yards white print
1½ yards red print
1½ yards blue print
2¼ yards red
1 yard white
6 yards fabric for backing
Queen-size batting

Cutting

Measurements include ¼" seam allowances. Patterns are on page 299.

From white print, cut:
• 10 (12½"-wide) strips. Piece strips to make 2 (12½" x 80") border strips and 2 (12½" x 110") border strips.
• 8 (14"-wide) strips. Cut strips into 15 (14") background squares for appliqué.

From red print, cut:
• 3 (14"-wide) strips. Cut strips into 38 (3" x 14") sashing strips.

From blue print, cut:
• 2 (3"-wide) strips. Cut strips into 24 (3") sashing squares.
• 60 As.

From red, cut:
• 60 Bs.
• 15 Ds.
• 1 (36") square for bias binding.

From white, cut:
• 60 Cs.
• 15 Es.

Block Assembly

1. Fold 1 background square in quarters and then diagonally. Press to make appliqué guidelines (*Folding Diagram*).
2. Referring to *Appliqué Placement Diagram,* appliqué in order: 4 As, 4 Bs, 4 Cs, 1 D, and 1 E.
3. Make 15 Lancaster Rose blocks.

Quilt by Meg Irizarry

Folding Diagram

Appliqué Placement Diagram

Quilt Assembly

1. Lay out blocks, sashing strips, and sashing squares as shown in *Quilt Top Assembly Diagram.* Join into rows; join rows to complete quilt center.

2. Center 1 border strip on each side of quilt and join. Miter corners.

3. Mark scalloped edge for border using template on page 299. Do not trim until binding is applied to front of quilt.

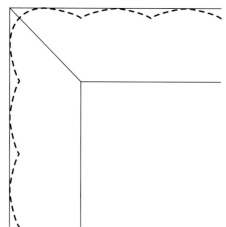

Scalloped Edge Placement

Quilting and Finishing

1. Divide backing fabric into 2 (3-yard) lengths. Cut 1 piece in half lengthwise. Sew 1 narrow panel to each side of wide panel. Press seam allowances toward narrow panels.

2. Layer backing, batting, and quilt top; baste. Quilt as desired. Quilt shown is outline-quilted in blocks, with fans and diagonal fill. Sashing has a chained heart pattern, featured on the opposite page, and scalloped borders are echo-quilted with a heart added at each point. Borders are filled with straight-line quilting.

3. Make 12½ yards of 2¼"-wide bias strip from 36" red square. Fold and press to make bias French-fold binding. Sew binding to quilt front. Trim scallops, turn binding to back, and stitch.

Quilt Label
Trace, scan, or photocopy this quilt label to finish your quilt.

Quilt Top Assembly Diagram

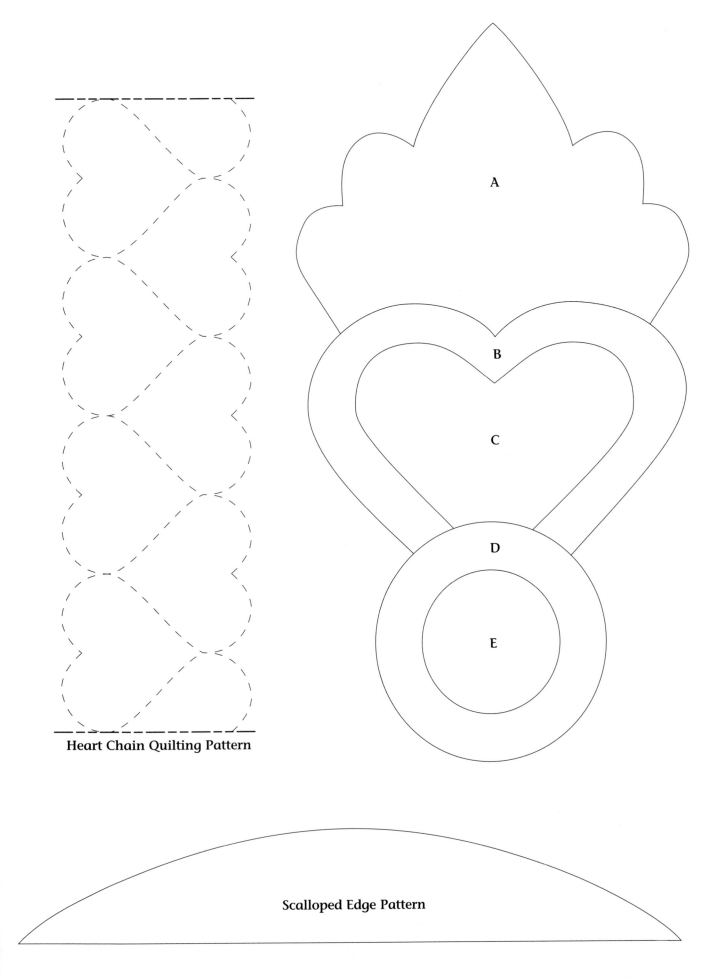

Heart Chain Quilting Pattern

A

B

C

D

E

Scalloped Edge Pattern

Appliqué 299

Whig Rose

Women have often named quilt patterns in support of their political beliefs, making their voices heard before being allowed to vote. The Whig Rose indicated support for the American Whig party, founded in 1834 and pulled apart by issues such as slavery and national expansion.

Finished Quilt Size
81" x 75"

Number of Blocks and Finished Size
9 (23") Whig Rose Blocks

Materials
6 yards muslin
1½ yards red
4 yards green
1 (3" x 22") strip gold
5 yards fabric for backing
Full-size batting

Cutting
Measurements include ¼" seam allowances. Border strips are exact length needed. You may want to cut them longer to allow for piecing variations. Patterns are on page 304.

From muslin, cut:
- 2 yards. Cut yardage into 1 (23½"-wide) lengthwise strip. Cut strip into 3 (23½") squares for appliqué.
- From remainder, cut 2 (6½"-wide) lengthwise strips. Cut strips into 2 (6½" x 69½") side borders.
- 2 yards. Cut yardage into 1 (23½"-wide) lengthwise strip. Cut strip into 3 (23½") squares for appliqué.
- From remainder, cut 2 (6½"-wide) lengthwise strips. Piece to make 1 (6½" x 81½") bottom border.
- 2 yards. Cut yardage into 1 (23½"-wide) lengthwise strip. Cut strip into 3 (23½") squares for appliqué. You will need 9 squares total.

From red, cut:
- 53 Bs.
- 108 Es.
- 36 Gs.
- 49 Js.

From green, cut:
- 9 (2¼"-wide) strips for binding.
- 1 (40") square. Make 35 yards of ¾"-wide bias from square. Cut 36 (14"-long) strips and 36 (7"-long) strips. Fold under ¼" on long sides and press to make bias strips for blocks. Cut 28 (6"-long) strips. Press as before to make bias strips for border. Cut 3 (90"-long) strips and press to make long border strips.
- 36 As.
- 108 Ds.
- 9 Fs.
- 99 Hs.
- 100 Hs reversed.
- 49 Is.

From gold, cut:
- 53 Cs.

Block Assembly
1. Fold squares into quarters and press to make appliqué guidelines (*Folding Diagram*).
2. Position 8 Hs and 8 Hs reversed as shown in *Appliqué Placement Diagram*. Position 4 (14"-long) stems and 4 (7"-long) stems, with stems overlapping H ends. Appliqué.

Folding Diagram

Quilt from Hanna Antiques, Birmingham, Alabama

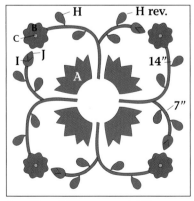

Appliqué Placement Diagram

3. Appliqué in position: 4 As, 4 Bs, 4 Cs, 4 Is, and 4 Js.

4. Join 12 Ds and 12 Es as shown in *D/E Assembly Diagram* to make 1 pieced circle. Appliqué circle in center of block.

D/E Assembly Diagram

5. Join 1 F and 4 Gs as shown in *F/G Assembly Diagram*. Appliqué to center of block to complete 1 Whig Rose block *(Block Diagrams)*.

6. Make 9 Whig Rose blocks.

F/G Assembly Diagram

Block Diagram 1

Block Diagram 2

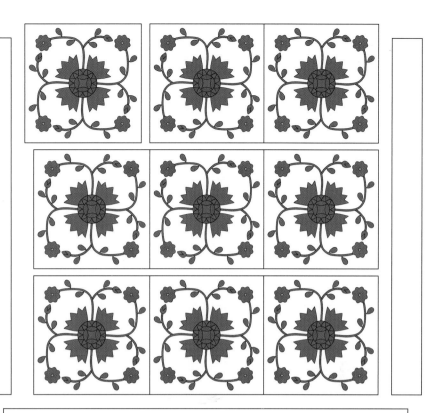

Quilt Top Assembly Diagram

Quilt Assembly

1. Referring to *Quilt Top Assembly Diagram,* lay out blocks in 3 rows of 3 blocks each. Join into rows; join rows to complete quilt center.

2. Add side borders to quilt. Add bottom border. *Note:* Quilt shown has no top border. You may add one if desired.

3. Referring to *Border Diagram* and to photo, position long stems on borders. Position short stems and leaves as shown, tucking under long stem. Appliqué in place.

4. Appliqué in order on borders: 17 Bs, 17 Cs, 13 Is, and 13 Js.

Quilting and Finishing

1. Divide backing fabric into 2 (2½-yard) lengths. Cut 1 piece in half lengthwise. Sew 1 narrow panel to each side of wide panel. Press seam allowances toward narrow panels. Seams will run horizontally.

2. Layer backing, batting, and quilt top; baste. Quilt as desired. Quilt shown is echo-quilted in blocks and borders, with leaf patterns between blocks.

3. Join 2¼"-wide green strips into continuous piece for straight-grain French-fold binding. Add binding to quilt.

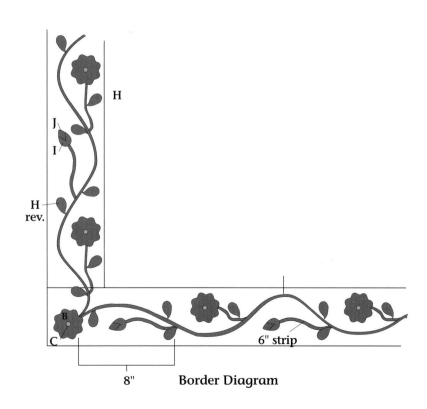

Border Diagram

Pansy

Pansies became a popular appliqué motif in the 1930s.
Several pattern companies offered their own versions,
including the Sears Roebuck catalog in 1934.
The buttonhole appliqué method you see in this quilt
was also extremely popular in the 1930s.

Quilt by Cecilee M. Lewis

Finished Quilt Size
80" x 82"

Number of Blocks and Finished Size
28 (10") Pansy Blocks

Materials
3½ yards pale green
5 yards dark green
1 yard purple
½ yard lavender
½ yard yellow
1 (3" x 22") strip yellow print
7½ yards fabric for backing
Full-size batting
Embroidery floss in purple, green, and black

Cutting
Measurements include ¼" seam allowances. Border strips are exact length needed. You may want to cut them longer to allow for piecing variations. Patterns are on page 308.

From pale green, cut:
• 2¾ yards. Cut yardage into 2 (3½"-wide) lengthwise strips. Trim strips to make 2 (3½" x 80½") border strips.
• 3 (10½"-wide) lengthwise strips. Cut strips into 27 (10½") squares for appliqué.
• 1 (10½"-wide) strip. Cut strip into 1 (10½") square for appliqué. You will need 28 total.

From dark green, cut:
• 2¾ yards. Cut yardage into 2 (3½"-wide) lengthwise strips. Trim strips to make 2 (3½" x 80½") border strips.
• 3 (10½"-wide) lengthwise strips. Cut strips into 27 (10½") squares for appliqué.
• 1 (10½"-wide) strip. Cut strip into 1 (10½") square for appliqué. You will need 28 total.
• 84 As.
• 100" total of 1"-wide bias strip. Cut bias strip into 28 (3½"-long) pieces. Press under ¼" on each long side to make 28 stems.
• 9 (2¼"-wide) strips for binding.

From purple, cut:
• 56 Bs.

From lavender, cut:
• 48 Cs.

From yellow, cut:
• 36 Cs.

From yellow print, cut:
• 28 Ds.

Block Assembly
1. Referring to *Appliqué Placement Diagrams*, appliqué in order: 1 stem, 3 leaves A, 2 petals B, 3 lavender petals C, and 1 center D.

2. Blanket-stitch around pieces with 2 strands of floss as follows: purple around petals, yellow around center, and green around leaves. Make 5 French knots in black in center to complete 1 Pansy block.

3. Make 16 Pansy blocks with lavender C petals and 12 Pansy blocks with yellow C petals.

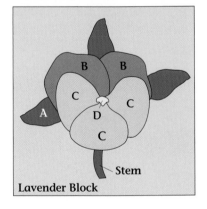
Lavender Block

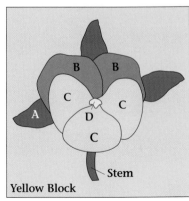
Yellow Block

Appliqué Placement Diagrams

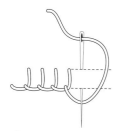

Blanket Stitch Diagram

French Knot Diagram

Quilt Assembly

1. Referring to *Quilt Top Assembly Diagram,* alternate 4 setting blocks and 4 lavender Pansy blocks. Join to make 1 lavender block row. Make 4 lavender block rows.

2. Alternate 4 yellow Pansy blocks and 4 setting blocks. Join to make 1 yellow block row. Make 3 yellow block rows.

3. Alternate lavender and yellow block rows. Join to complete quilt center.

4. Join 1 pale green and 1 dark green border strips to make top border. Add to top of quilt. Repeat for bottom border.

Quilting and Finishing

1. Divide backing fabric into (2½-yard) lengths. Cut 1 piece in half lengthwise. Sew 1 narrow panel between wide panels. Press seam allowances toward narrow panel. Remaining panel is extra and may be used to make a hanging sleeve. Seams will run horizontally.

2. Layer backing, batting, and quilt top; baste. Quilt as desired. Quilt shown is outline-quilted around appliqué, with leaves added in block corners. Setting blocks are quilted in appliqué pattern with leaves. Borders have a leaf design.

3. Join 2¼"-wide dark green strips into 1 continuous piece for straight-grain French-fold binding. Add binding to quilt.

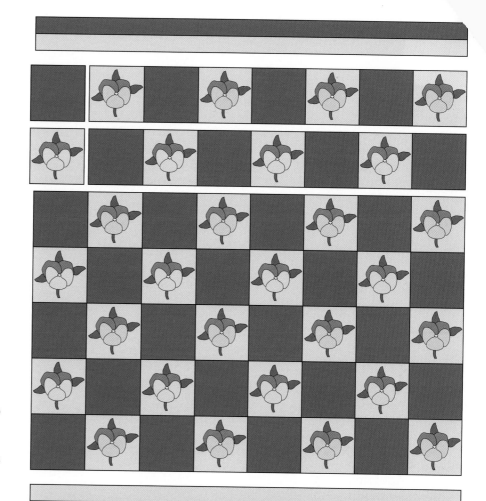

Quilt Top Assembly Diagram

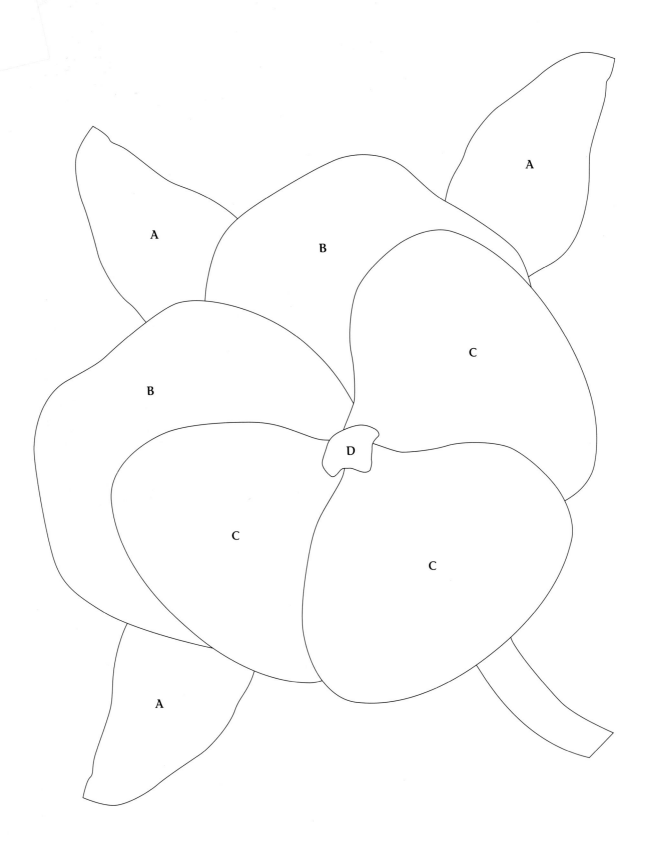

Dogwood

A welcome harbinger of spring in the South, the dogwood tree's blooming season is quite short. Perhaps the brevity of this season inspired a quilter to capture its beauty more permanently in this stunning medallion quilt.

Quilt from the Antique Quilt Source, Carlisle, Pennsylvania

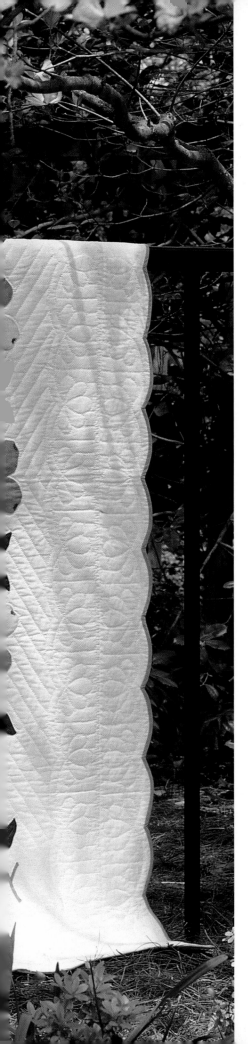

Finished Quilt Size
76" x 95"

Materials
3 yards 90"-wide white muslin
(6 yards if using 42"-wide fabric)
2 yards rose
1 yard pink
1 (4" x 22") strip yellow
½ yard green
1 yard brown
3 yards 90"-wide white muslin
(6 yards if using 42"-wide fabric)
for backing
Full-size batting
Embroidery floss in rose and brown

Cutting
Measurements include ¼" seam
allowances. Patterns are on pages
312–313.

From white, cut:
• 1 (82" x 101") rectangle. If using
42"-wide fabric, cut 2 (3-yard)
lengths. Cut 1 piece in half
lengthwise. Sew 1 narrow panel to
each side of wide panel. Press
seam allowances toward narrow
panels. Trim to 82" x 101".

From rose, cut:
• 22 As.
• 22 Bs.
• 4 Fs.
• 1 (36") square for bias binding.

From pink, cut:
• 22 As.
• 22 Bs.
• 4 Es.

From yellow, cut:
• 22 Cs.

From green, cut:
• 64 Ds.
• 4 Gs.

From brown, cut:
• 1 (30") square. Make 450" total of
¾"-wide bias strip. Cut into strips:
4 (28"-long), 2 (85"-long), 1 (50"-
long), and 33 (2¾"-long). Press
under ¼" on each long side to
make bias strips for appliqué.

Quilt Assembly
1. Beginning in center, position
bias strips as shown in *Quilt Top
Assembly Diagram*. Appliqué in
place.

2. Appliqué 8 flowers and 16
leaves in center as shown. Each
flower has 1 A and 1 B in the same
color, and 1 A and 1 B in opposite
color.

3. Position outer bias strips and
appliqué. Appliqué 14 flowers,
48 leaves, and 4 E/F/G blooms as
shown.

4. Embroider French knots and
center veins of flowers in rose.
Embroider outer edge veins of
flowers in brown.

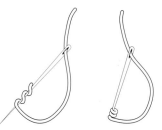

French Knot Diagram

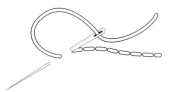

Backstitch Diagram

Quilting and Finishing
1. If using 42"-wide fabric, divide
backing fabric into 2 (3-yard)
lengths. Cut 1 piece in half lengthwise. Sew 1 narrow panel to each
side of wide panel. Press seam
allowances toward narrow panels.

2. Layer backing, batting, and
quilt top; baste. Quilt as desired.
Quilt shown is outline-quilted
around appliqué. Border is quilted
with shell scallop design as shown
on page p312. Background is filled
with diagonals.

3. Make 400" of 2¼"-wide bias
strip from rose square. Fold and
press to make bias binding. Use
quilting pattern as a guide for
scalloped edges. Add binding to
quilt. Trim scallops and stitch
binding to back.

Quilt Top Assembly Diagram

Measurements shown: 2¾", 28", 15½", 27", 13¾", 8¼", 13", 6", 8", Center, 50"

Labels: A, B, C, D, E, F, G

Shell Scallop Quilting Pattern

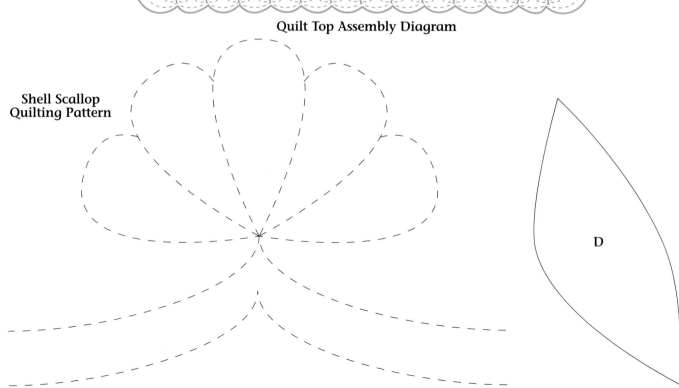

D

Appliqué 313

Mountain Rose

Many quilters designed their own rose quilts. Such lovely floral patterns were often reserved for the "best quilts" that were made as wedding presents and only used when company was coming. Therefore, antique examples, like the one shown here, are usually in excellent condition.

Finished Quilt Size
71" x 71"

Number of Blocks and Finished Size
25 (9") Mountain Rose Blocks

Materials
5 yards muslin
1½ yards dark pink
1¼ yards light pink
1 yard green
4¼ yards fabric for backing
Full-size batting

Cutting
Measurements include ¼" seam allowances. Patterns are on page 316.

From muslin, cut:
• 2⅛ yards. Cut yardage into 4 (4½"-wide) lengthwise border strips.
• From remainder, cut 2 (9½"-wide) lengthwise strips. Cut strips into 16 (9½") squares for appliqué.
• 9 (9½"-wide) crosswise strips. Cut strips into 33 (9½") squares for appliqué and setting squares. You will need 49 squares total.

From dark pink, cut:
• 8 (2¼"-wide) strips for binding.
• 25 As.
• 100 Ds.

From light pink, cut:
• 25 Bs.

From green, cut:
• 100 Cs and 100 Cs reversed.

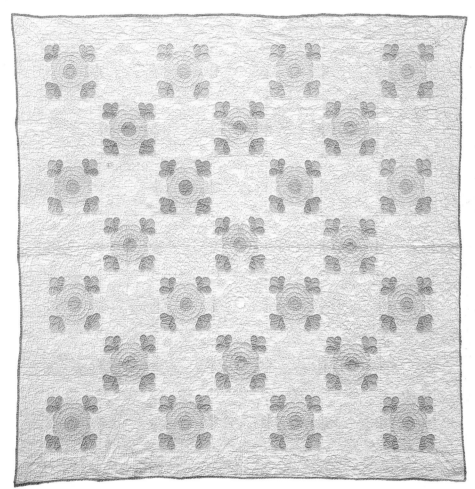

Quilt from The Antique Quilt Source, Carlisle, Pennsylvania

Block Assembly
1. Fold 1 appliqué square in quarters and then diagonally. Press to make placement guidelines (*Folding Diagram*).

2. Referring to *Appliqué Placement Diagram* on page 316, appliqué in order: 4 Ds, 4 Cs, 4 Cs reversed, 1 B, and 1 A.

3. Make 25 Mountain Rose blocks.

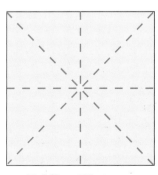

Folding Diagram

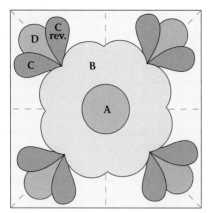

Appliqué Placement Diagram

Quilt Assembly

1. Referring to *Quilt Top Assembly Diagram,* lay out blocks and setting squares in 7 rows of 7 blocks each, alternating blocks and setting squares. Join into rows; join rows to complete quilt center.

2. Center 1 border strip on each side of quilt and join. Miter corners.

Quilting and Finishing

1. Divide backing fabric into 2 (2⅛-yard) lengths. Cut 1 piece in half lengthwise. Sew 1 narrow panel to each side of wide panel. Press seam allowances toward narrow panels.

2. Layer backing, batting, and quilt top; baste. Quilt as desired. Quilt shown is outline-quilted in blocks with concentric circles in Bs. Setting squares have a feathered wreath pattern, and background is filled with stipple quilting.

3. Join 2¼"-wide dark pink strips into 1 continuous piece for straight-grain French-fold binding. Add binding to quilt.

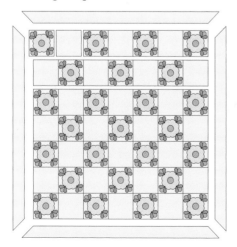

Quilt Top Assembly Diagram

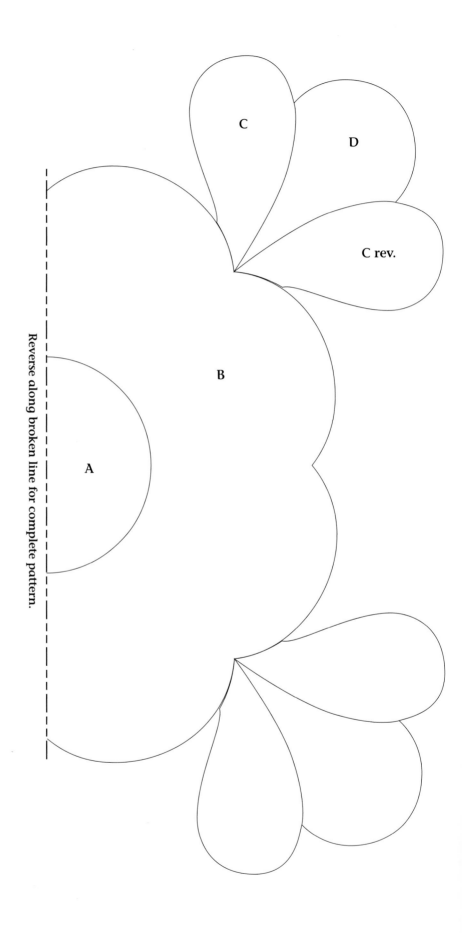

Reverse along broken line for complete pattern.

Currants & Coxcombs

This beautiful quilt, made around 1835, is a wonderful example of the red-and-green appliqué quilts popular in the mid-1800s. Notice how the green fabric used in the floral blocks has faded to yellow-green, while the green used for the birds and the diamonds has become blue-green.

Quiltmaker unknown; owned by Virginia E. Kane

Finished Quilt Size

92½" x 92½"

Number of Blocks and Finished Size

9 (18½") Currants Blocks
4 (18½") Coxcombs Blocks

Materials

9 yards white
1 fat quarter (18" x 22") yellow
2 yards red
2 yards light green
1½ yards dark green
8¼ yards fabric for backing
King-size batting
Embroidery floss in black and yellow

Cutting

Note: Measurements include ¼" seam allowances. Patterns are on pages 319–321.

From white, cut:

- 10 (7½"-wide) strips. Piece to make 4 (7½" x 95") border strips.
- 7 (19"-wide) strips. Cut strips into 13 (19") squares for appliqué blocks.
- 2 (27½") squares. Cut squares in quarters diagonally to make 8 side setting triangles.
- 1 (14"-wide) strip. Cut strip into 2 (14") squares. Cut squares in half diagonally to make 4 corner setting triangles.
- 10 (2¼"-wide) strips for binding.

From yellow, cut:

- 4 Fs.
- 36 Ks.
- 8 Ns.

From red, cut:

- 9 As.
- 36 Ds.
- 108 Es.
- 28 Gs.
- 16 Hs and 16 Hs reversed.
- 36 Ls and 36 Ls reversed.
- 36 Ms.

From light green, cut:

- 36 (1" x 6½) bias strips. Fold in ¼" on long sides and press to make 36 stems.
- 36 Bs.
- 36 Cs.
- 144 Es.

From dark green, cut:

- 20 Gs.
- 16 Is and 16 Is reversed.
- 36 Js.

Block Assembly

Folding Diagram

1. Fold 1 square in quarters and then diagonally. Press to make appliqué guidelines (*Folding Diagram*).

2. Referring to *Currants Appliqué Placement Diagram,* appliqué in order: 4 Ds, 4 Cs, 4 Bs. Position and appliqué: 12 red Es, 16 light green Es, 4 bias stems. Applique 1 A in center to complete 1 Currants block.

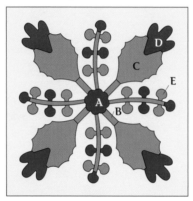

Currants Appliqué Placement Diagram

3. Make 9 Currants Blocks.

4. Fold 1 square in quarters and then diagonally. Press to make appliqué guidelines (*Folding Diagram*).

5. Referring to *Coxcombs Appliqué Placement Diagram,* appliqué in order: 3 red Gs, 3 dark green Gs, 1 F. Position and appliqué: 2 Hs, 2 Hs reversed, 2 Is, 2 Is reversed. Using 3 strands floss and using stitches indi-

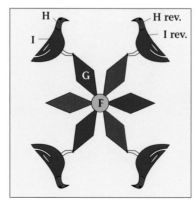

Coxcombs Appliqué Placement Diagram

cated on patterns, embroider eyes, eyebrows, and beaks in black. Outline-stitch legs in black. Satin-stitch wing patches in yellow to complete 1 Coxcombs Block.

6. Make 4 Coxcombs Blocks.

7. Referring to *Side Triangle Appliqué Placement Diagram,* appliqué in order: 2 red Gs, 1 dark green G, 1 H, 1 H reversed, 1 I, 1 I reversed, 1 N. Embroider as above to complete 1 side triangle block.

8. Make 8 side triangle blocks.

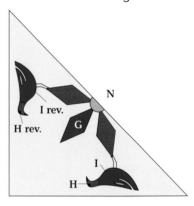

Side Triangle Appliqué Placement Diagram

Quilt Assembly

1. Lay out blocks, side triangles, and corner triangles as shown in *Quilt Top Assembly Diagram.* Join into diagonal rows; join rows to complete quilt center.

2. Center 1 border strip on each side of quilt and join. Miter corners.

3. Referring to *Border Appliqué Placement Diagram,* appliqué to border: 36 Js, 36 Ls, 36 Ls reversed, 36 Ms, 36 Ks.

Quilting and Finishing

1. Divide backing fabric into 3 (2¾-yard) lengths. Cut 1 piece in half lengthwise. Sew 1 narrow panel between wide panels. Press seam allowances toward narrow panel. Remaining panel is extra and may be used to make a hanging sleeve. Seams will run horizontally.

2. Layer backing, batting, and quilt top; baste. Quilt as desired. Quilt shown is outline-quilted in blocks, with detail quilted in. Background is filled with feathered vines.

3. Join white strips into 1 continuous piece for straight-grain French-fold binding. Add binding to quilt.

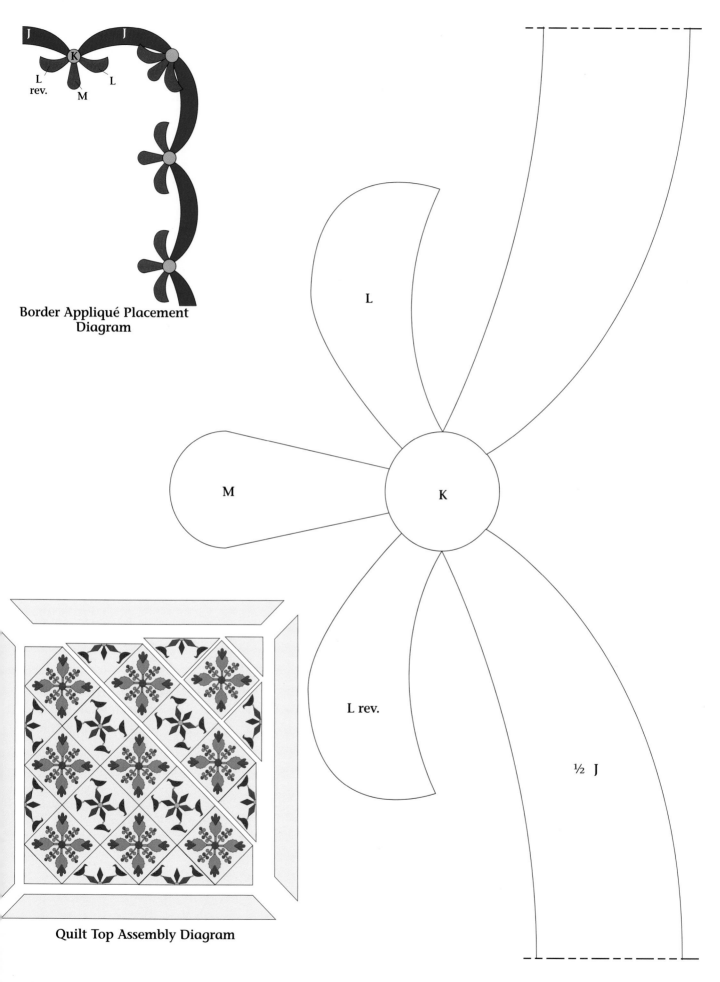

Border Appliqué Placement Diagram

J

J

K

L

L

rev.

M

L

M

K

L rev.

½ J

Quilt Top Assembly Diagram

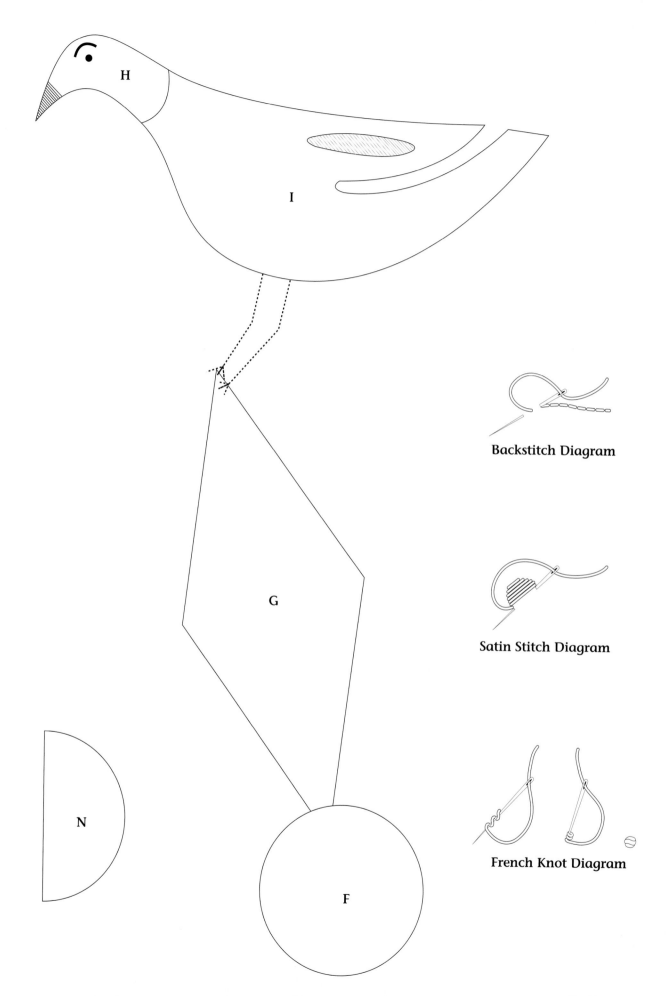

Backstitch Diagram

Satin Stitch Diagram

French Knot Diagram

Chapter 8

Special Techniques

Special technique quilts do not fit neatly into any generalized quilting category. Most are fairly easy— they just require their own, unique assembly.

• Probably one of the most popular of the quilts in this chapter is the *Crazy Quilt* on page 341. This technique, which saw its heyday during the Victorian era, has enjoyed renewed popularity as quilters explore stitch options on their fancy sewing machines.

• The *Cathedral Window* on page 324 is another perennial favorite. Once the muslin units are made, the quilt is ideal as a portable project.

• *Yo-yo* quilts, like the one on page 332, were popular during the Depression era, perhaps because each unit could be made from a small scrap of fabric. It also does not use costly batting or backing fabric.

• *Job's Tears* on page 337 is a string-pieced quilt that makes use of even the tiniest fabric scrap.

Peruse this chapter to find the next technique you want to try. You'll enjoy adding these new skills to your quilting repertoire.

Cathedral Windows

Cathedral Windows represents a wall of brilliant stained glass. Made with no batting and no quilting, the dimensional effect is achieved by folding fabric squares and stitching smaller contrasting squares into the folds.

Finished Quilt Size

Twin: 66" x 78"
Full: 72" x 84"
King: 96" x 108"

Materials

Muslin: Twin 23 yards, Full 27
  yards, King 45 yards
2" colored squares: 1096 Twin,
  1292 Full, 2236 King

Cutting

Measurements include ¼" seam
allowances.

• For twin size, cut muslin into 115
  (7"-wide) strips. Cut strips into 572
  (7") squares.
• For full size, cut muslin into 135
  (7"-wide) strips. Cut strips into 672
  (7") squares.
• For king size, cut muslin into 231
  (7"-wide) strips. Cut strips into
  1152 (7") squares.

Block Assembly— Hand Sewing

1. Fold under ¼"
on all sides of 1
muslin square and
press *(Diagram 1)*.

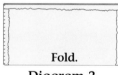

Diagram 1

2. Fold in half with right sides
facing. Whipstitch ends together,
stitching through fold only *(Diagram
2)*. Turn right side out.

Fold.

Diagram 2

3. Refold into a
square with seams
meeting at center.
Whipstitch open
edges together
through top layer
only *(Diagram 3)*.

Diagram 3

4. Fold corners in
so that points meet at center where
seams cross *(Diagram 4)*. Tack
through all layers to secure. Square
should measure 3".

Tack corners
through all
layers.

Diagram 4

A bed-size Cathedral Windows Quilt requires a lot of
muslin—usually around 30 yards. To make sure the
fabric is consistent throughout your quilt, buy a whole
bolt of fabric at once. Practice making one 4-unit block
first before purchasing extensive yardage.

5. Make 4 folded squares.

6. Place 2 squares together, open
sides facing, and whipstitch along 1
side through top layer. Repeat.
Open out and place 2 (2-square)
units facing; whipstitch to make 1
(4-square) block *(Diagram 5)*. Center
1 (2") colored square over diamond
shape formed by 2 squares and pin
(Diagram 5).

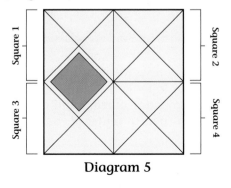

Diagram 5

7. Roll 1 folded edge over edge of
colored square, curving as shown,
and slipstitch in place *(Diagram 6)*.
Roll remaining 3 edges over colored

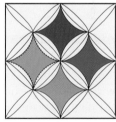

Diagram 6

square and slipstitch. Repeat for 3
more colored squares to make 1
Cathedral Windows block.

8. Make 143 blocks for twin size,
168 blocks for full size, and 288
blocks for king size.

Quilt Assembly

1. Join 11 blocks for twin size,
12 for full size, or 16 for king size to
make 1 row. Make 13 rows for twin
size, 14 rows for full size, or 18 rows
for king size. Add colored squares in
diamonds formed by adjacent blocks.

2. Join rows. Add colored squares
in diamonds formed by adjacent
rows.

Block Assembly—Machine Sewing

Note: *We used contrasting thread in photography for clarity, but you will want to use matching thread.*

1. Fold 1 muslin square in half and press. Stitch ¼" seam across each short end *(Photo A).*

2. Pull unsewn edges apart and flatten unit into square so that sewn edges meet at center. Press unit so that corners are crisp and square and seams are pressed in opposite directions *(Photo B).*

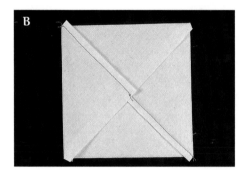

3. Sew remaining raw edges together with ¼" seam from corner to corner to just past center seam. Then sew from opposite corner just far enough to leave 1" opening (see arrow in *Photo C).*

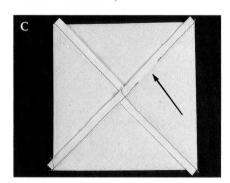

4. Turn square right side out through opening and press flat *(Photo D).* You don't need to sew the opening closed, because it will be

concealed inside the finished unit.

5. Working with seam side of unit facing up, fold each corner to center and pin; press fold to form guidelines *(Photo E).* Repeat steps to make 3 more units.

6. Place 2 units together with unseamed sides facing, aligning corners carefully. Stitch units together on folded guidelines to make rows *(Photo F).* Make 2 (2-unit) rows.

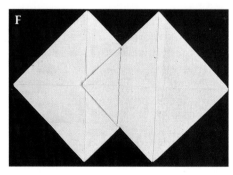

7. Join rows together in same manner to make 1 (4-unit) section. Once rows are joined, handtack loose corners at center of each unit *(Photo G).*

8. Place 2" fabric square over seam that joins units *(Photo H).*

9. Roll folded muslin edges over raw edges of insert and blindstitch in place, sewing through all layers *(Photo I).* Taper muslin edges at corners. Repeat with remaining inserts to complete section.

Completed Block

Orange Starburst

While browsing through her mother's attic,
Jo Ann Steiner discovered the embroidered blocks in this
quilt. Her grandmother had stitched them sometime before
1955. Jo Ann matched the orange embroidery with orange
fabric to complete the quilt.

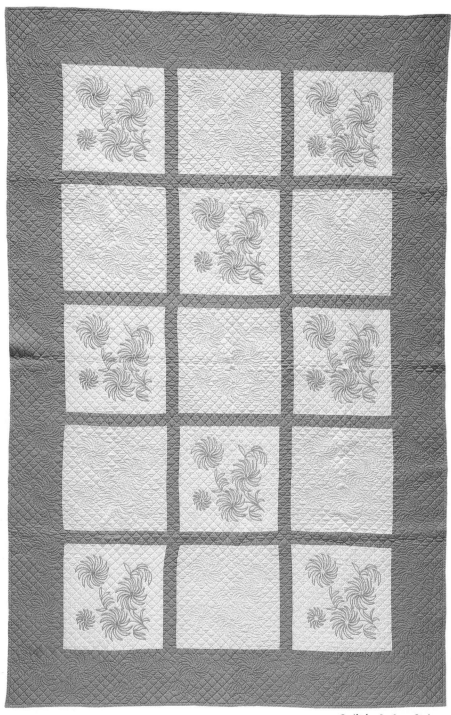

Quilt by Jo Ann Steiner

Finished Quilt Size

67½" x 102½"

Number of Blocks and Finished Size

8 (15½") Orange Starburst Blocks

Materials

4 yards muslin
4½ yards pumpkin orange solid
6 yards fabric for backing
Queen-size batting
3 skeins #5 pumpkin orange pearl
cotton

Cutting

Measurements include ¼" seam
allowances. Border strips are exact
length needed. You may want to cut
them longer to allow for piecing
variations. Patterns are on pages
329–331.

From muslin, cut:
- 8 (16"-wide) strips. Cut strips into
  15 (16") squares.

From pumpkin orange, cut:
- 2½ yards. Cut yardage into
  4 (9"-wide) lengthwise strips. Trim
  strips to make 2 (9" x 86") side
  borders and 2 (9" x 68") top and
  bottom borders.
- 11 (2½"-wide) strips. Piece to
  make 4 (2½" x 51") horizontal
  sashing strips. Cut remainder into
  10 (2½" x 16") vertical sashing
  strips.
- 10 (2¼"-wide) strips for binding.

Block Assembly

1. Transfer Orange Starburst pattern to 1 muslin square. Embroider using 1 strand pearl cotton. Embroider leaves and petals in chainstitch, stems in outline stitch, and center of flowers in French knots *(Stitch Diagrams)*.

2. Make 8 Orange Starburst blocks.

3. Transfer Orange Starburst pattern to remaining 7 muslin squares for quilting design.

Block Diagram

Quilt Assembly

1. Lay out blocks, vertical sashing strips, and horizontal sashing strips *(Quilt Top Assembly Diagram)*. Join into rows; join rows to complete quilt center.

2. Add side borders to quilt. Add top and bottom borders to quilt.

Quilting and Finishing

1. Divide backing fabric into 2 (3-yard) lengths. Cut 1 piece in half lengthwise. Sew 1 narrow panel to each side of wide panel. Press seam allowances toward narrow panels.

2. Layer backing, batting, and quilt top; baste. Quilt as desired. Quilt shown is quilted in Orange Starburst pattern in setting squares and borders. Background is filled with diagonal grid.

3. Join 2¼"-wide orange strips into 1 continuous piece for straight-grain French-fold binding. Add binding to quilt.

Joining old embroidered blocks together is a wonderful way to create an heirloom quilt. If you don't think you have enough blocks to make a large quilt, consider using plain alternate blocks, as shown here. In this example, the quiltmaker duplicated the embroidery pattern in quilting stitches. But you can also showcase special quilting stencils or create your own design.

Quilt Top Assembly Diagram

Outline Stitch Diagram

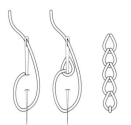

Chain Stitch Diagram

French Knot Diagram

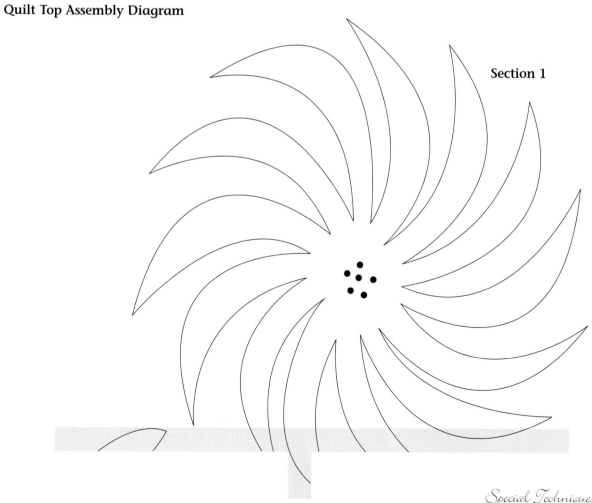

Section 1

Section 2

Section 3

Yo-yo

Although gathering circles of fabric into yo-yos dates back to pre-Victorian times, its popularity peaked during the Depression because it required only small bits of fabric. Stitching yo-yos to a white cotton foundation creates an interesting look that also makes the quilt more durable.

Quilt by Patsy Cobble

Finished Quilt Size
40" x 50"

Number of Blocks and Finished Size
456 (2") Yo-yos

Materials
1 3/8 yards lavender
1 3/4 yards blue
1 5/8 yards pink
1 3/8 yards green
1 1/8 yards yellow
1 3/8 yards white for backing
5 1/4 yards of pre-gathered (1"-wide) eyelet lace

Cutting
Measurements include 1/4" seam allowances. Trace pattern or draw 1 (4 1/2") circle on template material for yo-yo circle pattern.

From white, cut:
• 1 (38 1/2" x 48 1/2") backing piece.

From lavender, cut:
• 88 yo-yo circles.

From blue, cut:
• 116 yo-yo circles.

From pink, cut:
• 100 yo-yo circles.

From green, cut:
• 84 yo-yo circles.

From yellow, cut:
• 68 yo-yo circles.

Block Assembly
1. Turn under 1/4" along edge of yo-yo circle. Make running stitches around circle through both layers *(Diagram 1).*

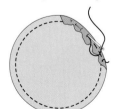

Diagram 1

2. Pull up tightly, gathering edges to center. Secure with a knot *(Diagram 2).*

Diagram 2

3. Center opening in circle, arrange gathers, and press to complete 1 Yo-yo *(Diagram 3).*

Diagram 3

4. Make yo-yos from all circles.

5. To join yo-yos, place 2 yo-yos with gathered sides facing. Whipstitch together on 1 edge *(Diagram 4).* Repeat to make rows; join rows in same manner.

Diagram 4

Quilt Assembly
Referring to *Quilt Top Assembly Diagram,* stitch together 24 horizontal rows of 19 yo-yos each.

Quilt Top Assembly Diagram

Quilt Finishing
1. Turn in 1/4" on all sides of backing and stitch. With back of yo-yos facing wrong side of backing, center yo-yos and stitch outer yo-yos to backing.

2. Topstitch lace around edge of quilt with bound edge just covering hem.

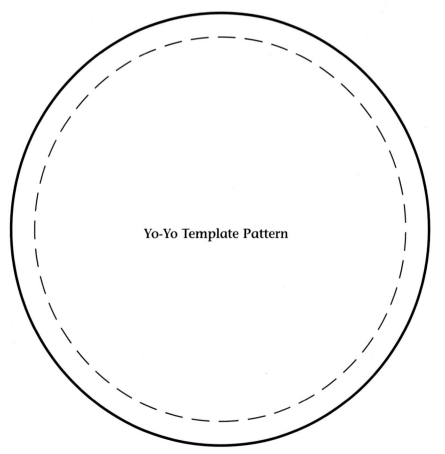

Yo-Yo Template Pattern

Rail Fence

Rail Fence is one of the simplest forms of strip piecing,
yet the results are so interesting that the technique appeals
to novice and veteran quilters alike.

Quilt by Marjorie Faris

Finished Quilt Size
58½" x 63"

Number of Blocks and Finished Size
182 (4½") Rail Fence Blocks

Materials
¾ yard print #1
¾ yard print #2
1½ yards print #3
¾ yard print #4
¾ yard print #5
3½ yards fabric for backing
½ yard of any above print for binding
Twin-size batting

Cutting
Measurements include ¼" seam allowances.

From print #1, cut:
• 12 (2"-wide) strips.

From print #2, cut:
• 12 (2"-wide) strips.

From print #3, cut:
• 24 (2"-wide) strips.

From print #4, cut:
• 12 (2"-wide) strips.

From print #5, cut:
• 12 (2"-wide) strips.

From binding print, cut:
• 7 (2¼"-wide) strips for binding.

Strip Set Assembly
1. Join 1 strip each of prints 1, 2, and 3 in order as shown in *Strip Set 1 Diagram.* Make 12 Strip Sets 1.

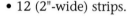

Strip Set 1 Diagram

2. Cut strip sets 1 into 92 (5"-wide) segments for Block 1 *(Block 1 Diagram).*

Quilt Top Assembly Diagram

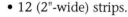

Block 1 Diagram

3. Join 1 strip each of prints 4, 5 and 3 in order as shown in *Strip Set 2 Diagram.* Make 12 Strip Sets 2.

Strip Set 2 Diagram

4. Cut strip sets 2 into 90 (5"-wide) segments for Block 2 *(Block 2 Diagram).*

Block 2 Diagram

Quilt Assembly
1. Lay out blocks as shown in *Quilt Top Assembly Diagram,* noting carefully the rotation of each block.

2. When satisfied with placement, join blocks into rows. Join rows to complete quilt top.

Quilting and Finishing
1. Divide backing fabric into 2 (1¾-yard) lengths. Cut 1 piece in half lengthwise. Sew 1 narrow panel to each side of wide panel. Press seam allowances toward narrow panels. Seams will run horizontally.

2. Layer backing, batting, and quilt top; baste. Quilt as desired. Quilt shown is quilted in alternating diagonals through blocks.

3. Join 2¼"-wide binding strips into 1 continuous piece for straight-grain French-fold binding. Add binding to quilt.

Finished Quilt Size
39" x 48"

Number of Blocks and Finished Size
48 (4½") Rail Fence Blocks

Materials
6 different 2" x 42" strips of dark fabrics in color #1
6 different 2" x 42" strips of light fabrics
6 different 2" x 42" strips of dark fabrics in color #2
¼ yard fabric for inner border
1½ yard fabric for outer border
⅜ yard fabric for binding
1½ yards backing fabric
Crib-size batting

Cutting
Measurements include ¼" seam allowances.

From inner border fabric, cut:
• 4 (2"-wide) strips.

From outer border fabric, cut:
• 4 (5"-wide) lengthwise strips.

From binding fabric, cut:
• 5 (2¼"-wide) strips for binding.

Block Assembly
1. Join 1 strip each of dark #1, light, and dark #2 to make a strip set *(Diagram 1)*. Make 6 assorted strip sets.

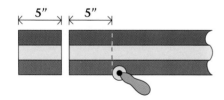

Diagram 1

2. Cut each strip set into 8 (5"-wide) segments, as shown in *Diagram 2*, to make 48 Rail Fence blocks.

Diagram 2

Quilt by Rhonda Richard

Quilt Assembly
1. Referring to *Row Assembly Diagrams,* join 6 blocks in each row, turning blocks as shown. Make 4 of Row 1 and 4 of Row 2.

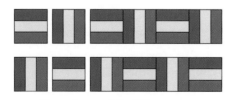

Row Assembly Diagrams

2. Join into rows, using photo as a guide.
3. Measure length of quilt through the middle. Trim 2 inner border strips to this measurement and add to quilt sides.
4. Measure width of quilt, including borders. Trim 2 inner border strips to size and add to quilt top and bottom.
5. Repeat with outer borders.

Quilting and Finishing
1. Layer backing, batting, and quilt top; baste.
2. Quilt as desired. Quilt shown has an overall leaf design.
3. Join 2¼" binding strips into 1 continuous piece for straight-grain French-fold binding. Add binding to quilt.

Job's Tears

Frugal quilters sometimes stitched irregular pieces
of scraps onto newspaper or catalog pages.
Though such thriftiness may not be necessary today,
string piecing is a fabulous way to use the
smallest pieces from your scrap bag.

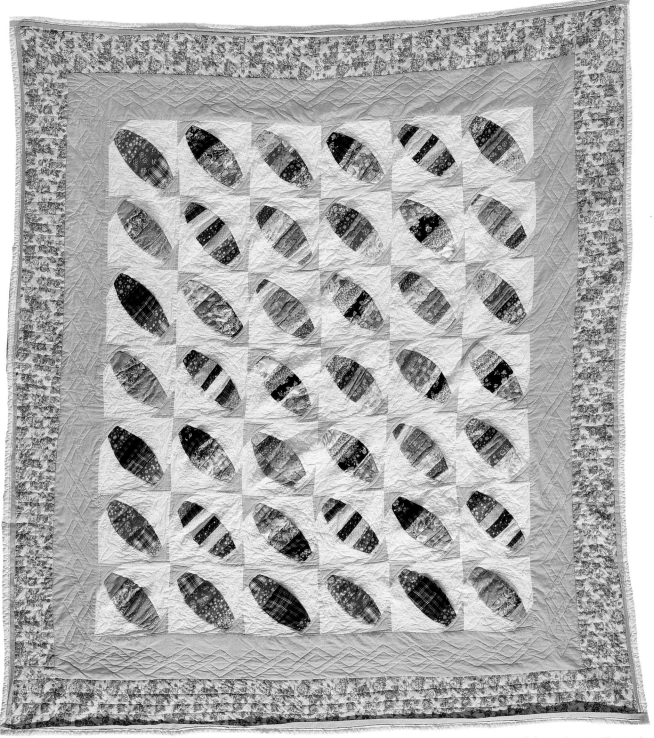

Quilt by Roslyn Oneille Hardy

Finished Quilt Size
68" x 76"

Number of Blocks and Finished Size
42 (8") Job's Tears Blocks

Materials
2½ yards green
1¾ yard yellow print
3½ yards muslin
4 yards total scraps, cut or torn into random-width strips
⅝ yard yellow for binding
4 yards fabric for backing
Twin-size batting
42 (5" x 9") rectangles foundation material for string piecing: paper, tear-away stabilizer, or muslin

Cutting
Measurements include ¼" seam allowances. Border strips are exact length needed. You may want to cut them longer to allow for piecing variations. Patterns are on page 340.

From green, cut:
- 6 (4½"-wide) strips. Piece to make 4 (4½" x 56½") border strips.
- 8 (2"-wide) strips. Piece to make 2 (2" x 76½") side piping strips and 2 (2" x 68½") top and bottom piping strips. Fold strips in half longways, wrong sides facing, and press.
- 84 Cs.

From yellow print, cut:
- 8 (6½"-wide) strips. Piece to make 2 (6½" x 64½") side borders and 2 (6½" x 68½") top and bottom borders.

From muslin, cut:
- 84 As.

From yellow, cut:
- 8 (2¼"-wide) strips for binding.

Block Assembly

1. Referring to *Diagram 1*, place 1 strip of scrap fabric right side up on 1 foundation rectangle and pin. Ends should extend past edges. Place second scrap strip right side down atop first strip, aligning long raw edges. Stitch with ¼" seam allowance. Remove pin.

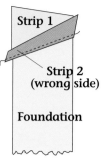

Diagram 1

2. Flip second strip right side up and press (*Diagram 2*).

Diagram 2

3. Repeat until foundation rectangle is covered (*Diagram 3*).

Diagram 3

4. Center template B on string pieced rectangle (*Diagram 4*).

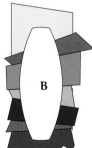

Diagram 4

Trace and cut out to make 1 string-pieced B (*Diagram 5*).

Diagram 5

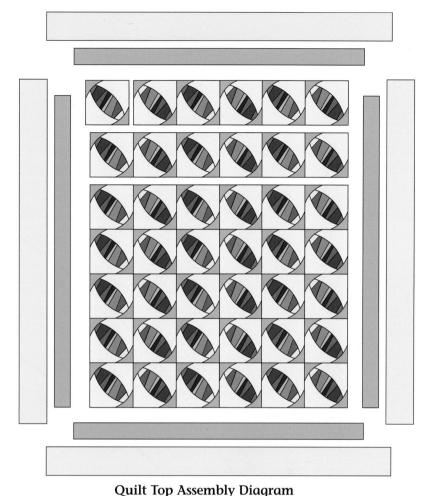

Quilt Top Assembly Diagram

5. Make 42 string-pieced Bs. If using paper or tear-away stabilizer for foundation, remove after block is pieced.

6. Referring to *Block Assembly Diagram*, join 1 A to each side of 1 B. Add 1 C to each end to make 1 Job's Tears block.

7. Make 42 Job's Tears blocks.

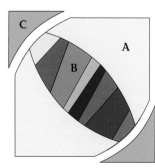

Block Assembly Diagram

Quilt Assembly

1. Referring to *Quilt Top Assembly Diagram*, lay out blocks in 7 rows of 6 blocks each. Join into rows; join rows to complete quilt center.

2. Add green side borders to quilt. Add green top and bottom borders.

3. Add yellow print side borders to quilt. Add yellow print top and bottom borders.

Quilting and Finishing

1. Divide backing fabric into 2 (2-yard) lengths. Cut 1 piece in half lengthwise. Sew 1 narrow panel to each side of wide panel. Press seam allowances toward narrow panels. Seams will run horizontally.

2. Layer backing, batting, and quilt top; baste. Quilt as desired. Quilt shown is outline-quilted in blocks with a fleur de lis pattern fill. Green border features a chain pattern, and outer border has a grid pattern.

3. Baste piping in place on all sides of quilt, beginning with sides.

4. Join 2¼"-wide yellow strips into 1 continuous piece for straight-grain French-fold binding. Add binding to quilt.

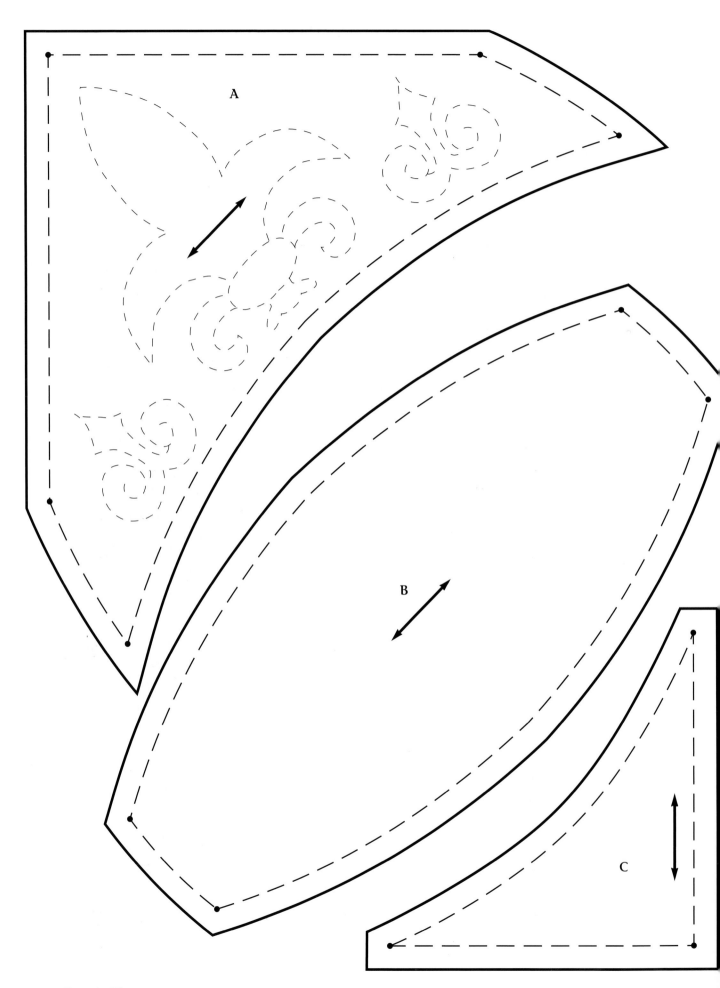

A

B

C

Crazy Quilt

Crazy quilting was all the rage in the 1880s. Women of leisure stitched crazy quilts for display in the parlor to show off their fine embroidery skills. Computerized sewing machines let quilters experiment with different stitch features and embroidery capabilities for today's crazy quilts.

Quilt by Eva Perkins Coleman

In Victorian times, intricate embroidery in a crazy quilt served as a status symbol. Only ladies of the moneyed class had enough leisure time to execute this type of elaborate needlework.

Crazy Quilt Tips

- Make crazy quilts in blocks. Blocks can then be sewn together or joined with sashing or setting squares.
- Mix large and small patches to achieve the random quality essential in crazy quilts.
- To prevent puckering, smooth the fabric in place without stretching it or the foundation.
- If possible, trim seam allowances to $\frac{1}{8}$". This will make embroidering through heavy fabrics much easier.
- Don't limit yourself to patchwork. Appliquéd pieces of fabric or lace can add an interesting touch and help cover raw edges or gaps in the design.
- Cut the foundation piece larger than the desired finished size and then trim it when you are finished embellishing the block. Embroidering will cause the blocks to pull in and reduce in size.

Finished Quilt Size
70" x 84"

Number of Blocks and Finished Size
30 (14") Crazy Quilt Blocks

Materials
7 yards muslin
15 yards assorted velvet scraps
5 yards fabric for backing
Assorted embroidery floss
Assorted pearl cotton

Cutting
Measurements include ¼" seam allowances.

From muslin, cut:
• 15 (16"-wide) strips. Cut strips into 30 (16") foundation blocks. Draw 1 (14½") square centered in each foundation block (Diagram 1).

Diagram 1

Block Assembly
1. Place first patch right side up on 1 corner of 1 foundation square and pin in place (Diagram 2).

Diagram 2

2. Place second patch atop first patch, right side down and aligned with raw edge (Diagram 3). Stitch through all layers.

Diagram 3

3. Trim seam allowance to ⅛" and flip open (Diagram 4).

Diagram 4

Continue in this manner until foundation square is covered to edges (Diagram 5). If you have an awkward angle, appliqué edges in place.

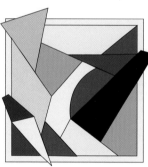

Diagram 5

4. Staystitch around block just inside 14½" marking (Diagram 6).

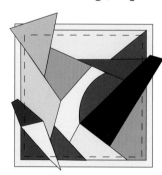

Diagram 6

5. Using 3 strands of embroidery floss, embroider fancy stitches over each seam. (See *Stitching Diagrams* on page 345.)

6. Trim block to 14½" to complete 1 Crazy Quilt block (Diagram 7).

7. Make 30 Crazy Quilt blocks.

Diagram 7

Quilt Assembly
1. Referring to photo, lay out blocks in 6 horizontal rows of 5 blocks each. Join into rows; join rows to complete quilt center.

2. Embroider fancy stitches over seams.

Quilting and Finishing
1. Divide backing fabric into 2 (2½-yard) lengths. Cut 1 piece in half lengthwise. Sew 1 narrow panel to each side of wide panel. Press seam allowances toward narrow panels. Trim backing to 76" x 90".

2. Layer backing and quilt top. To tie quilt, cut pearl cotton into 16" lengths. Thread needle with doubled length of thread. Beginning at center, tie square knots at center and corners of each block. Trim ends to 1" long (Tying Diagram).

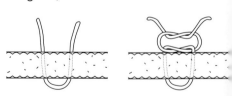

Tying Diagram

3. For self-binding, fold 2" of backing to front of quilt. Turn under ¼" seam allowance and slip-stitch to quilt top, mitering corners.

Stitching Diagrams

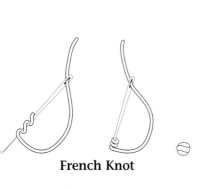

French Knot

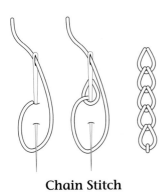

Chain Stitch

Chain Stitch Swag

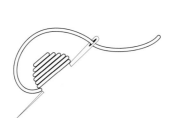

Outline Stitch

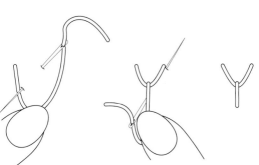

Fly Stitch

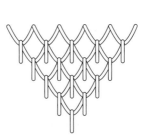

Stacked Fly Stitch

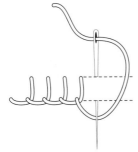

Satin Stitch

Blanket Stitch

Bargello Blanket Stitch

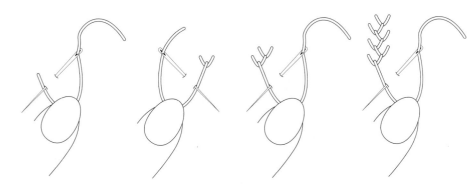

Feather Stitch

Feather Stitch Vine

Chapter 9

Quilter's Workshop

In this chapter, you'll learn all the techniques you need to know to make every quilt in this book.

- If you're new to quiltmaking, we suggest that you read this entire chapter before beginning your first quilt. You may discover new tools or techniques that will make the quilting process easier for you.

- If you are an experienced quiltmaker, you'll find this chapter a handy reference for techniques you don't use every day.

- How-to photographs guide you through important steps.

- Throughout the book, some quilt projects may refer you to pages within this chapter that demonstrate a particular technique.

Whether you are a beginner or a seasoned quilter, you'll find the latest tools, tricks, and techniques in our workshop. Consider it your own private quilting lesson!

Taking Stock

Enjoy quilting more and improve your accuracy with the right tools. Below is a list of must-have items to get you started. Many quilt shops have registry services, so make a wish list of supplies.

Cutting Tools

Rotary Cutter: Purchase a cutter with at least a 2"-diameter blade. The larger cutters allow you to cut through more layers. Look at the instructions on the back of the package to see the proper way to hold the brand you bought.

Large and regular rotary cutters on a cutting mat

Cutting Mat: Purchase the largest mat you can afford. Make sure you at least have one that measures 18" x 24".

Cutting Rulers: The longer you quilt, the more of these you will buy. Start with a 6" x 24" ruler. Later you may want to add a 6" square, a 12½" square, and a triangle ruler.

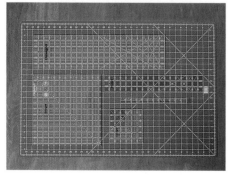

Assorted rulers on a cutting mat

Cutting Table: Make your worktable a comfortable height for standing while you cut and work. Most people like a cutting table about 36" high. Some tables are available with collapsible sides to conserve space when not in use.

Thread Clippers: Trim threads quickly with this spring-action tool.

Fabric Shears: A fine pair of sharp fabric shears will become one of your treasured possessions. To keep them sharp, do not cut anything but fabric with them.

Paper Scissors: Use an inexpensive pair of large, sharp scissors to cut paper, template plastic, and cardboard—everything except fabric.

Appliqué Scissors: The duckbill piece at the bottom helps you to trim background fabrics away from appliqué shapes.

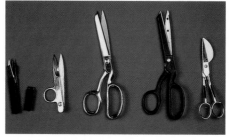

Scissors: Spring-action thread clippers, regular thread clippers, fabric shears, paper scissors, and appliqué scissors

Sewing Tools

Sewing Machine: Unless you plan to do machine appliqué, a good straight-stitch sewing machine is all you'll need.

Needles: Replace the needle in your sewing machine regularly. Size 80/12 is just right for machine piecing. For handwork, use a size 10 or 11 sharp for hand appliqué and a 10 or 12 between for hand quilting.

Walking Foot: If you plan to machine-quilt, you must have a walking foot to feed the layers through your machine evenly.

Thread: Use cotton thread for

Bernina® walking foot

piecing and quilting. You'll find that neutral colors—white, beige, or gray—work with most quilts.

Pins: Spend a few extra dollars to get fine silk pins. These pins are so thin, you can usually keep them in your fabric and sew over them with most sewing machines. *Note: Never sew over pins with a computerized sewing machine.*

Pressing Tools

Iron: Look for a steam iron that produces plenty of steam.

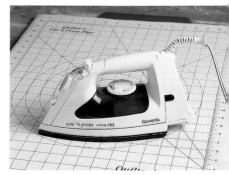

Rowenta® iron

Plastic Squirt Bottle: Some fabrics need a spray of water in addition to the steam from the iron.

Ironing Board: An ironing board or large pressing pad at one end of your cutting table will enable you to stand and to press at a comfortable height. Specialty ironing boards are now available that are equal width on both ends or extra-large in the traditional shape. Quilters love these large boards because they make pressing the backing and the quilt top easier. Look for these ironing boards in quilting catalogs, or try the Martha Stewart Living® large board available at K-Mart.

Planning the Quilt

Once you've selected a quilt pattern, prevent multiple trips to the fabric store with a little planning. Decide if you need to adjust the size, change the color scheme, or make templates.

How to Use Our Patterns

We give rotary-cutting instructions wherever possible. When patterns are needed, they are printed full size. Patterns for pieced blocks show the seam line, or sewing line, dashed, and the cutting line solid.

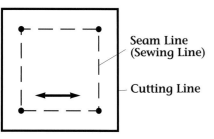

Sample Piecing Pattern

Appliqué patterns do not include seam allowances. If you are working with paper-backed fusible web, or if you are making freezer-paper patterns, you will want to trace the pattern finished size, as it appears in the book. For hand appliqué, cut out the fabric pieces slightly larger than needed. The less fabric you have to turn under, the less bulky your appliqué pieces will be.

Sample Appliqué Pattern

Adapting the Quilt Size

If the quilt you plan to make from this book is not the size you want, there are several ways to adapt the design.

To make a smaller quilt, eliminate a row of blocks, set the blocks without sashing, and/or narrow the border widths.

To make a larger quilt, add rows of blocks, sashing, and/or multiple borders. Each addition requires extra yardage, which you should estimate before you buy fabric. A good rule of thumb is to buy more fabric than you think you'll need, in case the quilt shop sells out of the bolt you're using.

To make a smaller quilt: Eliminate a row of blocks, set the blocks without sashing, and/or narrow the border widths.

To make a larger quilt: Add rows of blocks, sashing, and/or multiple borders.

Making Templates

Many of the quilts in this book can be made with rotary-cutting techniques. However, a few do require templates. You can make templates from traditional template plastic or from cardboard.

However, we have found a product that allows you to make your own templates and still use a rotary cutter to cut the fabric! Designed by John Flynn, the Cut-Your-Own Templates™ kit (see page 368) includes several sheets of formica and everything you need to make any template shape. The formica is thick enough that you can use your rotary cutter to cut along its edge.

John Flynn's Cut Your Own Templates kit

Appliqué

Appliqué is the process of sewing pieces onto a background to create a fabric picture. Choose the one that works best for you from the four methods shown here.

Needle-Turned Appliqué

For traditional hand appliqué, make templates for the shapes using the template material of your choice. Using a pen or pencil, draw around these shapes on the right side of the appliqué fabric (Photo A).

Cut out the fabric shape, adding a scant seam allowance—less than ¼" (Photo B).

Glue or pin-baste the shape to the background fabric. Use the needle to turn under the seam allowance as you sew, making sure the drawn line is completely turned under (Photo C). This is called needle-turned appliqué.

Slipstitch around each piece, using

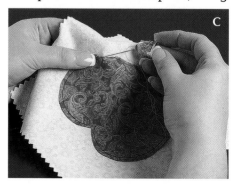

thread that matches the appliqué (not the background). Pull the needle through the background and catch a few threads on the fold of the appliqué. Reinsert the needle into the background and bring the needle up through the appliqué for the next stitch. Make close, tiny stitches that do not show on the right side.

Matching silk thread becomes nearly invisible when used in appliqué, as we used in Photo C.

Freezer-Paper Appliqué

In using this technique, the finished appliqué will be a mirror image of the pattern. So if the pattern is an irregular shape (not symmetrical), first reverse the pattern.

Trace a full-size pattern onto the paper (nonwaxy) side of the freezer paper (available in grocery stores near the aluminum foil). Cut out each freezer-paper template along the drawn lines.

When you press the seam allowances over the freezer paper, we recommend using a product called GluTube®. If you've ever used a glue stick with freezer paper to temporarily "baste" the seam allowances, you'll discover that GluTube® works much the same way. However, it is not gooey once it dries, and it will not stick to your fingers and make a mess like a glue stick can. It also allows you to create sharp, smooth edges on your appliqué. Here's how it works:

1. Press the freezer-paper template to the wrong side of the appliqué fabric waxy side down (Photo A).

2. Apply GluTube® in a circular motion, covering approximately ¼' of the edges along both the template and the fabric (Photo B). Let the glue dry for a few minutes.

3. Cut out the template, adding ¼" seam allowance (Photo C). Don't worry about cutting into the glue—once dry, it has the same consistency as the adhesive on yellow sticky notes.

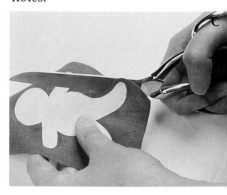

4. Clip curves or points as needed. Using a straight pin, fold the seam allowances over the edge of the template. Use your fingers to gently set the temporary bond (Photo D). You may lift and reposition the fabric as needed.

5. Appliqué the shape to the background as usual *(Photo E)*.

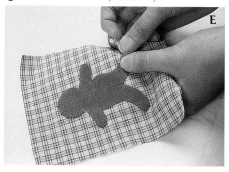

Clip the background fabric from behind the appliquéd shape and gently remove the freezer paper with tweezers. The template will release easily.

GluTube is available in quilt shops, or see our Resources on page 368.

Fusible Appliqué

If you do not enjoy handwork, fusing appliqué shapes with paper-backed fusible web may be an option for you. Follow manufacturer's instructions on the packages, as there are slight differences among brands.

You will still need to cover the fabric edges so that they will not ravel when the quilt is washed. You can do this with a machine satin stitch or with a hand blanket stitch, as shown in the diagram below, or by machine, as described in the following text. Note: if the quilt will be used and laundered a good deal, the raw edges will still fray over time if the seam allowances are not turned under. However, these techniques are ideal for wall hangings or display pieces.

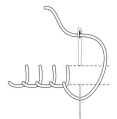

Hand Blanket Stitch Diagram

Machine Blanket Stitch (or Buttonhole Appliqué)

Although the technical term for this stitch is the **blanket stitch**, the method has become known popularly as **buttonhole appliqué.**

Bernina® sewing machines are probably the best known for their perfect buttonhole appliqué stitches.

For fray-proof edges and sturdy appliqué, follow the steps below. We sewed our sample on the Bernina Artista 170 Quilter's Platinum Edition.

1. Trace the pattern onto the paper side of the fusible web.

2. Following manufacturer's instructions, fuse the webbing to the wrong side of the fabric.

3. Cut out the fabric shapes along the drawn line *(Photo A)*.

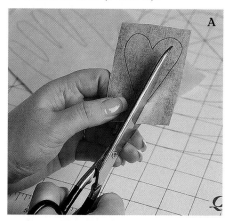

4. If you are working with multiple pieces, fuse the smaller shape onto the larger one first. Remove paper backing and fuse the smaller shape onto the other shape *(Photo B)*.

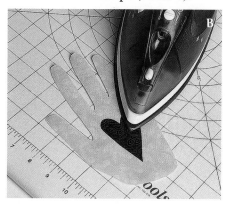

5. Remove the paper backing from the larger piece and fuse it to the background fabric *(Photo C)*.

6. Attach an open toe foot (#20 Bernina) and select the buttonhole stitch (#329). Select the "needle down" function *(Photo D)*.

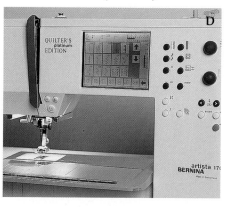

7. Stitch around the edges of the shape *(Photo E)*. Stitch slowly going around curves. For points, stop (the needle will be down to secure the fabric), raise the presser foot, and pivot the block.

8. Stitch around all raw edges to complete the block *(Photo F)*. If desired, put a drop of FrayCheck® at the beginning and ending stitching points.

Machine Blanket Stitching

Organizing a Signature Quilt

Planning a memory quilt in which blocks have signatures
of friends and family may seem like a daunting task, but
following the ten tips below can help the process go smoothly.

Although this book features only a few signature quilts, any block with a large open area can be made into a signature quilt. Just make sure to use light fabrics in the signature area for easy readability.

1. Plan well in advance. Setbacks often occur in large group projects, and having a tight deadline will only add to your stress level.

2. Choose a fairly simple block pattern, like the one shown on this page. People often postpone projects they think are challenging.

3. If the quilt will be a gift, try to use colors to suit that person's taste, not yours.

4. Decide how many blocks you need and make a list of all participants.

5. If you will be making all the blocks yourself, stabilize the signature pieces with freezer paper on the wrong side and distribute them to your friends to sign.

6. If multiple quilters are making blocks, set a color or fabric theme for the quilt. If not, you'll end up with neons, reproduction prints, and novelty prints, and the quilt will lack cohesion.

7. If the quilt will have a uniform background (as opposed to a quilt that uses many background fabrics), buy more of that fabric than you need. That way, you can cut more pieces if some get lost or soiled.

8. Purchase several Pigma™ pens. We recommend using the .05 width. The tip is wider than the .01 size, making the writing more visible and less likely to fade. Mark people off your list as they return their signature piece or quilt block.

9. While waiting for blocks to arrive, make a few extra blocks, since some people may not meet the deadline. Also, make a fancy

The Friendship Album, featured on page 187, is an example of a signature quilt.

quilt label including information on who the quilt is for, why it was made, and the date of presentation. For more on quilt labels, see page 366.

10. Sewing skills vary with each person, so some blocks may be off measurement. A good solution is to use sashing strips, as shown in the white rectangles in the quilt above. By making the sashing strips a tad larger or a tad smaller in key places, you can often compensate for misshapen blocks. If a block is

distorted beyond use, carefully remove the signature area with a seam ripper and remake the rest of the block.

Signing and Stamping Fabric

Whether you are signing a quilt block or making a fancy quilt label, these tips will help you embellish the fabric successfully.

Fabrico® Ink and Pigma Pens®

Signing Blocks

To sign blocks, you will need freezer paper (available in grocery stores near the aluminum foil) and colorfast, fabric-safe pens like Pigma™ pens.

1. To stabilize the fabric for writing, press a piece of freezer paper to the back.
2. Use a thick-pointed permanent pen to draw a line on the paper side of the freezer paper to give you a writing guideline that will be visible through the fabric.
3. Using a .05 colorfast, fabric-safe pen, write lightly and slowly to allow the ink to flow evenly and to prevent the pen from catching in the weave of the cloth (fabric is rougher than paper). Let the ink dry.
4. Heat-set the ink with a hot, dry iron on the back of the fabric.

Using Rubber Stamps

Stamping is a fun and easy way to add decoration and documentation to your quilts. To successfully stamp on fabric, the stamp design must be deeply etched into the rubber. Many stamps designed for paper stamping are not deeply etched. As a result, the image may be pale and the details lost on fabric. Stamps made by Susan McKelvey (see Resources, page 368) meet these requirements.

Make sure that the ink you use is colorfast and fabric-safe. We recommend Fabrico™ ink, which is available in 12 colors on preinked pads.

Stamping Blocks

Practice on a fabric scrap to see how much ink you need and how much pressure to apply. Stamp on a hard, flat surface.

1. When inking the stamp, hold the stamp up and the stamp pad down as shown in *photo*. This enables you to control how much ink you put on the stamp.
2. Tap the pad gently against the stamp. Press lightly several times, rather than hard once, to prevent applying excess ink.

Gently press the ink pad to the stamp with the ink pad on top. This distributes the ink evenly.

3. Stamp the fabric by pressing firmly; don't rock the stamp.
4. Let the ink dry. It dries quickly to the touch.
5. Heat-set the ink with a hot, dry iron on the back of the fabric.

This quilt label includes a stamped image.

Quilters of the mid-nineteenth century used stamps to embellish their signature quilts.

Set-In Seams

Some blocks, such as the LeMoyne Star, require set-in seams in addition to continuous, straight seams. Photos below illustrate how to use special machine features for that task.

If you have a high-end model sewing machine, such as a Bernina Artista 170 Quilter's Platinum edition shown in these photos, you can follow these steps. If you have a regular straight-stitch sewing machine, you can still follow the guidelines below for backstitching, pivoting, and staying out of the seams.

1. Select the "needle down" position on your sewing machine *(Photo A).*

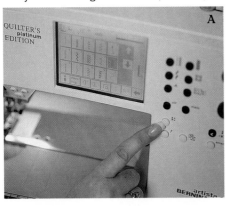

2. Select the straight stitch (Stitch #1) and the "stitch in place" function, located in the function keys at the bottom of the screen *(Photo B).* *Tip:* Use the blunt end of an object, rather than your fingers, to select an option and you won't get smudge marks on your computerized screen.

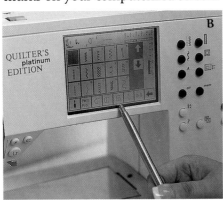

3. Select 2 diamond pieces and stack them with right sides facing. Attach the #37 presser foot, which allows you to sew a perfect ¼" seam. Beginning at the intersection where the drawn lines form an elongated X, make about 3 stitches in place *(Photo C).*

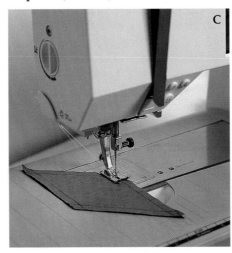

4. Touch the "stitch in place" function key again to turn it off and then stitch down the seam line. When you reach the next intersection, stitch in place again to secure. Clip the thread tails and remove the piece from the machine *(Photo D).* Press the seam open.

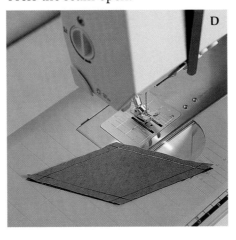

5. The next step is to attach the triangle between the 2 diamonds. This is where it is especially important to not sew within the seam allowance, and you will need to pivot. By using a knee lift, you can use your knee to raise the presser foot for the pivot, leaving both hands free to manipulate the block pieces *(Photo E).*

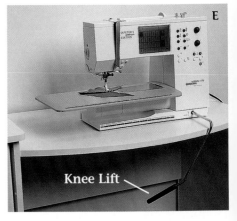

6. Align the triangle between the 2 diamonds. Begin stitching at the seam intersection for both pieces, securing stitches as above. Sew down the seam until you reach the diamond intersection. Use the knee lift to raise the presser foot *(Photo F).*

7. Pivot the unit and sew down the next seam line *(Photo G)* until you reach the intersecting lines. Stitch in place to secure.

Cut diamonds quickly and easily with your rotary cutter.

Rotary Cutting Diamonds

Although you can use the templates if you are more comfortable with that method, you will find that rotary cutting will greatly speed your cutting time.

In the photo example above and in the text below, we are cutting a 2⅝" diamond. However, each set of instructions will give you the correct measurements to use. You will still position the ruler and cut in a similar manner.

1. Begin with a 2⅝"-wide strip (or the strip width called for in the instructions).
2. Cut the left end of this strip at a 45° angle by aligning the 45° line on your ruler with the bottom edge of the fabric strip.
3. Cut at a 45° angle every 2⅝" to make diamonds. (The recently-cut edge of the diamond will align with the 2⅝" measurement on your ruler.)

To check your accuracy in cutting, lay your rotary-cut diamond on top of the diamond template in the book. The two pieces should be the same size.

Setting-In Pieces for a Lemoyne Star

The following diagrams show how to piece a LeMoyne Star. Use the needle-down position and the pivoting techniques shown on page 354.

1. Follow instructions on page 354 to make 4 of Unit 1 using diamonds and triangles.

Unit 1

2. To make Unit 2, place a square atop right edge of Unit 1, with right sides facing. Stitch in place at seam intersection; then sew to raw edge *(Diagram A)*. Press seam allowances toward diamonds. Make 4 of Unit 2.

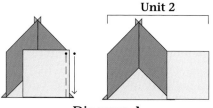

Unit 2

Diagram A

3. With right sides facing, match square of 1 unit with diamond of second unit *(Diagram B)*. With square on top, stitch from outside edge to seam intersection. Stitch in place.

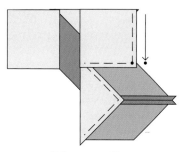

Diagram B

4. With right sides facing, align unstitched edges of diamonds, folding other pieces out of the way. Pin-match diamonds. Stitch in place at inner seam line to edge of fabric *(Diagram C)*. Press diamond seams

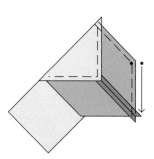

Diagram C

open and corner-square sec toward center of block. Make 2 Unit 3 *(Diagram D)*.

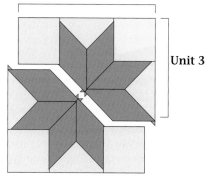

Unit 3

Diagram D

5. To join units, sew squares to diamonds as described in Step 3.
6. With right sides facing, use a positioning pin to match diamonds at center *(Diagram E)*. Stitch in place

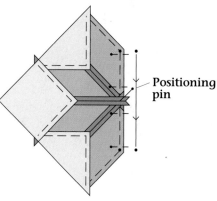

Positioning pin

Diagram E

at top seam intersection and stitch precisely through center, removing pins as you sew, and stitching in place at end of seam. Press seam allowance open.
7. Press corner seam allowances toward diamonds *(Diagram F)*.

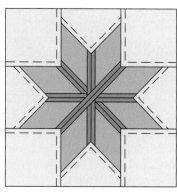

Diagram F

Piecing Curves

Some quilters believe that curved seams are best sewn by hand, while others prefer to use the machine. With a little practice, you can sew curved seams quickly on the sewing machine.

As a general rule, the larger the curved seam, the easier it will be to sew it on the machine. The main secrets for success are carefully pinning and gently tugging the fabric as you sew. We suggest using fine silk pins for pinning, because they are very thin and will reduce buckling in your block.

1. After you've cut out the block pieces, fold each one in half and make a finger crease to find the center. With right sides facing, pin at the center match points *(Photo A)*.

2. Next, align the raw edges of your inner and outer curved pieces along the left side and pin *(Photo B)*.

3. Aligning the curved edges, pin the loose area between the left side and the center *(Photo C)*.

4. Repeat Steps 2 and 3 for the right side of the curve. When you're done, the unit should look like Photo D. The block will look buckled.

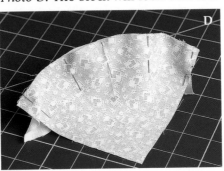

5. It is crucial to have a ¼" seam guide on your sewing machine to keep your seam even. Sew slowly. Every few stitches, pause to turn the unit and give the bottom piece a little tug. That will prevent puckers and tucks as you sew. However, you must take care to keep the raw edges of the curves aligned.

6. Remove the pins. Make small clips along the curved seam allowance *(Photo E)*. This will make the curve lie flat.

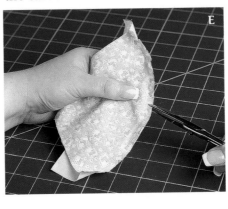

7. Using a steam iron, press the seam allowance toward the darker fabric *(Photo F)*.

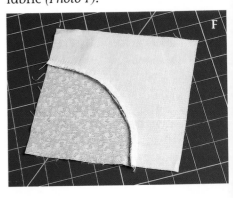

8. You should have a beautiful curve with no tucks or puckers *(Photo G)*.

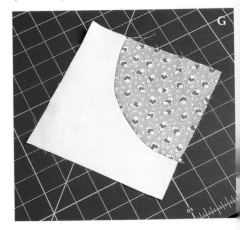

Drunkard's Path *on page 125 is made with curved seams.*

Setting Blocks

Once you've made your quilt blocks, it's time to decide how you want to set them. A set is the arrangement in which blocks are sewn together.

Joining Blocks

Arrange blocks and setting pieces on the floor, on a large table, or on a design wall. Identify the pieces in each row and verify the position of each block. This is the fun part—move the blocks around to find the best balance of color and value. Don't begin sewing until you're happy with the placement of each block. The choice of set is very important. The same blocks can look very different in various sets.

Press seam allowances between blocks in a **straight set,** where the blocks are arranged side-by-side, in the same direction. From row to row, press in opposite directions so that seam allowances will offset when you join rows *(Straight Set Diagram).*

In an **alternate straight set,** two blocks alternate across the rows checkerboard style *(Alternate Straight Set Diagram).* The alternate block can be a different quilt block or a plain setting square, as shown in the diagram.

In an **alternate diagonal set,** press seam allowances between blocks toward setting squares or triangles *(Alternate Diagonal Set Diagram).* This creates the least bulk and always results in opposing seam allowances when you join adjacent rows.

Sashing, strips that separate blocks, eliminates questions about pressing. Just remember to always press toward the sashing. Assemble rows with sashing strips between blocks, pressing each new seam allowance toward the sashing *(Sashing Diagram).* If necessary, ease the block to match the strip. Assemble the quilt with sashing rows between block rows.

Straight Set Diagram

Alternate Diagonal Set Diagram

Alternate Straight Set Diagram

Sashing Diagram

Borders

Most quilts have borders, which help frame the quilt. They can be plain, pieced, or appliquéd, with square or mitered corners. The guidelines below will help you measure, cut, and attach accurate borders.

Measuring

It's common for one side of quilt top to be slightly different from the measurement on the opposite side. Even small discrepancies in cutting and piecing add up across the quilt. Sewing borders of equal length to opposite sides will help square up the quilt again.

When you cut lengthwise strips for borders, you'll want to measure your quilt before trimming the strips to the size indicated in the instructions. When you measure, measure down the center of the quilt rather than along the edges. If your quilt is slightly off measurement, it will be most obvious at the edges of the quilt top. If you just sew on borders without measuring or by just measuring down the side, your borders will have what's called a "lettuce leaf" effect—they will be wavy. It

will be especially obvious when you quilt the piece, as there will likely be puckers in the borders where you have to take up the slack.

Square Corners

Measure from top to bottom through the middle of the quilt as shown in *Square Corners Diagram*. Trim side borders to this length and add them to the quilt sides. You may need to ease one side of a quilt to fit the border and stretch the opposite side to fit the same border length. In the end, both sides will be the same. Unless you're using a walking foot, your sewing machine naturally feeds the bottom layer through the feed dogs faster than it does the top layer. So always put the longer side (the side that needs to be eased in) on the bottom as you sew.

For top and bottom borders, measure from side to side through the middle of the quilt, including the side borders you just added and their seam allowance. Trim to this measurement and add to the quilt.

Mitered Corners

Mitered corners create the illusion of a continuous line around the quilt. They are ideal for striped borders, some pieced borders, or multiple plain borders. Sew multiple borders together first and treat the resulting striped unit as a single border for mitering. Follow the instructions below to miter.
1. Determine the finished outer dimensions of the quilt, as shown by the outer arrows in the *Mitered Corners Diagram*. Cut borders to this length, adding an extra 5" for seam allowances and ease of matching.

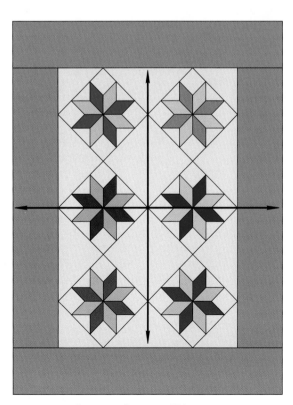

Square Corners Diagram

Mitered Corners Diagram

2. Place a pin on the center of the quilt side and another pin on the center of the border.

3. With right sides facing and raw edges aligned, match the pins on the border to the quilt. Working from the center out, pin the border to the quilt. The border will extend beyond the quilt edges. Do not trim.

4. Sew the border to the quilt, backstitching at each end. Press the seam allowance toward the border. Join the remaining borders in the same manner.

5. With right sides facing, fold the quilt at one corner to align adjacent borders. Pin the quilt center out of the way. Press the borders flat.

6. Align the 45° angle on your rotary ruler with the quilt/border seam line *(Photo A)*.

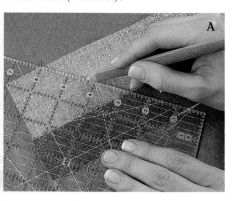

Along the edge of the ruler (which is at a 45° angle to the border), draw a line from the end of the seam allowance to the outside edge of the border. This is the sewing line for the miter. Pin borders together along the sewing line *(Photo B)*.

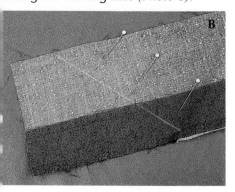

7. Beginning with a backstitch at the inside corner, stitch on the drawn line to the outside edge. Check the right side of the quilt to see that the seam lies flat and fabrics match up as desired *(Photo C)*.

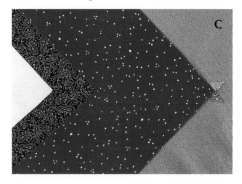

8. When satisfied with the mitered seam, trim excess fabric to a ¼" seam allowance. Press this seam open *(Photo D)*.

Preparing to Quilt

Before you begin quilting your top, you must select a quilting pattern, mark the quilt design if needed, choose a batting, and make a backing. Following are suggestions to guide you in these decisions.

Selecting a Quilting Pattern

The quilting design is an important part of any quilt, so choose it with care. The hours you spend stitching together the layers of your quilt create shadows and depths that bring the quilt to life, so make the design count.

In our "Quilting and Finishing" instructions, we tell you to "quilt as desired," but then we also tell you how the project shown was quilted. Since most of the intricate quilting designs were used from purchased stencils, we cannot reproduce the patterns within the book. However, we have given patterns wherever possible.

Many quilting catalogs feature quilting stencils you can buy for both hand and machine quilting. (See Resources on page 368.)

Quilting Without Marking

There are several ways to quilt that do not require you to mark the quilt top:

• **In-the-ditch:** Quilting right in the seam, where fabric pieces meet. This stitching adds dimension to the quilt, but the stitching itself is not highly visible.
• **Outline Quilting:** Quilting ¼" from the seam line. You can "eyeball" this measurement or use ¼"-wide masking tape as a guide.
• **Grid Quilting:** Quilting in straight, diagonal lines, usually 1" apart. Using the 45° line on your ruler to get you started, place 1"-wide masking tape on your quilt and quilt along its edge. Never keep the tape on your quilt for long periods of time—if you must set your project aside for a time, remove the tape.
• **Stippling:** Freestyle, meandering lines of quilting worked closely together to fill open areas.

Using a stencil to mark a quilting design

Using Stencils

To find a stencil for a quilting design, check your local quilt shop or mail-order catalogs (see Resources, page 368) for one that suits your quilt. Measure the area you want to quilt, such as a 12" block, and look for a stencil the same size.

To transfer a design to the quilt top, position the stencil on the quilt and mark through the slits in the stencil. Connect the lines after removing the stencil. You will find it much easier to mark the quilt top at this point rather than waiting until it is basted.

Before using any marker, test it on scraps to be sure the marks will wash out. Don't use just any pencil. There are many pencils and chalk markers available that are designed to wash out. If you plan to enter your quilt into competition, it is important that your marking lines do not show.

Batting

Precut batting comes in six sizes—craft, crib, twin, full, queen, and king. The batting listed for each quilt is the most suitable for the quilt's finished size. Some stores sell 90"-wide batting by the yard, which might be more practical for your quilt.

Loft is the height or thickness of

the batting. For a traditional, flat look, choose low-loft cotton batting. Thick batting is difficult to quilt, unless you plan to machine quilt it.

Polyester batting is easy to stitch and can be washed with little shrinkage. However, look for the word "bonded" when selecting polyester batts. Bonding keeps the loft of the batt uniform and reduces the effects of bearding (migration of loose fibers through the quilt top). Avoid bonded batts that feel stiff.

Cotton batting provides the flat, thin look of an antique quilt, making it ideal for most of the projects in this book. Some seasoned quilters shy from cotton batting because older types were difficult to quilt. But today's cotton batts are needle-punched and are very easy to quilt. Cotton shrinks slightly when washed, giving it that wrinkled look characteristic of all quilts.

Cotton batting swatches

Wool batting is made of 100% wool fibers that are punched with hundreds of needles through a strong, thin base material to prevent tearing, shifting, or migration. Quilting through wool batting is like quilting through butter.

You'll find wool an excellent insulator, ideal for colder climates. As a natural fiber, wool lets your quilt breathe without adding weight. Wool batts are thin like cotton and don't seem to hold wrinkles.

Wool shrinks about 3%. If you're concerned about shrinkage, hand-wash the batt in cold water and dry it in a dryer before quilting. Otherwise, use it as you would a cotton batt.

Wool batting

Backing

The instructions in this book tell you how to cut and piece standard 42"-wide fabric to make backing. The backing should be at least 4" larger than the quilt on all sides.

For a large quilt, 90"- or 108"-wide fabric is a sensible option that reduces waste and eliminates backing seams. Quilters are no longer limited to muslin; new wide fabrics are available in lovely prints.

Some quilters treat the backing as another design element of their quilt, choosing to piece interesting designs or appliqué large shapes. Sometimes a quirky print bought on the clearance table adds just the right punch.

Layering

Lay the backing right side down on a large work surface—a large table, two tables pushed together, or a clean floor. Use masking tape to secure the edges, keeping the backing wrinkle-free and slightly taut.

Smooth the batting over the backing; then trim the batting even with the backing. Center the pressed quilt top right side up on the batting. Make sure the edges of the backing and quilt top are parallel.

Do *not* baste on a carpeted floor! It is easy to get the basting threads caught in the carpet. After all your hard work, you may find that your quilt is stitched to the floor!

Layering the backing, batting, and quilt top

Basting

Basting keeps the layers from shifting during quilting, so take time to baste carefully to avoid lumps and pleats in your finished quilt. If your quilt is large, a large frame can aid your basting. Look for a guild with one.

For **thread basting**, use a long needle and white thread. Colored thread can leave a residue on light fabrics. Start in the quilt center and baste a line of long stitches to each corner, making a large X. Then baste parallel lines 6" to 8" apart. Finish with a line of basting ¼" from the edge.

For **pin basting,** use nickel-plated safety pins. Pin every 3" to 4". One handy way to judge spacing is to use your fist as a guide. Don't close the pins as you go, as this can pucker the backing. When all pins are in place, remove the tape at the quilt edges. Gently tug the backing as you close each pin so that pleats don't form underneath.

Another popular method is to use a **basting gun,** which shoots plastic tabs through the quilt layers, similar to price tags attached to retail clothing. Use a basting grate underneath the quilt so you're not trying to tack against a solid surface. Use paper-cutting scissors to trim the tabs away after the quilting is done.

Thread basting

Pin basting

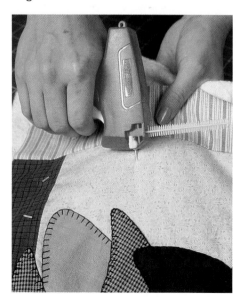

Basting gun

Quilting

The choice of quilting by hand or by machine depends on the quilt design, how much time you have, and the quilt's intended use. Another option is to have your project quilted with a professional quilting machine. Check your quilt shop or guild for local sources.

Hand Quilting

1. To make a stitch, first insert the needle straight down *(Photo A)*. With your other hand under the quilt, feel for the needle point as it pierces the backing.

2. Roll the needle to a nearly horizontal position *(Photo B)*.

Use the thumb of your sewing hand and the underneath hand to pinch a little hill in the fabric as you push the needle back through the quilt top. Gently tug the thread to pop the knot into the quilt.

3. Then rock the needle back to an upright position for the next stitch. Load 3 to 4 stitches on the needle before pulling it.

4. With 6" of thread left, tie a knot close to the quilt top. Backstitch; then pop the knot into the batting. Run the thread through the batting and out the top to clip it *(Knot Diagram)*.

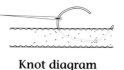

Knot diagram

Machine Quilting

If you plan to machine quilt, you must have a walking foot for your sewing machine *(Photo A)*. This allows all the quilt layers to feed through your machine evenly.

Use this foot for straight-line quilting, such as quilting in-the-ditch *(Photo B)*.

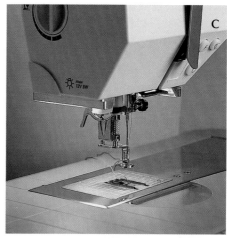

For free-motion quilting or stippling, you will need a darning foot *(Photo C)*.

Lower the feed dogs or cover them. You control the stitch length by manually moving the fabric *(Photo D)*.

Binding

Binding encloses the raw edges of your quilt. You may choose from straight-grain or bias binding. The only times a quilt must have bias binding is when it has curved edges or rounded corners or if you use a plaid binding and want the plaid to appear on point.

Bias Binding

1. To cut bias binding, start with a square. (For a queen-size quilt, a 32" square is sufficient.) Center pins at the top and bottom edges with the heads toward the **outside.** At each side, center a pin with the head toward the **inside** edge (*Diagram 1*).

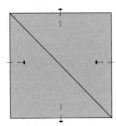

Diagram 1

2. Cut the square in half diagonally to make 2 triangles.

3. With right sides facing, match the edges with the pin heads pointed to the **outside.** Remove the pins and join the triangles with a ¼" seam. Press the seam open (*Diagram 2*).

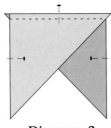

Diagram 2

4. On the wrong side of the fabric, mark cutting lines parallel to the long edges. Space the lines 2¼" apart, or the desired width of your binding (*Diagram 3*). (Space the lines

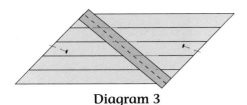

Diagram 3

at 2½" apart when working with thicker fabric, like flannel, or thicker batting.)

5. Match the edges with the pin heads pointing to the inside, right sides facing, offsetting 1 width of binding strip as shown. Join the edges with a ¼" seam to make a tube. Press the seam open.

6. Begin cutting at the extended edges. Follow the drawn lines, rolling the tube around as you cut, until all the fabric is cut into a continuous strip (*Diagram 4*).

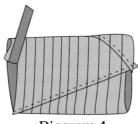

Diagram 4

7. Fold the binding in half lengthwise with wrong sides facing. Press.

Self Binding

Many Depression-era quilts use self binding—that is, the backing fabric is trimmed, folded, and stitched to the front to enclose the quilt edges. Although this type of binding is not as sturdy as a separate fabric binding, it does conserve fabric and is true to early techniques.

1. Trim the batting even with the quilt top.

2. Trim the backing to 2" around all sides of quilt.

3. Fold backing in half toward quilt and press. Fold in half again and then fold to front and slipstitch in place to make ½"-wide binding. Miter corners.

Straight-grain Binding

1. Cut the needed number of strips from selvage to selvage. Cut the strips 2¼" wide when working with thin batting and 2½" wide when working with thicker fabric (like flannel) or thicker batting.

2. Join the strips end to end to make a continuous strip. To join 2 strips, layer them perpendicular to each other with right sides facing. Stitch a diagonal seam across the strips as shown in *Joining Diagram.* Trim the seam allowances to ¼" and press open.

3. Fold the binding in half lengthwise with wrong sides facing. Press.

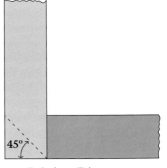

Joining Diagram

Adding Binding

Sew the binding to the front of the quilt first by machine. Begin stitching in the middle of any quilt side. Do not trim excess batting and backing until after you stitch the binding to the quilt.

1. Matching raw edges, lay the binding on the quilt. Stitch the binding to the quilt, using a ³⁄₈" seam and leaving about 2" unstitched at the top *(Diagram A)*.

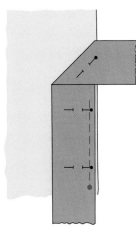

Diagram A

2. Continue stitching down the side of the quilt. Stop ³⁄₈" from the corner and backstitch. Remove the quilt from the machine and clip the threads.
3. Fold the binding strip straight up, away from the quilt, making a 45° angle *(Diagram B)*.

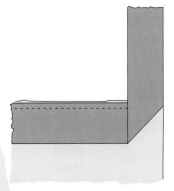

Diagram B

ld the binding straight down
the next side to be stitched,
ng a fold that is even with the
lge of the previously stitched

in stitching at the top edge of
w side *(Diagram C)*. Stitch

Fold.

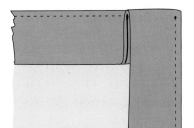

Diagram C

down the length of the new side. Continue until all 4 corners and sides are joined in this manner.
6. Stop stitching 1" from the point where the binding began. Trim the excess binding, leaving a 2" tail. Join the 2 tails with diagonal seams *(Diagram D)*. Trim the excess

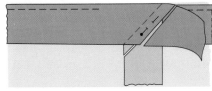

Diagram D

binding beyond the diagonal stitching and press open. Stitch a straight line over this area to secure the open space *(Diagram E)*.

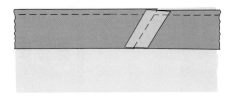

Diagram E

7. Trim the excess batting and backing even with the binding's raw edge.
8. Turn the binding over the raw edge of the quilt. Slipstitch the binding in place on the backing with matching thread. At each corner, fold the binding to form a miter. The miter should form naturally when you turn the corners to the back of the quilt. Whipstitch the miter closed *(Diagram F)*.

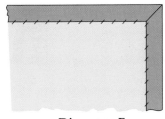

Diagram F

Prairie Points

Use prairie points instead of binding to add another design element to your quilt.
1. To make prairie points, fold 3³⁄₄" squares in half *(Diagram A)*.

Diagram A

2. Fold each piece in half again to make a small triangle *(Diagram B)*.

Diagram B

3. On the right side of the quilt, arrange prairie points along each side, with each triangle overlapping its neighbor as needed to fit *(Diagram C)*. Align the raw

Diagram C

edges of the triangles with the quilt border. Space prairie points evenly and baste through the top and batting only, keeping the backing free.
4. Folding the backing out of the way, stitch the prairie points in place through the quilt top and the batting *(Diagram D)*.

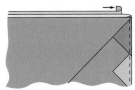

Diagram D

5. Trim the batting even with the quilt top. Trim the backing to 1" on all sides. Turn under the edges of the backing, covering the edges of the prairie points, and blindstitch backing in place *(Diagram E)*.

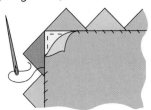

Diagram E

Quilt Labels

It is unfortunate to come across any quilt with no record of the quilt's history. Include a quilt label with every quilt you make. Appliqué or piece the label to the back, or include it in a block on the front.

At a minimum, your quilt label should include:
- the name of the quilt
- your name
- your city and state
- the date of completion, or the date of presentation.

Additional information can include the story behind the quilt, the maker, and/or the recipient. Consider recording how old you were when you made the quilt.

There are numerous ways to embellish your quilt label. You can use Pigma® pens, rubber stamps, cross-stitch, embroidery, or even your computer. If a quilt label is designed on your computer, you can make a quilt label with photo transfer paper or with Computer Printer Fabric™ by June Tailor. Instructions come with the package.

You can add more labels if the quilt is displayed, published, or acknowledged with an award.

If you make a quilt as a gift, be sure to record that you made it, who it was for, the date, and the occasion.

Even if you purchase an antique quilt, make a label.

June Tailor makes computer printer fabric, which you can feed directly into your printer. This package is for black ink only, but it is also available for using colors.

Research the pattern to see if you can determine the approximate date the quilt was made, or simply put "unknown." But at least put your name and the date and place you purchased it for future reference.

If you are adept at other types of needlework, use that in your quilt label. Here, the quiltmaker designed and cross-stitched her own label.

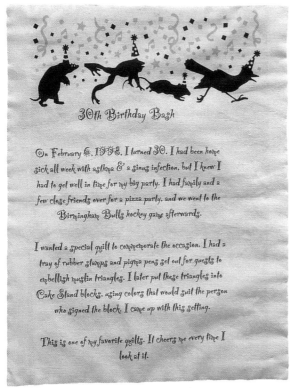

This quilt label was generated on the computer using computer clip art and a fancy font.

Sometimes an extra quilt block can be used on the back to make a label.

Resources

General Quilt Supplies

Contact the following companies for a free catalog.

Connecting Threads
P.O. Box 8940
Vancouver, WA 98668-8940
1-800-574-6454

Hancock's of Paducah
3841 Hinkleville Road
Paducah, KY 42001
1-800-845-8723
Fax: (502) 443-2164
www.Hancocks-Paducah.com

Keepsake Quilting™
Route 25B, P.O. Box 1618
Centre Harbor, NH 03226
1-800-865-9458
www.keepsakequilting.com

Photo Transfer

Photos-to-Fabric™
Mallery Press
4206 Sheraton Drive
Flint, MI 48532-3557
1-800-278-4824
www.quilt.com/amisimms

Rotary-cutting Rulers and Mats

Prym-Dritz Corporation
14 Westover Avenue
Stamford, CT 06902
1-800-845-4948

Rubber Stamps, Pigma™ Pens, Ink

Wallflower Designs
Susan McKelvey
P.O. Box 307
Royal Oak, MD 21662
Send $3.00 for catalog.

Template Material

Cut-Your-Own Templates
Flynn Quilt Frame Company
1000 Shiloh Overpass Road
Billings, MT 59106
1-800-745-3596
www.flynnquilt.com

Hanging Sleeve

If you plan to hang your quilt on a wall or display it in a quilt show, you will need to add a hanging sleeve. A sleeve distributes the weight of your quilt evenly and allows it to hang straight and flat.

Never hang a quilt with nails, staples, or tacks. They will not support the weight of the quilt, and even if you can get them to hold the quilt to the wall, the quilt's weight will pull holes around the tacks. A hanging sleeve distributes the weight evenly across the width of the quilt.

You can slip a dowel or a curtain rod through the sleeve and hang it from brackets attached to the wall. Or you can use an "invisible" method that works well for large quilts. Have a length of 2"- or 3"-wide board cut the length of your sleeve (not the quilt). Insert eye screws into each end (see *photo*).

Eye screws at each end allow you to fasten the quilt securely to the wall.

Then hang the quilt through the eye screws with strong nails, or even better, toggle bolts. Toggle bolts allow you to hang a quilt on drywall. They make a pretty big hole, so make sure you want that quilt there before you drill the inserts into the wall. Although fairly permanent, this method is ideal because it will support the quilt's weight and you cannot tell how the quilt is hung—the hardware is invisible.

Follow these steps to make a hanging sleeve:

1. Cut an 8"- or 9"-wide strip of left-over backing fabric that is the same length as the quilt edge.

2. Turn under ½" on each end of the strip. Then turn under another ½". Topstitch to hem both ends.

3. With wrong sides facing, fold the fabric in half lengthwise and stitch the long edges together. Press the seam allowances open and to the middle of the sleeve *(Diagram A).*

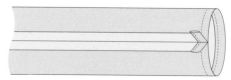

Diagram A

4. Center the sleeve on the quilt ½" to 1" below the binding with the seam against the backing. Hand-stitch the sleeve to the quilt through the backing, making sure no stitches show through the quilt top *(Diagram B).*

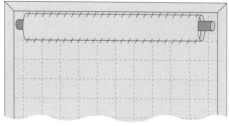

Diagram B